It's tempting to follow the Hermione Grangers of the classroom - the students who always have a hand up, who make lessons look smooth, who already know the answers. But our job isn't limited to designing instruction for the kids who find school easy. We're here to make sure every child gets a turn to engage in the great conversation - the most interesting ideas our species has made. This book refuses to confuse nodding along with understanding, or busy activity with learning. It treats checking for understanding not only as what it is - the engine of responsive teaching - but as an expression of an ethical commitment: that every child can succeed when we support them to shine and show what they know.

Zach Groshell, *PhD, USA. Former teacher, author, instructional coach, podcaster, chief learning scientist*

This is a generous, thoughtful guide to the most important question in teaching: what are they thinking? David Goodwin shows, with clarity and warmth, how to make students' thinking visible and their learning real. Given David's deep understanding of the science of learning, *What Are They Thinking?* is research-rich, practical, and deeply humane. An essential book for every teacher and the basis for ongoing CPD. I'll be recommending it widely.

Mary Myatt, *education writer and speaker*

This excellent book by David Goodwin covers a lot of ground: cognitive science, desirable difficulties, formative assessment, motivational theory, questioning, scaffolding, adaptive teaching . . . and a lot more besides. Its scope and detail are impressive. Importantly, it also offers a great deal of exemplification across a wide range of subject areas, supporting teachers to understand how principles might be applied in practice. For all of these reasons, it should be a very valuable resource to anyone interested in developing their teaching practice.

Bruce Robertson, *Next Level Educational CEO, and author of* The Teaching Delusion *trilogy and Power Up series*

Checking for understanding is at the heart of great teaching, and yet it's also one of the most complex aspects of our job. *What Are They Thinking?* does a brilliant job of explaining why this part of teaching is so complex; considering the role that prior knowledge plays, how poor proxies can give us an illusion of learning, and what great checks for understanding actually look like as part of an adaptive teaching framework. The book distils the research in an accessible but thorough way, and yet this is also an eminently practical book. The sections on strategies such as hinge questions, cold call and the use of mini whiteboards are filled with helpful examples from a range of subjects as well as classroom vignettes which bring the strategies to life. This book not only gave me a wider depth of knowledge but it really made me think hard. *What Are They Thinking?* is a highly recommended read for any classroom teacher who wants to find out more about what their students know and understand.

Rachel Ball, *PD Specialist at Steplab, Co-author of* The Scaffolding Effect

What a magnificent book! Goodwin does a wonderful job of explaining the theory behind checking for understanding and applying it to the classroom to improve learning outcomes. I don't care what age you teach, what the subject matter is, or how long you've been in the teaching profession, *What Are They Thinking?* will deepen your knowledge and appreciation for what great teaching looks and sounds like in the classroom; how to efficiently and effectively assess student thinking and move students forward in the process of learning.

Blake Harvard, *Classroom Teacher and Author of* Do I Have Your Attention?

This book offers a clear, research-informed guide to checking for understanding and responding to what students actually know. Goodwin explains key cognitive principles in practical classroom terms and shows how they connect to responsive teaching.

Strategies are presented with strong rationale and concrete guidance, making them easy to implement consistently. The result is a book that strengthens everyday practice, improves the accuracy of assessment in the moment, and helps teachers make better instructional decisions lesson by lesson.

Professor Haili Hughes, *Professor of Educational mentoring and coaching, Academica University of Applied Sciences*

In *What Are They Thinking?*, David Goodwin tackles one of the most uncomfortable truths in teaching: we are often less certain about students' understanding than we think. This book goes beyond surface-level questioning strategies and digs into the cognitive science of prior knowledge, misconceptions, and memory, showing why learning is so easy to misjudge and so hard to secure. What makes this book stand out is its insistence that checking for understanding is not a routine but a responsibility. Hinge questions, cold call, and mini whiteboards are treated not as engagement tools but as instruments for better instructional decisions. This is a thoughtful, rigorous book every teacher will find beneficial to read.

Sarah Cottinghatt, *Research Lead at Steplab*

WHAT ARE THEY THINKING?

Teachers make decisions every lesson based on what they think students understand. However, without reliable ways to check understanding, teachers risk teaching to an illusion, and those most likely to be left behind are often the most vulnerable. ***What Are They Thinking?*** tackles one of the most consequential questions in teaching: how can we reliably find out what students actually understand, and use that insight to decide what to do next?

The book explores the research behind checking for understanding and shows why it is central to so much of what we know about how learning happens. Drawing on evidence from cognitive science and formative assessment, it provides practical guidance to help teachers design checks that include every student, reveal misconceptions early, and allow teachers to respond thoughtfully to the evidence they provide. Examining checking for understanding across key areas of teaching and learning, the chapters cover:

- Prior knowledge, including schema theory, meaning-making, and consolidation;
- The science of learning, including desirable difficulties, learning versus performance, and assessment;

- Practical classroom techniques, such as cold calling, mini whiteboards, hinge questions, and exit tickets applicable from early years education to post-16 and beyond; and
- Applying checks for understanding in SEND, adaptive teaching and oracy.

Part of the Teacher CPD Academy series from InnerDrive, ***What Are They Thinking?*** is essential reading for teachers and school leaders who want to move beyond reassurance, make learning visible, and teach with greater precision, confidence, and impact. Checking for understanding is framed as a moral and professional imperative, making it more likely that teaching is guided by evidence rather than well-intentioned intuition.

David Goodwin is a trust-wide Teaching and Learning Lead in the East of England, working with colleagues across Early Years to Key Stage 4. He writes, speaks, and occasionally illustrates ideas about teaching and learning. He remains, first and foremost, a learner.

The Teacher CPD Academy

Series editors: Bradley Busch and Edward Watson

The Homework Conundrum
How to Stop the Dog From Eating Homework
Jovita M. Castelino

Do I Have Your Attention?
Understanding Memory Constraints and Maximizing Learning
Blake Harvard

Creativity for Teachers
A Cognitive Science Approach
Claire Badger and Jonathan Firth

The Scaffolding Effect
Supporting All Students to Succeed
Rachel Ball and Alex Fairlamb

Evidence Informed Wisdom
Making Better Decisions in Education
Bradley Busch, Edward Watson and Matthew Shaw

Unlocking Oracy
Enhancing Student Learning and Personal Development
Nikki Sullivan, Kelly Heaton and Lucy Lowde

Demystifying Adaptive Teaching
How to Teach to the Top
Jade Pearce

Fail Better
How Teachers can Help Students Overcome Failure, Perfectionism, Procrastination, Impostor Syndrome and Test Anxiety
Mark Roberts

Coaching for Adaptive Expertise
Sarah Cottinghatt, Haili Hughes and Adam Kolhbeck

What Are They Thinking?
The Ultimate Guide to Checking for Understanding
David Goodwin

WHAT ARE THEY THINKING?

The Ultimate Guide to Checking for Understanding

David Goodwin

Routledge
Taylor & Francis Group
LONDON AND NEW YORK

Designed cover image: Courtesy of InnerDrive

First published 2027
by Routledge
4 Park Square, Milton Park, Abingdon, Oxon OX14 4RN

and by Routledge
605 Third Avenue, New York, NY 10158

Routledge is an imprint of the Taylor & Francis Group, an informa business

British Library Cataloguing-in-Publication Data
A catalogue record for this book is available from the British Library

ISBN: 978-1-041-10826-9 (hbk)
ISBN: 978-1-041-10823-8 (pbk)
ISBN: 978-1-003-65701-9 (ebk)

DOI: 10.4324/9781003657019

Typeset in Interstate
by Apex CoVantage, LLC

CONTENTS

ACKNOWLEDGEMENTS

I have been fortunate to co-author three previous books, each with generous collaborators (Oliver Caviglioli, Emma Turner, and Michael Chiles) whose thinking stretched my own, and for whose influence I remain deeply grateful. For a long time, I said that if I were ever to write another book, I would do so alone.

But no work of value is created in isolation. While my name sits on the cover, this book exists because of the insight, encouragement, and professional generosity of many others, each of whom helped refine the ideas that follow.

My thanks to Brad, Edward, Claire, and the InnerDrive team for welcoming me into the InnerDrive community and for their trust throughout this process. They offered encouragement and challenge in equal measure, while giving me the space to wrestle with the ideas and shape the book in my own way.

This book stands on the shoulders of many thoughtful educators whose work has informed, challenged, and refined my own. I owe a particular debt to Carl Hendrick, Mary Myatt and Dylan Wiliam; to Rachel Ball, Doug Lemov, and Blake Harvard; to Haili Hughes, Paul Kirschner, and Tom Sherrington; to Sarah Cottinghatt, Oliver Caviglioli, and Efrat Furst; to Peps McCrea, Rob Coe, and Daisy Christodoulou; and to David Didau, Harry Fletcher-Wood, Adam Boxer, Craig Barton, Michael Chiles, Alex Quigley, Zach Groshell, Bruce Robertson, and Kate Jones.

I am equally grateful to the thoughtful colleagues who contributed spotlight sections to this book: Alex Fairlamb, Jamie Clark, Adam Lamb, Elliot Morgan, Miriam Hussain, Sarah Robertson, Rachel Ashfield, and Nikki Sullivan. Each brought clarity from lived classroom experience, grounding the ideas in practical wisdom and reminding me that the most powerful professional learning is always rooted in real classrooms.

Finally, nothing meaningful is achieved without the quiet strength of family. Thank you to my wife, Marie, for your patience, generosity and constant support, and to our daughter, Maddison, who keeps me grounded by reminding me that her poem in the Robin Hood's Bay local newsletter secured her status as a published author long before mine.

FOREWORD

I was five years into my teaching career before anyone told me what cognitive science had to say about how learning actually works. Five years of well-intentioned but largely improvised instruction, built on intuition, imitation, and whatever I happened to pick up along the way. When I finally encountered the research on memory, attention, and knowledge acquisition, it was not merely informative; it was a rebuke. I had been operating in the dark, and the worst part was that I hadn't known it.

That experience has stayed with me, and it is one reason this book matters so much. David Goodwin has written what I wish someone had placed in my hands during those early years: a rigorous, practical, and intellectually serious guide to one of the most consequential acts a teacher performs, the act of finding out what students are actually thinking.

On the surface, checking for understanding seems unremarkable. Every teacher does it, or believes they do. We ask, "Does everyone understand?"[1] We scan the room for nodding heads. We take the confident hand that shoots up and treat it as a proxy for the whole class. But as Goodwin shows with characteristic precision, these habits are not checks at all. They are rituals of reassurance, comforting to the teacher and largely uninformative about the learner. The nodding heads may conceal deep confusion. The confident volunteer may be the only student in the room who grasps the material. And the silence that follows "Any questions?" tells us almost nothing, except that students have learned it is safer to say nothing than to reveal what they do not know.

Dylan Wiliam has described the essence of formative assessment as creating "moments of contingency," which refer to points in a lesson at which the teacher's next instructional move is genuinely dependent on what the student reveals. This is the animating idea of Goodwin's book. Teaching without these moments is like navigating without a compass; you may be moving, but you have no reliable way of knowing whether you are heading in the right direction. The gap between what a teacher teaches and what a student learns is not incidental. It is the fundamental problem of instruction. Everything else, the quality of explanation, the design of practice tasks, the architecture of the curriculum, depends on whether the teacher can create and act upon these moments of contingency with precision and purpose.

What makes this book distinctive is not merely its theoretical grounding but its refusal to remain at the level of abstraction. Each chapter moves from principle to practice, offering teachers concrete strategies, from cold calling and mini whiteboards to hinge questions and exit tickets, that are not presented as gimmicks but as instruments calibrated to the realities of human cognition. Goodwin understands something that too many professional development programmes miss: that a strategy without a rationale is just a trick, and a rationale without a strategy is just a lecture. He provides both.

I am particularly struck by the book's treatment of prior knowledge. As Goodwin notes, students do not arrive as blank slates; in any given classroom, the variation in what students already know is enormous and largely invisible unless the teacher deliberately surfaces it. This is not an abstract concern; it is an equity imperative. Students from disadvantaged backgrounds often lack the prior knowledge that their more privileged peers absorb at home, from dinner table conversations, from books, from travel. If the teacher does not check for and activate that prior knowledge, they are building on foundations that may not exist, and the students who suffer most are precisely those who can least afford to fall behind.

There is something else here worth emphasising. Every time a teacher runs a well-designed check for understanding, every time they require all students to think and respond rather than relying on willing volunteers, they are not merely assessing. They are teaching. As Dan Willingham has observed, *memory is the residue of thought*.[2] Checking for understanding, done well, dissolves the artificial boundary between assessment and instruction. It makes the act of finding out what students know an act of deepening what they know.

David Goodwin has written a book that respects both the science and the craft. He treats teachers as professionals capable of engaging with complex ideas and translating them into daily practice. In a profession too often subjected to fashionable interventions with little evidence to support them, this book offers something far more valuable: the tools to see clearly, to act wisely, and to teach in a way that genuinely serves every student in the room.

Carl Hendrick, Professor of Learning Science at Academica University of Applied Sciences.

References

1. Black and Wiliam (2009) "Developing the theory of formative assessment," *Educational Assessment, Evaluation and Accountability*, 21(1), p. 6.
2. Willingham, D.T. (2009) *Why don't students like school?: A cognitive scientist answers questions about how the mind works and what it means for the classroom*. San Francisco: Jossey-Bass.

SERIES EDITORS' FOREWORD

What Are They Thinking? is an incredible addition to InnerDrive's Teacher CPD Academy Series. This series is based on the philosophy that if evidence is made accessible and paired with practical strategies, then it can be transformational. This book embodies that.

Teaching is often described as a craft, a science, or an art. In reality, it is probably all three, and at the heart of each lies a deceptively simple question: what are my students thinking? In this book, David Goodwin tackles this question head-on, reminding us that learning is rarely neat, linear, or predictable. Instead, it is messy, complex, and often hidden. What students take away from a lesson is often not the same as what you carefully planned or explicitly taught. Assumptions about understanding can be comforting, but they are also one of the greatest barriers to effective teaching. If future teaching decisions are built on shaky and inaccurate foundations, learning suffers.

Students may appear confident while holding fragile misconceptions, or struggle outwardly while making meaningful progress internally. Unless we actively seek to understand what students are thinking, we risk teaching to an illusion rather than a reality. Knowing what students are thinking transforms teaching. When teachers have genuine insight into students' understanding, misconceptions, and reasoning, they are far better placed to decide what to do next. Should you revisit a concept? Provide a scaffold? Increase the level of challenge? Or simply give students more time to think?

Checking for understanding is not an add-on or a box-ticking exercise. It is the engine of responsive, adaptive teaching, guiding instruction by evidence rather than instinct alone. Crucially, David explores what students are thinking in two complementary senses. First, he emphasises the importance of fostering a culture where students feel safe and willing to share their thoughts. Without trust, curiosity, and psychological safety, even the best questioning techniques will fall flat. Second, he provides practical strategies to elicit students' thinking more accurately and more efficiently.

What Are They Thinking? is a practical guide for teachers at every stage of their career. It challenges us to be more curious about our students' minds and more deliberate in our responses. For those looking to deepen these ideas further, this book sits alongside a dedicated course available on InnerDrive's Teacher CPD Academy, offering structured professional learning to support the principles explored here.

Ultimately, *What Are They Thinking?* reminds us that great teaching begins not with what we say, but with what our students think, and what we choose to do once we truly understand it. We have no doubt that this will become the ultimate guide to checking for understanding for teachers and educators.

Bradley Busch and Edward Watson, Directors of InnerDrive

INTRODUCTION

What is the role of a teacher? In her book *Mastery Teaching* (1982), Madeline Hunter answered this question concisely, " . . . *the job of the teacher is to inspire, not perspire.*" She suggested that too many teachers were working late into the night, identifying and correcting students' work after the fact.[1]

Hunter's message is as relevant today as it was nearly fifty years ago. Reliable checks for understanding help teachers to unearth gaps, confusion, and misconceptions during instruction, allowing teachers to address these when it matters, in-the-moment. In doing so, teachers can shift their effort away from retrospective correcting towards a more efficient and responsive form of teaching.

An amusing insight, likely to raise a wry smile for many readers, is Hunter's claim that teachers tend to commit one of three common errors when checking for understanding.

The first is the rhetorical "**OK?**" Having explained and modelled the steps to solving a problem, the teacher smiles and asks, "So those are the steps . . . OK?" Few students are brave enough to reply, "No, it is not OK. It doesn't make sense." Students' silence is mistaken for understanding.

The second is the classic, and totally ineffective, "**Do you understand?**" Again, very few students would be willing to admit publicly that they do

DOI: 10.4324/9781003657019-1

not understand. There is a much deeper issue here, too: students at this stage do not yet know what they have misunderstood. Until they have to articulate their thinking or are required to attempt a task, they have little way of judging the security of their own understanding.

Finally, there is the frequently used, "**Does anyone have any questions?**" In this situation, one of two things tends to happen. Either students refrain from asking because the question implies that having a question indicates they weren't listening, or a question is asked that bears little relation to the learning itself: "Miss, what do you think the score will be tonight?"

And so a central message of this book is that, if teachers are to avoid *covering the curriculum* while leaving many students behind, they need reliable ways to answer the question, "What are they thinking?", and to use those insights to make *better-founded* instructional decisions.

Another central tenet of this book is that learning is often far less visible than teachers assume. Busy students, engaging lessons, fluent answers, and confident volunteers can easily give teachers the impression that learning is secure. Yet, as you will read in Chapter 4, these are fairly unreliable proxies for durable learning. What students can do during a well-structured lesson, particularly when tasks are heavily scaffolded, may tell the teacher very little about what their students will remember or be able to apply later.

Checking for understanding, then, is not about measuring learning. It is about generating formative inferences that help teachers to see how students are thinking, where there is confusion, and what needs to happen next.

However, not all checks for understanding are created equally. If the teacher expects only a small number of students to respond, they risk making decisions based on a narrow, unrepresentative sample of the class. Voluntary participation tends to privilege the most confident voices and conceals uncertainty elsewhere. In such classrooms, thinking is unevenly distributed, and evidence is correspondingly thin.

For these reasons, another central message of this book is that checks for understanding must be designed to involve all students, not just the confident volunteers. When it is expected that all students think and respond, teachers gain a more complete and reliable picture across the class, which supports their decision-making.

An additional, often overlooked benefit of checking for understanding is that each time a teacher runs a cold call, mini whiteboard, or hinge question routine, students are rehearsing their thinking. Each check draws on Dan Willingham's often-quoted observation that "memory is the residue of thought."[2] When all students are expected to think and respond, they are not simply revealing what they know; they are making sense of new concepts and beginning to consolidate them. Seen in this way, checking for understanding helps to avoid the artificial separation of assessment from teaching.

This book, while dense, is practical in the truest sense of the word. Checking for understanding is familiar territory for most teachers, yet its impact depends on how thoughtfully it is designed and enacted. For this reason, the book takes a deliberately deep dive into the practice, examining the decisions that underpin it and the conditions that enable it to function well.

Checking for understanding deserves this attention because it is central to so much of what we know about how learning happens. It shapes what students attend to, how much cognitive load they experience, and how securely concepts are encoded in memory through rehearsal and retrieval. It supports explanations, practice, feedback, and adaptation, acting as the connective tissue between what is taught and what students learn. When teachers and leaders invest the time to develop and implement a culture of checking for understanding, they are investing in something that strengthens almost every aspect of teaching.

References

1. Hunter, M. (1982) *Mastery teaching*. El Segundo, CA: Corwin Press.
2. Willingham, D.T. (2009) *Why don't students like school?: A cognitive scientist answers questions about how the mind works and what it means for the classroom*. San Francisco: Jossey-Bass.

SECTION 1

Checking for Understanding and Prior Knowledge

1 Prior Knowledge and Schema Theory

When we ask, "What are they thinking?", the answer depends greatly on what students already know. Simply put, prior knowledge shapes students' perception, thinking, and learning.

Prior knowledge is powerful: it can serve as a foundation for new learning or hinder it if misconceptions remain unchallenged.[1] Checking for understanding plays a critical role in this process. First, it helps to identify gaps and inaccuracies that might impede learning. Second, when teachers intentionally design checks that surface and link this knowledge, they are guided to draw on the prerequisite knowledge that underpins the new learning. By confirming students are making the intended connections, teachers make it more likely that new information connects meaningfully to existing schema.

Recognising the role of checking for understanding in connecting new material to existing knowledge structures is key to securing meaningful learning. Failing to check what students already know risks trying to build on shaky foundations, allowing misconceptions to persist, and missing opportunities to activate knowledge that would otherwise support new learning.

Prior Knowledge *Can Be* Velcro for New Content

Eminent psychologist David P. Ausubel famously said, "The most important single factor influencing learning is what the learner already knows.

DOI: 10.4324/9781003657019-3

Ascertain this and teach him accordingly."[2] Building on this insight, his work in cognitive science and educational psychology highlights two key principles. First, meaningful learning occurs when students connect and integrate new material with their existing knowledge (schemas in long-term memory). Second, before introducing new content, teachers must assess the accuracy and strength of existing cognitive networks to determine students' readiness to integrate new material.

Jean Piaget (1952) shared this view. He described learning as a process of assimilation and accommodation. New information is either connected to existing knowledge (assimilation) or modifies existing schemas to make room for new material (accommodation).[3]

Given how foundational prior knowledge is in the learning process, the field has widely treated it as almost axiomatic. Yet, a recent study by Buchin and Mulligan (2025)[4] challenges this assumption. Through a carefully controlled experiment, they found that students with greater domain-specific knowledge did not automatically learn new content in that domain any better than peers with little prior knowledge. In other words, prior knowledge on its own did not guarantee additional learning gains.

Crucially, the study did not include an explicit activation phase in which new learning was deliberately linked to existing knowledge. While the study was well designed, it is worth noting that students studied the material for only three days. As Carl Hendrick points out, this hardly constitutes 'prior' knowledge in any meaningful educational sense.[5] Therefore, the null result can be interpreted as an example of what happens when prior knowledge is left dormant.

This study tells us that unless teachers actively activate relevant prior knowledge, by first surfacing it and then explicitly showing students how new learning connects, it risks remaining inert. Students are unlikely to make these links on their own. This is where prerequisite checks for understanding can help resurface the relevant prior knowledge needed to connect with new content.

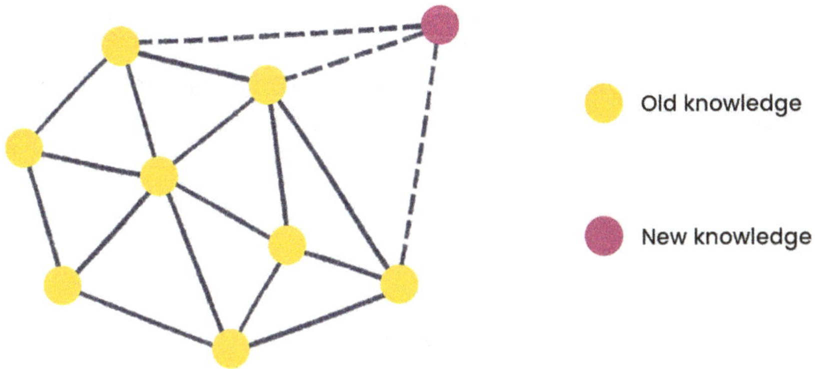

In discussing how a teacher can determine whether their instruction has been effective, Nuthall beautifully captures the interplay between checking for understanding and prior knowledge: " . . . in order to know if you have been effective, you must have some way of knowing what your students believed, knew, could do, or felt before you taught them and what your students believed, knew, could do, or felt after you taught them."[6]

Yet, as Nuthall explains, this is not as simple as it seems. His research highlights vast disparities in students' prior knowledge: while students collectively know about 50% of the curriculum content before it is taught, no single student knows the entire 50%. On average, each student begins with only a small portion, around 15%, of what the teacher intends them to learn. Prior knowledge is unevenly and unpredictably distributed.

In any given classroom:

- Around 20% of students may already grasp most of what is about to be taught;
- About 50% have partial or patchy knowledge that loosely relates to the topic;
- And roughly 20% may have little to no understanding at all.

This breakdown isn't a precise mathematical division; it's a heuristic, a way to capture the challenge teachers face when trying to pitch instruction to a room full of students all starting from different places. How can a teacher build new knowledge when the foundations are so varied?

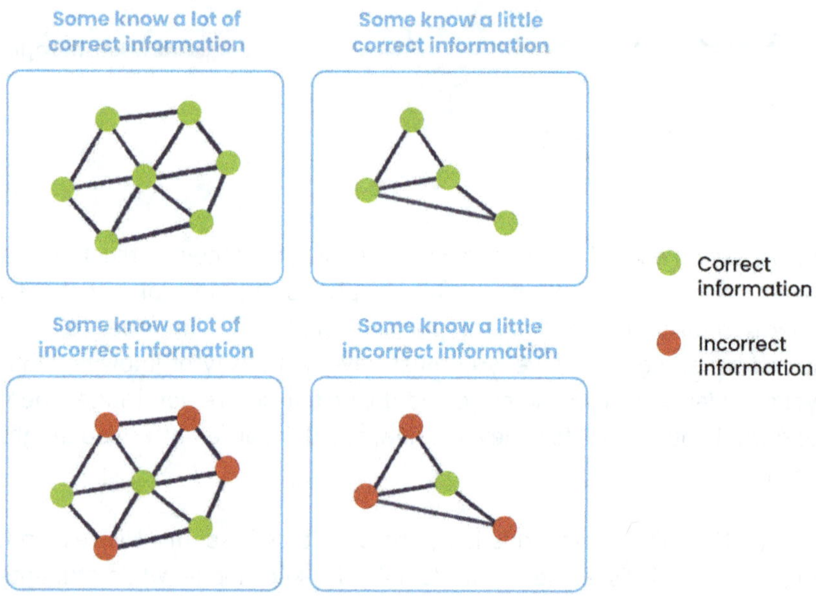

The challenge for teachers is ensuring the classroom experience is equitable, allowing all students, regardless of their starting point, to access the same ambitious curriculum.

Another challenge is that in thematic subjects like language, history, and geography, students acquire much of their knowledge outside of school, often in vastly different ways depending on their socioeconomic background.[7] The rise of social media and the internet as primary sources of information, coupled with the impact of COVID-19 on learning experiences, has only exacerbated these disparities.[8]

This tells us that students do not enter the classroom as blank slates. This is why schema theory is proving helpful to teachers. Properly understood, it helps explain how knowledge is organised and why some students integrate ideas more seamlessly than others.

Schema Theory

Schema theory helps teachers understand the role of prior knowledge in the learning process. The theory has academic utility, leading teachers to recognise the analogous nature of cognition: how knowledge is structured and recalled. While there are many definitions of schemas, it is generally accepted that they contain the following features:

- Generalised and Abstract: Formed from multiple experiences, schemas capture patterns while omitting unique contextual details of these experiences.
- Networked and Interconnected: Schemas exist in a web of related concepts, shaping perception and thought.
- Adaptive and Predictive: They help us interpret new situations and guide behaviour based on past knowledge.[9]

Students who possess robust schemas for a topic retain and recall new information more effectively, while those lacking prior knowledge struggle to integrate it. For teachers to optimise learning, they must first identify the extent and accuracy of students' prior knowledge to reveal misconceptions and gaps.[9,10,11]

Schema theory asserts that new information is more likely to be understood and remembered when it connects to existing knowledge structures. It's as though knowledge stored in long-term memory gives new information a helping hand through the bottleneck of working memory.

The following examples illustrate how teachers can enact schema theory in practice by actively checking for and activating prior knowledge before introducing new concepts. In each case, the teacher deliberately brings to the surface what students already know, diagnoses gaps or misconceptions, and then helps students link the new material to existing schemas.

EARLY YEARS PHONICS (AGE 4-5)

New content: Introduce the digraph "sh" (/sh/)

Prior knowledge: Students' knowledge of individual letter sounds, blending skills, and familiarity with oral language patterns.

Teacher moves:

- **Letter-sound correspondences**: Before introducing the digraph "sh," the teacher checks whether students can correctly identify and pronounce the individual sounds of the letters *s* and *h*. She displays flashcards and invites the class to rehearse the sounds together through a choral response, then cold calls a small number of students individually, deliberately selecting those whose prior knowledge may be less secure. These checks are important in determining if the children possess the foundational grapheme-phoneme correspondence knowledge necessary to combine the two letters meaningfully.
- **Phonemic awareness**: The teacher uses oral blending games to check that students can hear and manipulate phonemes. For instance, she says "/s/ - /u/ - /n/," prompting students to blend it as "sun." She begins with a choral practice, followed by cold calls to several pupils, sampling widely to gather feedback. This gives clear evidence of students' confidence in blending and segmenting sounds, a key step before fluent decoding.
- **Previous phonics recall**: The teacher revisits previously taught consonant-vowel-consonant (CVC) words like "sat" or "hop." She directs students to decode them to reinforce the idea that known sounds can combine into words.
- **Connecting to new learning**: Only after confirming this prior knowledge is secure does the teacher introduce the new digraph "sh"

using familiar words like "shop" and "shoe." She emphasises how the combination of *s* and *h* creates a new, single sound, linking it to known vocabulary and sounds.

This approach ensures that the new digraph doesn't appear in isolation but is integrated into an active, accurate phonics schema.

KS2 MATHEMATICS (AGES 7-11)

New content: Add fractions with unlike denominators (e.g., ½ + ¼)

Prior knowledge: Students' understanding of part-whole relationships, equivalence, and previous experience with adding like fractions.

Teacher moves:

- **Understanding denominators**: The teacher uses a visual model (e.g., shaded circles) to check whether students understand that the denominator indicates the number (and therefore the size) of equal parts. She poses the question, "Which is bigger: ½ or ¼? Why?" and asks students to record their answers on mini whiteboards. This approach enables her to collect responses from all thirty students almost simultaneously, rather than relying on a few volunteers, providing a more comprehensive and diagnostic insight into the class's understanding.
- **Equivalent fractions**: The teacher prompts students to find fractions equivalent to 1/2 (e.g., 2/4) to see whether they can recall and manipulate equivalent forms. A quick number line activity or fraction wall helps refresh this concept.
- **Adding like fractions**: The teacher gives students problems like 1/4 + 1/4 and asks them to explain their reasoning aloud. She checks for misconceptions, such as students incorrectly adding denominators.
- **Introducing new content**: Only after these schema checks does the teacher model how to add 1/2 + 1/4 by converting 1/2 to 2/4, then

adding 2/4 + 1/4 = 3/4. She explains that we're building on what they already know about counting like parts.

By anchoring the new method in the prior schema, the teacher reduces cognitive load and promotes conceptual understanding.

KS3 ENGLISH LITERATURE (AGES 11-14)

New content: Begin study of *A Midsummer Night's Dream*

Prior knowledge: Students' understanding of literary genres, themes, Elizabethan culture, and dramatic conventions.

Teacher moves:

- **Genre knowledge**: The teacher begins by checking what students already know about Shakespearean comedy, asking, "What do you expect to find in a comedy?" She gathers ideas such as mistaken identity, love triangles, and magical elements. Students first record their initial thoughts on mini whiteboards, then refine them through think-pair-share, before the teacher uses cold calling to sample responses. This layered approach helps reveal the depth and accuracy of students' existing knowledge structures while giving them two opportunities to rehearse and clarify their thinking before sharing with the whole class.
- **Thematic connections**: To activate their thematic schema, the teacher asks students to recall what they can about previous texts with similar themes, such as *Romeo and Juliet* (love and conflict) and *The Highwayman* (forbidden love).
- **Cultural background**: The teacher probes for recall of the Elizabethan worldview. Questions like, "What did people in Shakespeare's time believe about fate or magic?" help reactivate relevant cultural context.

- **Dramatic devices**: She reviews common techniques like soliloquy, dramatic irony, and rhyming couplets. Students might identify these from earlier texts or spot them in short excerpts.

Students are ready to engage meaningfully with the play because the new material feels more familiar. The teacher has been intentional in activating the most relevant prior knowledge.

These examples demonstrate the dual benefit of checking for understanding when activating prior knowledge. Each check serves to identify gaps and misconceptions. Additionally, by strategically revisiting relevant prior knowledge, students can build new learning on existing structures. As a result, it becomes more likely that new material is understood, retained, and ready for application when needed.

Ensuring that this essential knowledge is learned meaningfully increases the likelihood that students will retain it within their schemas. This connection leads naturally to our next critical intersection of prior knowledge and checking for understanding: moving students beyond rote memorisation towards meaningful learning.

2 Prior Knowledge and Meaning-making

This chapter focuses on meaning-making and the role of advance organisers in scaffolding fragile prior learning. At first, this may feel like a brief detour. However, the ideas explored here align with this book's central messages.

One core message is that effective checks for understanding increase participation, deepen thinking, and support students in making sense of the material. Meaning-making occurs when students successfully connect new concepts to what they already know. When those connections are weak or inaccurate, learning becomes fragile. An advance organiser is one way of supporting students when their prior knowledge is insufficient to sustain new learning.

Strong checks for understanding also rely heavily on a teacher's domain-specific knowledge. Designing an effective advance organiser requires teachers to analyse content at a level they might not otherwise consider. This process sharpens teachers' understanding of the conceptual structure of a topic and, in turn, supports the creation of better questions; the type that provides a clearer window into students' thinking.

Finally, this chapter reinforces an important principle: checks for understanding are not measures of learning (a distinction explored later in the book). They are diagnostic tools intended to inform what happens next. When teachers identify that students are working from a fragile base,

DOI: 10.4324/9781003657019-4

they need a way to firm up understanding. Advance organisers are designed to fill in any gaps.

Why Knowing Isn't Enough: The Shift to Meaningful Learning

Canadian-American cognitive psychologist and psycholinguist Steven Pinker once said:

> "Cognitive psychology has shown that the mind best understands facts when they are woven into a conceptual fabric, such as a narrative, mental map, or intuitive theory. Disconnected facts in the mind are like unlinked pages on the Web: They might as well not exist."[12]

Meaningful learning occurs when new information is integrated into existing knowledge structures by forging non-arbitrary connections. [2,13] When this happens, students can retrieve and apply knowledge flexibly rather than simply reciting facts under controlled conditions.

When teachers focus on how students organise knowledge, students are more likely to recall prior knowledge and integrate new ideas. Many view organising knowledge as administrative or superficial, but it is crucial for effective learning. Thoughtful organisation prevents knowledge from becoming isolated facts that lack clarity or meaning.

Empirical evidence from cognitive science supports these claims. Emeritus professor Frederick Reif noted that the recall and application of knowledge depend on how it is structured. He claimed, "Poorly organised knowledge cannot be readily remembered or used. But students don't know how to organise their knowledge effectively."[14]

What role, then, does checking for understanding play in shaping students' knowledge organisation? To answer this, we must return to Ausubel's landmark insight: effective teaching begins by recognising and activating what students already know. Consider students beginning their study of *A Midsummer Night's Dream*. By first administering a low-stakes quiz or diagnostic check, a teacher can assess students' prior knowledge of anchoring concepts vital to Shakespearean comedy. These are concepts students have likely encountered elsewhere in the curriculum. Such an assessment might reveal significant disparities in students' prior knowledge.

When faced with these knowledge gaps, the teacher may worry that some students lack the background to access and integrate the new material into their schema. Rather than diluting the expectations of some, the teacher can intervene strategically. This means explicitly "creating" and scaffolding the prior knowledge that students need.[7]

In many ways, we can prime students for meaningful learning by first checking the knowledge in their existing schemata. Where there are significant prior knowledge gaps, we might scaffold students' knowledge organisation by creating an advance organiser, as Ausubel called it.

To understand advance organisers and how they support weak prior knowledge, first consider how knowledge is structured.

The science of learning shows that the way students organise knowledge within their schemas directly shapes what they notice and learn. Your students' schemas affect their ability to learn new material. Students do not perceive knowledge in the same way as you do as an expert. Their novice schemas keep them from noticing essential content unless you guide them.

This distinction becomes even clearer when exploring the differences between expert and novice schemas. As an expert, you naturally possess richly structured, interconnected networks of concepts and facts. In contrast, students' schemas are typically fragmented, superficial, and incomplete. However, it's worth noting that the novice-to-expert journey is not a strict dichotomy but a continuum, as powerfully captured in the

Five-Stage Model of Adult Skill Acquisition developed by Stuart and Hubert Dreyfus (2004).[15] The Dreyfus model claims learners progress through five stages:

- Novice - dependent on rules and context-free facts;
- Advanced beginner - beginning to notice context-specific features;
- Competent - overwhelmed by complexity but starting to take ownership of decisions;
- Proficient - able to see patterns and important features without needing to rely solely on rules;
- Expert - acting intuitively, based on deep experience and well-developed schemas.

Note: Although the Dreyfus model describes adult skill acquisition, it can still provide a useful lens for considering how students move from novice towards expert.

Significantly, progress through these stages requires more than harvesting facts; it depends on experience, contextual understanding, and emotional involvement. Schema maturation involves moving from rigid, rule-based schemas to flexible, intuitive ones.

As this maturation unfolds, students progressively build more intricate schemas, automating key ideas and shifting attention from isolated facts to broader principles.

Understanding this progression helps teachers resist the "curse of knowledge," the tendency among experts to forget how challenging new concepts can be for novices to grasp. Schema, in this context, refers to students' mental models or frameworks used for understanding information. Overcoming the curse of knowledge requires teachers to frequently check for understanding in ways that probe students' schema for depth and flexibility.

To further illustrate how knowledge organisation shapes learning, consider research from two landmark studies. In 1946, A.D. de Groot explored chess masters' perception of chess problems.[16] Unsurprisingly, chess experts identified superior moves more rapidly and explored potential moves more deeply than their novice counterparts. Their schemata allowed them to quickly recognise meaningful patterns rather than viewing individual chess pieces in isolation.

De Groot's findings underscore a critical principle: *effective knowledge organisation depends on explicitly recognising and highlighting associative connections among ideas.*

Another illuminating study by Chi, Feltovich, and Glaser examined how physics experts and novices categorised problems.[17] Novices tended to group problems based on surface-level similarities, such as the objects involved or visual appearances. In contrast, experts categorised problems based on deeper underlying principles, such as Newton's Laws or the Conservation of Energy. Experts' knowledge was effectively indexed and anchored around these key principles, allowing rapid retrieval and application.

This research leads to a second principle: *teachers must help students firmly anchor new knowledge in the overarching concepts and foundational principles of a discipline.*

Although novice students initially lack the sophisticated, interconnected schemas of experts, these structures can, and must, be intentionally developed over time. One method that supports this process is Ausubel's advance organisers.

An Advance Organiser Can Act as a Scaffold for Weak Prior Knowledge

Advance organisers serve as ideational scaffolds that front-load and stabilise key concepts, enabling new knowledge to be organised effectively.[2,7,18] They can help students organise and connect ideas as they construct new knowledge.

We have already seen from Buchin and Mulligan (2025)[4] that prior knowledge, by itself, does not reliably boost learning. Teachers need to be intentional, taking deliberate steps to activate and link relevant prior knowledge to the concepts about to be introduced. Advance organisers provide a scaffold that transforms prior knowledge into what Gurlitt et al. (2011)[19] call a *proto-schema*: an initial mental framework that students can build upon. In this way, advance organisers become a living structure to which new content can meaningfully attach.

Advance organisers are fundamentally different from summaries. Summaries typically itemise or list the content to be covered, functioning as checklists without actively engaging students' existing schemas.[20] Advance organisers, however, act as pre-instructional frameworks, providing generalised and abstract concepts, known as subsumers, that anchor and organise new information as it is introduced. This crucial difference promotes meaningful learning by explicitly connecting new ideas to overarching themes and big-picture concepts.

Operating at a higher level of abstraction, advance organisers highlight the essential themes and patterns within a topic, allowing students to perceive underlying relationships. Their general and inclusive nature provides students with an effective cognitive structure for integrating seemingly discrete pieces of information into coherent, meaningful schemas.

Ausubel argued that knowledge is optimally structured hierarchically, with overarching concepts at the top and progressively more specific details arranged systematically below. Joseph Novak's influential work on concept maps reinforces this idea, demonstrating that meaningful knowledge develops through interconnected, hierarchical structures that move from general concepts to specific details. [20]

Extensive research supports the efficacy of advance organisers. Metastudies in Robert Marzano and colleagues' *Classroom Instruction that Works* indicate high effect sizes for advance organisers.[21] Marzano categorises them into four distinct types: expository, narrative, skimming, and graphic. All four have demonstrated strong effects. Expository organisers are particularly useful when students lack sufficient prior knowledge.[7,18] When teachers check for understanding, as a part of a formative range-finding to gauge students' prior knowledge, they may uncover gaps in the accuracy or extent of students' existing knowledge. In such cases, an expository organiser provides a structured scaffold. This scaffold enables students to access new material by helping them establish the conceptual foundations they may otherwise lack.

For this reason, this chapter focuses specifically on how expository organisers can support meaningful learning. Also, despite the strength of this research base, much of the practical guidance available to teachers focuses almost exclusively on graphic organisers, with far fewer concrete classroom examples of other forms.

Expository organisers usually take the form of short, descriptive texts introducing students to the overarching concepts of a topic. Sometimes students' existing knowledge is limited, and the curriculum sequencing has not prepared them for the new topic. In these situations, stories, analogies, or concrete examples can act as entry points.[18] The advance organiser must be accessible and presented at an appropriate conceptual level for students. It should bridge prior knowledge with new content, activate relevant existing schemas, and serve as a reference point. This helps orient students as they progressively deepen their understanding throughout the learning process.

To illustrate these ideas, show how advance organisers scaffold limited prior knowledge, and highlight the critical role of checking for understanding in their effective use, let's examine an example from KS3 geography (ages 11–14).

THE LIVING WEB: UNDERSTANDING THE TROPICAL RAINFOREST

Imagine a spider's web: complex, beautiful, and fragile. Every strand connects and supports another. Pull one thread and the rest begin to shift. Some strands stretch or break. That's what the tropical rainforest is like. It's more than a collection of trees and animals. It's a world of connections between plants and animals, people and places, the forest, and the climate itself.

In the rainforest, trees contribute to the creation of rain. Rain feeds the soil. Soil feeds the plants and trees. Plants feed insects. Insects feed birds. And on and on it goes. People are part of this web, too: gathering food, discovering medicines, and relying on the forest in ways they may not even realise.

But this web can be broken. When trees are cut down, the balance shifts. One change can lead to another. Sometimes, the damage spreads further than anyone expects.

As you explore the rainforest, keep some questions in the back of your mind:

- *How do living things survive here, and how do they depend on each other?*
- *What happens when one part of the web is disturbed?*
- *Why does it matter if species disappear?*
- *Is it possible for people to use the forest without harming it?*

The rainforest is full of connections. Plants, animals, and the environment all depend on each other in surprising ways. Let's explore how those connections work.

Introducing a High-level Concept Through Abstraction and Metaphor

Using abstract, inclusive ideas, such as the emotionally resonant spider's web, helps students grasp new content by making interdependence concrete and relatable. Ausubel's theory supports this: advance organisers such as the web metaphor model systems thinking, encompass relationships among all living and non-living components, and connect broad topics like biodiversity, food webs, climate change, and human impact.

Hierarchical Organisation of Knowledge

The organiser is structured hierarchically. The top-level concepts include interdependence and cause and effect, represented in the organiser by the phrases "Every strand is connected . . ." and "One change can lead to another . . ." respectively. Mid-level concepts, such as adaptations and biodiversity, are introduced through questions like "How do living things survive here and how do they depend on each other?" and "Why does it matter if species disappear?" Ausubel presented learning as a hierarchical process, beginning with broad, general concepts, and progressing to detailed, specific knowledge.

Subsumption and Anchoring

Subsumption occurs when students meaningfully connect new knowledge to prior ideas. The organiser *may* facilitate this process when introduced and engaged appropriately by linking organically to previously embedded knowledge:

- Adaptations of rainforest species slot under the question, "How do living things survive here and how do they depend on each other?"
- Deforestation and climate change are anchored to the principle: "One change can lead to another."
- Biodiversity loss is explored through the lens of the question: "Why does it matter if species disappear?"
- Sustainable practices are guided by the inquiry: "Is it possible for people to use the forest without harming it?"

The organiser ensures new learning does not occur in isolation. Every fact students encounter can be effectively "filed" under an existing conceptual category, thereby enhancing comprehension and memory.

Promoting Retention and Transfer

Because the metaphor, themes, and questions are clear, relatable, and emotionally anchored, students are more likely to retain new knowledge, revisit central questions, and apply their understanding to new issues.

For instance, a lesson on palm oil production isn't just about agriculture; it becomes a reflection on what happens when *one part of the web is disturbed*. A discussion about ecotourism connects directly to the idea of *using the forest without breaking it*.

The organiser builds mental "handles" that make later content easier to grasp, connect, and recall.

Using Checking for Understanding to Secure Big Ideas

Creating an advance organiser like the Living Web expository organiser requires the teacher to consider the hierarchical organisation of knowledge. It prompts greater attentiveness to overarching, inclusive concepts that serve as "holding baskets" for the more nuanced ideas, facts, and details that follow.

To "create" the prior knowledge students will require to access new material, students must first understand the concepts front-loaded by the advance organiser. Without this foundation, they are unlikely to make the meaningful conceptual links that lead to deep learning.

Like almost all techniques in a teacher's toolkit, advance organisers are not a stand-alone strategy. And like nearly all methods a teacher can call on, they are most effective when paired with checking for understanding. By firming up the top-level concepts in advance, students are primed to receive new material with greater accuracy and clarity.

To fully leverage the benefits of an advance organiser, it should be revisited at key moments across the topic. In *Teaching WalkThrus*, Sherrington and Caviglioli show the power of connecting specific details (small picture) to the overarching big picture.[22] This reflects Ausubel's subsumption theory.

The teacher can make explicit links between small-picture details, such as trees releasing water vapour through transpiration, and the overarching concept of interdependence. For example, the teacher can explain how trees not only rely on rain but also help produce it. Their role is central to the survival of everything else in the rainforest.

On the next page, you will see a reconstructed example of a student's work. While the original scanned version was too big to reproduce in full, the example retains a representative selection of their annotations to illustrate how the teacher engineered opportunities for students to revisit their organiser and fortify conceptual connections. Students stuck their advance organisers across a double-page spread. They revisited the organiser throughout the topic, adding annotations, rehearsing explanations of the story, and making explicit links between new learning and the unit's overarching themes.

Throughout lessons, the teacher uses cold calling to probe students' understanding, exit tickets to identify gaps and misconceptions at the end of the instructional sequence, and hinge questions and mini whiteboards to check whether all students are forging the intended links.

The key is to make these links explicit and ensure students understand them, allowing them to connect new information meaningfully to the conceptual anchors established by the organiser.

Advance organisers help set the stage for meaningful learning. They are only the beginning. As students engage in new material, building deep, transferable knowledge is not automatic. This is where the role of consolidation becomes critical. Organising knowledge provides an anchor for new material. Consolidation secures it, transforming fleeting perceptions into lasting, flexible understanding. This allows students to retrieve and apply their knowledge when it matters most.

The Amazon stores approximately 100 billion tonnes of carbon in its trees and soil. Cutting trees releases this carbon dioxide into the atmosphere, contributing to the enhanced greenhouse effect.

In the Amazon Rainforest, the constant temperature (around 27°C) and high annual rainfall (over 2000 mm) allow dense vegetation to flourish. These tall trees release water vapour through transpiration, forming rain clouds that sustain the same humid climate the trees depend on.

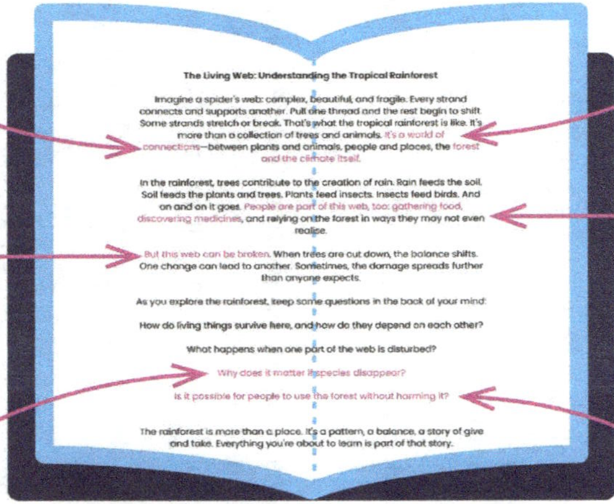

The Living Web: Understanding the Tropical Rainforest

Imagine a spider's web: complex, beautiful, and fragile. Every strand connects and supports another. Pull one thread and the rest begin to shift. Some strands stretch or break. That's what the tropical rainforest is like. It's more than a collection of trees and animals. It's a world of connections—between plants and animals, people and places, the forest and the climate itself.

In the rainforest, trees contribute to the creation of rain. Rain feeds the soil. Soil feeds the plants and trees. Plants feed insects. Insects feed birds. And on and on it goes. People are part of this web, too: gathering food, discovering medicines, and relying on the forest in ways they may not even realise.

But this web can be broken. When trees are cut down, the balance shifts. One change can lead to another. Sometimes, the damage spreads further than anyone expects.

As you explore the rainforest, keep some questions in the back of your mind:

How do living things survive here, and how do they depend on each other?

What happens when one part of the web is disturbed?

Why does it matter if species disappear?

Is it possible for people to use the forest without harming it?

The rainforest is more than a place. It's a pattern, a balance, a story of give and take. Everything you're about to learn is part of that story.

Deforestation for cattle ranching and soy farming reduces canopy cover, lowering transpiration and rainfall. Drier conditions lead to soil erosion, wildfires, and biodiversity loss.

Indigenous groups such as the Yanomami live sustainably, taking only what they need and allowing areas to regenerate. Many modern medicines originate from rainforest plants — for example, quinine from cinchona trees and the rosy periwinkle used to treat leukaemia.

If pollinators like bees or bats decline, fruit trees fail to reproduce, which then affects animals that rely on those fruits.

Selective logging, ecotourism, and sustainable agroforestry (growing coffee under tree canopies) can provide income without large-scale deforestation.

3 Prior Knowledge and Consolidation

To understand consolidation, it's helpful to consider how memories form. New memories begin as ephemeral and nebulous, their form indistinct; unless sufficiently rehearsed, they fade quickly. For information to be absorbed into schemata, it requires consolidation, a process that takes time, retrieval practice, and, counterintuitively, forgetting. (More on that later.)

Consolidation is the process of shifting from knowing something to understanding it and then applying it meaningfully. Inspired by the work of Efrat Furst, the following example illustrates this shift:

STAGE 1: KNOWING (MEMORISATION WITHOUT DEEP UNDERSTANDING)

A student remembers that $\frac{1}{2} + \frac{1}{2} = 1$ because they can recall the rule: "When adding fractions with the same denominator, add the numerators." The student can solve similar problems but struggles to explain their reasoning beyond simply repeating the rule. If presented with a word problem, they may fail to see the connection to fractions.

STAGE 2: EARLY CONSOLIDATION (CONNECTING TO MEANING)

The student is asked to visualise fractions using a number line or fraction bars. They explain in their own words how two halves make a whole, reinforcing conceptual understanding rather than just procedural recall.

DOI: 10.4324/9781003657019-5

When encountering a different but related problem, like "What is $3/4 + 1/4$?", they generalise the idea, rather than simply recall an isolated rule.

At this stage, early consolidation begins as the student builds meaningful connections.

STAGE 3: UNDERSTANDING (TRANSFERABLE KNOWLEDGE)

Now the student is ready to apply the concept to multiple contexts, such as measuring ingredients in a recipe or splitting a bill. They recognise fractions as representations of division, connecting the concept to other areas of the curriculum. They predict and explain new scenarios, such as why $1/2 \times 1/2$ is smaller than $1/2$, demonstrating true conceptual flexibility.

At this point, fractions are no longer just a rule to memorise; they are a deeply understood concept that can be applied flexibly.[23]

Checking for understanding is the teacher's tool for monitoring and guiding this consolidation process. It allows teachers to see whether a student is stuck in rote memorisation, making meaningful connections, or ready to apply knowledge. Without it, misconceptions may go unnoticed, or students may believe they understand something when, in reality, they are simply recalling isolated facts. Also, the very act of checking for understanding supports the rehearsal necessary for consolidation.

At the same time, while striving to help students make meaning, it is equally important to recognise that rote memorisation still plays a crucial role in their learning journey.

In her aptly titled article, "Understanding 'Understanding,'" Efrat Furst reminds us that meaning-making is "unequivocally an important teaching goal." However, Efrat also stresses that the process of consolidation builds on earlier, more surface-level stages of learning. Rote learning and memorisation might be considered a catalyst, stepping stones toward a deeper conceptual understanding.[23]

Memorisation can support working memory. Cognitive load theory notes that rehearsed, automated knowledge requires minimal working memory to retrieve. When such knowledge is automated, working memory is free for demanding tasks like reasoning and problem-solving.

Ultimately, rote learning is not the enemy of meaningful learning. It's the foundation on which it develops.

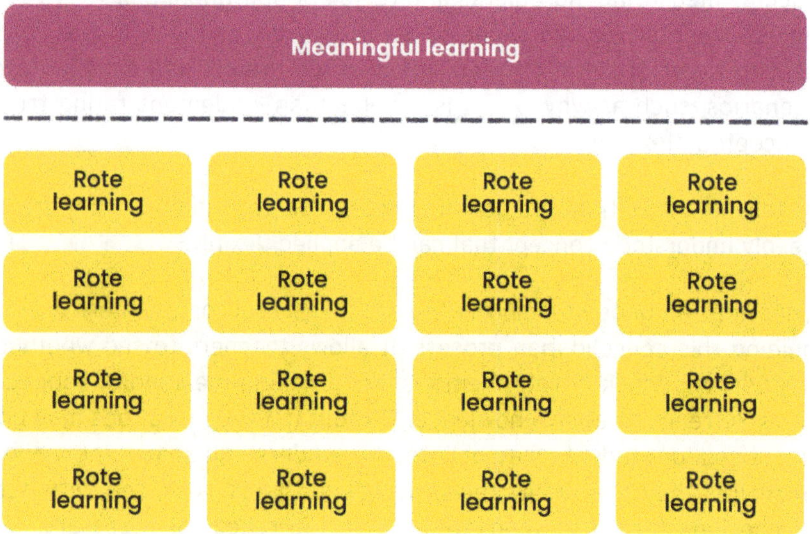

Making Thinking Visible

A powerful way to check for understanding is elaboration, or elaborative interrogation. Elaboration asks students to connect new material to what they already know and explain this in their own words.[24] It turns assumed understanding into visible thinking, making it less likely that students give the correct answer for the wrong reason (more on that later).

Elaborative interrogation involves asking questions that probe students' thinking. For example, prompts such as "Why is this true?" or "How does this connect to what we already know?" reveal students' thinking by surfacing the reasoning behind their responses. Such insights clarify whether students are drawing from secure or fragile schema and can help reveal misconceptions.

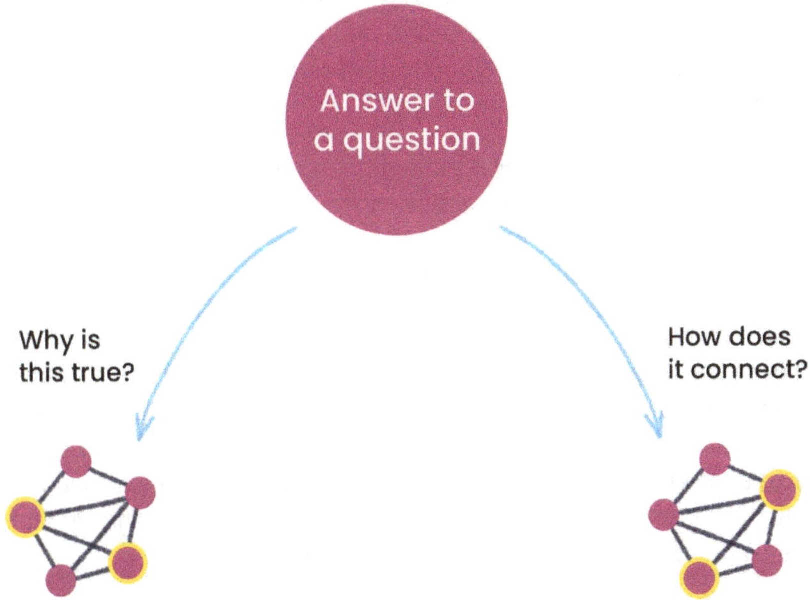

Elaboration also supports deep processing. When students compare and contrast similar concepts, principles, and strategies, they build richer, more distinct representations. As they learn to distinguish between related ideas, they gain conceptual clarity. This deeper processing makes retention and recall more likely because the material is meaningfully connected.

Studies by Martin and Pressley and by Dunlosky and colleagues show that elaborative interrogation, for example, answering "why" questions, helps students retain and apply knowledge more effectively.[25,26] This process requires students to verbalise and justify their thinking. By doing this, they support consolidation, transforming fragile, short-term memories into stable, long-term ones. Each explanation reconstructs memory, weaving new ideas into existing knowledge and reinforcing retrieval pathways. Elaboration helps students turn unclear or half-formed ideas into clear, lasting understanding.

Crucially, both studies found that effortfully trying to explain, even without arriving at a fully accurate explanation, can activate relevant schema and promote better recall. As Dunlosky and colleagues note, "Elaborative interrogation is effective even when learners don't produce adequate answers . . . the attempt itself activates prior knowledge supportive of the new fact."[26]

In other words, when students attempt to explain why something is true or compare it with what they already know, they activate relevant schemas, even if their reasoning is incomplete. In doing so, they begin the cognitive work of integrating new knowledge into existing mental frameworks and consolidating their understanding.

This has significant implications for checking for understanding. Surface-level recall questions can mislead teachers into thinking students have a better grasp of the material than they do. Students often recall isolated facts and yet still hold misconceptions or fail to connect ideas meaningfully. Because misconceptions often coexist with correct information, they may go undetected unless teachers probe deeper.

Elaborative interrogation makes students' thinking visible. It exposes the structure of their understanding, allowing teachers to respond with more precision.

Take this example. A teacher asks, "What is the climate like in a tropical rainforest?" A student might respond, "Hot and wet." While technically correct, the answer reveals little about their depth of understanding. A teacher using elaborative interrogation might follow up with:

- "Why do you think it's always hot and wet in tropical rainforests?"
- "How does the climate affect the types of vegetation that grow there?"
- "Can you think of other places in the world with similar conditions? Are they all rainforests?"

These questions prompt students to connect facts to overarching concepts such as latitude, convective rainfall, biodiversity, and adaptation. They reveal whether students can explain relationships, apply concepts across contexts, and distinguish between surface similarities and deep structures.

Of course, elaboration is effortful. These types of questions are cognitively demanding, and expecting all students to respond meaningfully in the moment may be unrealistic. That's why, later in this book, we'll explore how techniques such as wait time and mini whiteboards can help students rehearse and refine their thinking before sharing their contributions with the rest of the class.

The 3Cs: A Shortcut to Deep Thinking

Another strategy to help students connect new concepts to prior knowledge is Arthur Shimamura's 3Cs Technique (Categorise, Compare, and Contrast), from his book *MARGE: A Whole-brain Learning Approach for Students and Teachers*.[27] This technique invites students to organise knowledge, examine similarities and differences, and articulate conceptual boundaries, all core to schema development and deep learning.

The 3Cs draw on what students already know and help to build a bridge to new material. The technique helps students organise their knowledge by prompting them to classify ideas, make meaningful comparisons, and draw distinctions. When students categorise, compare, and contrast concepts, they begin to integrate knowledge more deeply by placing it within hierarchies, identifying relationships, and drawing conceptual boundaries.

In doing so, students go beyond surface-level familiarity by tackling questions requiring reasoning, relational thinking, and reflection on how ideas connect or diverge. These questions move them past mere recall, encouraging deeper understanding.

Let's look at how teachers might use the 3Cs across different subjects:

Science

- *Categorise:* "Which group does this type of rock belong to: igneous, sedimentary or metamorphic? How do you know?"
- *Compare:* "How are photosynthesis and respiration similar?"
- *Contrast:* "What makes endothermic and exothermic reactions different?"

History

- *Categorise:* "Would you place this event under political, economic, or social causes? Why?"
- *Compare:* "How was the American Revolution similar to the French Revolution?"
- *Contrast:* "What distinguishes the ideologies of fascism and communism?"

Maths

- *Categorise:* "Is this a linear or quadratic equation? How do you know?"
- *Compare:* "How is multiplying fractions like multiplying whole numbers?"
- *Contrast:* "What's the key difference between area and perimeter?"

These types of questions reveal where students are in their learning. Because they require a more nuanced understanding, they often surface knowledge gaps and misconceptions that would otherwise remain hidden. The 3Cs refine schema development by encouraging students to organise knowledge more efficiently and deeply. They also provide teachers with valuable insight into the structure and quality of student understanding.

Techniques such as elaboration and the 3Cs ensure that learning is not just about retention but about making knowledge usable, adaptive, and meaningful.

So far, we've explored how prior knowledge supports learning by providing anchors to help secure new material. When prior knowledge is effectively activated and links are made explicit, it promotes understanding and deep processing of new material. But there are situations where students' prior knowledge can hinder learning. The next section explores this issue and discusses potential solutions.

What Happens When Prior Knowledge Backfires?

Meaningful learning depends on teachers leveraging prior learning by activating appropriate and accurate prior knowledge. However, there are times when what students already know can impede learning. One way this happens is when students import everyday meanings into technical contexts.[1]

In their study about an introductory statistics class, Delmas and colleagues found that students' prior knowledge hindered learning.[28] They found students' understanding of everyday words, such as *random* and *spread,* interfered with learning. In everyday language, random often suggests a lack of pattern, haphazardness, or unpredictability. If you say, "I chose those songs at random," it might mean you picked them without any particular order or system. In statistics, however, the word "random" has a much more nuanced meaning. Random sampling, for example, is a method where every member of a population has an equal chance of being selected. This is a very structured process and therefore has a contradictory definition compared to the everyday meaning of the word "random."

This study highlights that prior knowledge, while essential, can sometimes disrupt learning. It also reinforces the importance of clarifying when technical definitions differ from everyday usage. Teachers should not assume that a correct answer reflects deep understanding.

One practical response to this study would be to identify and map the tier 3 vocabulary in your subject that carries alternative or even contradictory meanings in everyday language. Teach these differences explicitly, using clear examples from both contexts, then check for understanding, ensuring that students are not simply reciting definitions but genuinely grasping how meanings shift across domains.

The Danger of Overextended Analogies

Another example of prior knowledge interfering with learning occurs when analogies are used to help make abstract concepts concrete. Analogies are powerful cognitive tools that help students connect new learning to what they already know. However, analogies have limits. If students fail to recognise these, or if the teacher pushes an analogy too far, it can hinder learning and promote misconceptions.

Take the analogy that tectonic plates are like pieces of a jigsaw puzzle that fit together to form the Earth's crust. This analogy has limits: jigsaw pieces have fixed, rigid edges, while tectonic plate boundaries are dynamic, deforming, and interacting in complex ways (e.g., subduction zones). Also, plates don't just passively fit together; they constantly shift due to mantle convection and stress forces. This analogy can impede learning because students may assume plate boundaries are static and fixed rather than recognising continuous movement and deformation.

When using analogies, it is important to recognise their limits and constantly check students' understanding to ensure they are only committing the relevant analogous knowledge to their long-term memory.

Cross-curricular Pitfalls: When Knowledge Doesn't Transfer Well

Forging cross-curricular links has an intuitive appeal. But selecting inappropriate prior knowledge from other curriculum areas can also impede learning. Research by Anne Beaufort (2007) on Generic Writing and Its Limitations Across Domains found that college writing courses often teach writing as a one-size-fits-all approach.[29] Beaufort argues that writing conventions vary dramatically across disciplines (e.g., history, engineering, and business each has different expectations for structure, evidence, and argumentation). A student trained in general essay writing may struggle when asked to write a scientific report because they lack knowledge of discipline-specific genres.

Beaufort's study highlights that, when making cross-curricular links, teachers should check whether students are adapting their prior knowledge to support the learning of new, domain-specific content, or simply transferring it verbatim from another subject without adjustment.

Cross-curricular links can enrich learning by helping students draw on what they already know. But approach with care. Avoid tenuous connections, ensure the crossover promotes learning in both subjects, and, above all, frequently check for understanding to ensure the links are shaping students' understanding as intended.

Stubborn Misconceptions

Of all the ways checking for understanding helps students use prior knowledge to learn new ideas, arguably the most important is identifying erroneous knowledge and misconceptions.

Erroneous prior knowledge becomes especially problematic when new learning contradicts students' existing beliefs. Some errors are easily corrected through explicit refutation, for example, the misconception that Pluto is a planet.[1] However, inaccuracies deeply woven into students' conceptual networks, their schema, are incredibly resistant to correction. These inaccuracies have a name: misconceptions.

Misconceptions are stubborn and resilient. They persist because they've been reinforced over time. We've seen how meaningful learning occurs when students connect what they are learning to what they already know. Information that fits well with existing schema is congruent: it matches students' existing beliefs and understanding, integrates well, and is retained for a long time. However, research by Greve and colleagues indicates that schema-incongruent information, ideas and concepts that contradict prior knowledge, can sometimes be remembered just as well, or even better.[30] Such misconceptions are especially persistent because they blend accurate and inaccurate details, often appear in multiple contexts, and, in some cases, even help us make sense of the world.

To illustrate how misconceptions persist, consider the commonly held belief that the sun rises in the east and sets in the west. This misconception is practically useful: it has helped people plan their day around sunrise and sunset without understanding orbital mechanics. In fact, for most of human history, this simplified model worked well enough for agriculture, navigation, and religious calendars. However, this flawed belief breaks down when we try to explain phenomena like the seasons. Only by recognising the limitations of this misconception can we understand why the Earth's tilt, not our distance from the Sun, causes seasonal changes.

Deeply held misconceptions can take time to overcome, even with direct intervention. A study by Dunbar and Fugelsang tested students' understanding of seasonal change, finding that only 25% could accurately explain it.[31] The same students were tested again after watching an educational video explaining how seasons change. Only 2% of students revised their misconceptions. While the video improved students' understanding of Earth's orbit, it failed to help them grasp how the Sun's angle affects the seasons. Rather than restructuring knowledge, students often just adapt their misconceptions.

Addressing misconceptions requires patience and strategic intervention. If a misconception has been encountered on multiple occasions and in different contexts, it won't be corrected with a single explanation or refutation. Common misconceptions, and when and how they will be addressed, should be carefully mapped out across the curriculum. Just as students build knowledge over time, so too must teachers systematically dismantle misconceptions, ensuring that erroneous ideas are actively surfaced and corrected before they become deeply ingrained.

Breaking down a misconception requires more than a quick correction. Teachers must explicitly reveal why it is wrong, modelling examples that contrast the misconception with the correct understanding. A single explanation is rarely sufficient. Instead, students should engage in elaborative checking for understanding, explaining their reasoning so teachers can ensure the misconception is truly being overwritten. Revisiting the misconception over time is essential. Without frequent checks, students may slip back into old, faulty thinking. Only through repeated exposure and deliberate practice can we be confident that students' schema has truly shifted.

One of the most effective ways for surfacing misconceptions, hinge questions, is explored in detail in Chapter 10 of this book.

Ultimately, effective teaching isn't merely about "covering the content" but about ensuring students' existing cognitive frameworks are robust enough to absorb it. Regular and purposeful checks for understanding support this, ensuring that every student moves from superficial knowledge to meaningful, lasting learning.

Section 1 Checking for Understanding and Prior Knowledge Concluding Principles for Practice

1. **Checking for understanding must begin with prior knowledge.**

   Before teaching new content, teachers need reliable ways of surfacing what students already know, how secure that knowledge is, and how it is organised. Without this, instruction risks building on fragile or inaccurate foundations.

2. **Correct answers are not evidence of understanding.**

   Students can recall facts while holding misconceptions or failing to connect ideas meaningfully. Checks for understanding must probe reasoning and relationships and surface misconceptions, not just check for correctness.

3. **Prior knowledge must be activated and organised to support learning.**

   Existing knowledge does not automatically help students learn. Teachers must deliberately activate, refine, and, when necessary, construct the prior knowledge required for new learning to make sense.

4. **When prior knowledge is weak, teachers need a planned response, not lowered expectations.**

   Advance organisers provide one way of scaffolding fragile knowledge while preserving curricular ambition. They help students access complex material without simplifying it.

5. **Checking for understanding is diagnostic, not evaluative.**

   Its purpose is not to judge learning but to inform what happens next: whether to proceed, revisit, consolidate, or intervene. Effective teaching depends on responding intelligently to what checks reveal.

Section 1: Checking for Understanding and Prior Knowledge References

1. Ambrose, S.A., Bridges, M.W., DiPietro, M., Lovett, M.C., and Norman, M.K. (2010) *How learning works: Seven research-based principles for smart teaching*. San Francisco: Jossey-Bass.
2. Ausubel, D.P. (1968) *Educational psychology: A cognitive view*. New York: Holt, Rinehart and Winston.

3. Piaget, J. (1952) *The origins of intelligence in children*. New York: International Universities Press.
4. Buchin, Z.L. and Mulligan, N.W. (2025) "Prior knowledge and new learning: An experimental study of domain-specific knowledge," *Journal of Experimental Psychology: Applied*, 31(2), pp. 84–98. doi: 10.1037/xap0000520.
5. Hendrick, C. (n.d.) How much does prior knowledge really . . . [online]. Available at: https://carlhendrick.substack.com/p/how-much-does-prior-knowledge-really (Accessed: 27 September 2025).
6. Nuthall, G. (2007) *The hidden lives of learners*. Wellington: NZCER Press.
7. Kirschner, P.A. and Hendrick, C. (2020) *How learning happens: Seminal works in educational psychology and what they mean in practice*. Abingdon: Routledge.
8. Bryce, T.G.K. and Blown, E.J. (2023) "Ausubel's meaningful learning revisited," *Current Psychology*. [online] Available at: https://doi.org/10.1007/s12144-023-04440-4 (Accessed: 1 March 2025).
9. Cottingham, S. (2023) "Constructing schemas." In: K. Jones, ed. *The researchED guide to cognitive science: An evidence-informed guide for teachers*. Woodbridge: John Catt Educational, pp. 25–38.
10. Audrain, S. and McAndrews, M.P. (2022) "Schemas provide a scaffold for neocortical integration of new memories over time," *Nature Communications*, 13, p. 5795.
11. Ausubel, D.P. (2000). *The acquisition and retention of knowledge: A cognitive view*. Dordrecht: Springer.
12. Pinker, S. (2005) *How the mind works*. New York: W.W. Norton & Company.
13. Novak, J.D. (2002) "Meaningful learning: The essential factor for conceptual change in limited or inappropriate propositional hierarchies," *Science Education*, 86(4), pp. 548–571.
14. Reif, F. (2008) *Applying cognitive science to education: Thinking and learning in scientific and other complex domains*. Cambridge, MA: MIT Press.
15. Dreyfus, H.L. and Dreyfus, S.E. (2004) "The five-stage model of adult skill acquisition," *Bulletin of Science, Technology & Society*, 24(3), pp.177–181.
16. de Groot, A.D. (1946) *Het denken van den schaker: Een experimenteel-psychologische studie* [*The thinking process of the chess player: An*

experimental-psychological study]. Amsterdam: N.V. Noord-Hollandsche Uitgevers Maatschappij.

17. Chi, M.T.H., Feltovich, P.J., and Glaser, R. (1981) "Categorization and representation of physics problems by experts and novices,". *Cognitive Science*, 5(2), pp. 121–152.
18. Cottingham, S. (2023) *Ausubel's meaningful learning in action*. Woodbridge: John Catt Educational.
19. Gurlitt, J., Dummel, S., Schuster, S., and Nückles, M. (2011) "Differently structured advance organizers lead to different initial schemata and learning outcomes," *Instructional Science*, 40(2), pp. 351–369. doi:10.1007/s11251-011-9180-7.
20. Novak, J.D. (1998) *Learning, creating, and using knowledge: Concept maps as facilitative tools in schools and corporations*. Mahwah, NJ: Lawrence Erlbaum Associates.
21. Marzano, R.J., Pickering, D.J., and Pollock, J.E. (2001) *Classroom instruction that works: Research-based strategies for increasing student achievement*. Alexandria, VA: Association for Supervision and Curriculum Development (ASCD).
22. Sherrington, T. and Caviglioli, O. (2020) *Teaching walkthrus: Five-step guides to instructional coaching*. Woodbridge: John Catt Educational Ltd.
23. Furst, E. (n.d.) "Understanding 'understanding.' Teaching with learning in mind. Available at: https://sites.google.com/view/efratfurst/teaching-with-learning-in-mind/understanding-understanding (Accessed: 24 March 2025).
24. Brown, P.C., Roediger, H.L., and McDaniel, M.A. (2014) *Make it stick: The science of successful learning*. Cambridge, MA: Belknap Press of Harvard University Press.
25. Pressley, M., Symons, S., McDaniel, M.A., Snyder, B.L., and Turnure, J.E. (1992) "Encouraging mindful use of prior knowledge: Attempting to construct explanatory answers facilitates learning," *Educational Psychologist*, 27(1), pp. 91–109.
26. Dunlosky, J., Rawson, K.A., Marsh, E.J., Nathan, M.J., and Willingham, D.T. (2013) Improving students' learning with effective learning techniques: Promising directions from cognitive and educational psychology. *Psychological Science in the Public Interest*, 14(1), pp. 4–58.

27. Shimamura, A.P. (2018) *MARGE: A whole-brain learning approach for students and teachers*. North Charleston, SC: CreateSpace Independent Publishing Platform.

28. Delmas, R., Garfield, J., Ooms, A., and Chance, B. (2007) "Assessing students' conceptual understanding after a first course in statistics," *Statistics Education Research Journal*, 6(2), 28–58.

29. Beaufort, A. (2007) *College writing and beyond: A new framework for university writing instruction*. Logan: Utah State University Press.

30. Greve, A., Cooper, E., Tibon, R., and Henson, R.N. (2018) "Knowledge is power: Prior knowledge aids memory for both congruent and incongruent events, but in different ways," *Journal of Experimental Psychology: General*, 148(2), pp. 325–341.

31. Dunbar, K. N., Fugelsang, J. A., and Stein, C. (2007) "Do naive theories ever go away? Using brain and behaviour to understand changes in concepts." In: M. Lovett and P. Shah, eds *Thinking with data*. Psychology Press, p. 193.

SECTION 2

Checking for Understanding and the Science of Learning

4 The Illusion of Learning

There's an old joke that goes something like this:

> Two friends are sitting in a pub.
>
> One says, "I've taught my dog to speak French."
>
> The other raises an eyebrow. "Really? Let's hear her then."
>
> The first shrugs: "I said I taught her. I didn't say she'd learnt it."

It gets a laugh, but also lands an uncomfortable truth: teaching doesn't guarantee learning.

DOI: 10.4324/9781003657019-7

When we ask ourselves, "What are they thinking?", we explore the space between what we teach and what students learn. It is here where checking for understanding becomes essential. It is how teachers begin to close the gap between instruction and learning.

Learning is Not an Instantaneous Exchange of Knowledge

What is taught and what is learned are not always the same. When Wiliam says, "students do not learn what they are taught," he is not undermining the importance of teaching.[1] Rather, he reminds us that teaching is not an instantaneous exchange of knowledge from teacher to student: it is a form of disciplined improvisation: a performance shaped by continuous feedback and adjustments based on what students do or do not yet understand. Students bring prior knowledge, misconceptions, and varying levels of motivation to the learning process. Consequently, what students take away from a lesson often differs from what the teacher intended. This reality only reinforces the need to explore students' thinking and check their understanding before assuming they are ready to move on.

Such insights have led some to claim that teaching is more complex than medicine or brain surgery.[2,3] In his concise but commanding book *Developing Expert Teaching*, Peps Mccrea boldly and wittily argues that teaching is harder than brain surgery. He notes that while brain surgeons operate on one patient at a time, with access to advanced technology, expert support teams, and the ability to see the brains they're working on, teachers are often working alone, tasked with reshaping the minds of 20 to 30 students, without ever seeing inside those minds.

In the previous chapters, we discovered that students vary significantly in prior knowledge. And now we are confronted with the reality that student thinking is often invisible.

It's not all doom and gloom. We can look for evidence of learning. But it helps to know which signs truly reflect emerging understanding and which are misleading proxies masquerading as learning.

The Illusion of Learning: Poor Proxies

In 2015, Professor Rob Coe delivered a now widely cited speech to the Association of School and College Leaders (ASCL) on the problem of *poor proxies for learning*: classroom routines and behaviours that are often mistaken for evidence of learning.[4] Coe argued the following are poor indicators of learning:

- Students are busy: lots of work is done (especially written work);
- Students are engaged, interested, motivated;
- Students are getting attention: feedback, explanations;
- Classroom is ordered, calm, under control;
- Curriculum has been "covered" (ie presented to students in some form);
- (At least some) students have supplied correct answers, even if they
    - Have not really understood them
    - Could not reproduce them independently
    - Will have forgotten it by next week (tomorrow?)
    - Already knew how to do this anyway.

Of course, we want students to be engaged, our classrooms to be orderly, and for students to answer questions correctly. But the message here is that these things, while important, don't guarantee learning.

Take engagement. It's a common belief that visible participation reflects learning. Yet research tells a different story. Students can appear engaged without processing new material deeply. They become skilled at looking busy, especially when interacting with content they already understand. This is important: in many classrooms, students already know 40-50% of what is being taught.[5] Visible engagement can mislead teachers into overlooking which students feel challenged, who are coasting, and who might be falling through the cracks unnoticed.

Engagement can also tempt us into making lessons feel more exciting than they need to be. This is usually well-intentioned: no teacher wants students to find important content uninteresting. But when the activity becomes the hook, it can also become the memory. Students may remember searching the classroom for potatoes with questions about the Great Famine attached, or making a volcano in geography, while remembering far less about the causes of famine, migration, tectonic processes or the anatomy of a volcano itself.

Another way teachers can mistakenly believe that learning has occurred is when students supply the correct answers for the wrong reasons. Students sometimes arrive at correct answers not through understanding, but by unconsciously responding to cues and prompts from the teacher: a phenomenon Carl Hendrick aptly terms cognitive ventriloquism.[6]

These cues can be subtle. When students are on the verge of answering, teachers might unconsciously nod, shift their tone of voice, or change their facial expressions. These small, often unconscious signals can nudge students toward the expected answer, even if they haven't grasped the underlying concept. Even the structure of a question can do the heavy lifting. Take, for example, a teacher who says, "So if 3 x 2 = 6, what is 4 x 2?" The phrasing suggests a pattern, nudging students to respond with "8." But this isn't necessarily evidence of understanding multiplication; it may simply be pattern-spotting. What feels like learning is, in reality, a performance of correctness without understanding.

Again, we are reminded why checking for understanding is indispensable. A correct answer, on its own, is insufficient. Teachers must probe beneath the surface: How did the student arrive at the answer? Can they explain the reasoning in their own words? Can they apply the concept in a different context? These follow-up moves can help distinguish genuine understanding from guesswork, mimicry, or pattern recognition. It's crucial not to assume learning has taken place simply because students correctly answer low-tariff questions.

Without exploring how students arrived at a correct answer, teachers risk mistaking performance for learning, accepting the correct answer without recognising that it was reached for the wrong reasons. Because learning happens in the mind and is therefore invisible, teachers often conflate it with performance, which is often visible. But understanding the difference between the two is crucial.

Instructional Illusions: When Performance Masquerades as Learning

Learning is the long-term retention of knowledge and the ability to apply it in new contexts. Retention means the knowledge is long-lasting and retrievable when required. Application is about flexibility, using retrieved knowledge in different contexts, not just under the same conditions in which it was encountered. To determine whether learning has occurred, we need to wait and test that knowledge in different contexts.[7]

In contrast, performance is what teachers observe in the here and now. It's the temporary fluctuation in knowledge or behaviour, visible during and immediately after instruction. Teachers often use performance as a proxy for learning, but this is a highly unreliable indicator. Just because students can mimic desired responses during a lesson or shortly after does not mean they will retain and apply that knowledge in a week, a month, or a year later. It would be naive to assume so.

This distinction is crucial because while performance may be misleading, errors are far more reliable.[8] Misconceptions and mistakes reveal gaps in understanding. These are opportunities to intervene and address fragilities in students' schema. In fact, it's worth reconsidering the act of checking for understanding as *checking for misunderstanding*. This shift in perspective transforms checking for understanding from mere verification to diagnosis.

Conflating learning with performance increases the risk of assuming students have mastered concepts when, in fact, they have only performed well under structured and possibly scaffolded conditions. This creates what Soderstrom and Bjork call "instructional illusions": moments when both teacher and students falsely believe learning has occurred based on insubstantial signals.[9]

For example, imagine a student who solves a subtraction problem correctly right after the teacher's instructional input; the student now sees this as evidence of learning. A week later, the student is asked to apply the same concept independently, but they falter and cannot replicate the steps. What appeared to be learning was merely a temporary performance, propped up by recent exposure and teacher guidance.

But if we reframe the act as checking for misunderstandings, we can unearth the hidden misconceptions that sabotage learning. In these moments, students reveal not just what they know, but crucially, what they don't. Checking for understanding is not simply about verifying correctness. It should help surface misconceptions and gaps so the teacher can respond in real time.

The Curse of Knowledge

We briefly encountered the curse of knowledge when examining how novices and experts organise information differently. The curse of knowledge is the tendency to underestimate how long it takes others to learn something you've already mastered. For teachers, this can lead to overestimating what students know, understand, and can do because the material feels intuitive to them, the expert.

Traditionally, this phenomenon was thought to originate from experts over-relying on their own expertise and knowledge to make assumptions about novices. However, a recent study by Tullis and Feder offers a different explanation.[10] Their research suggests that the curse of knowledge may not result from egocentric perspectives or inhibition but from a lack of valid, diagnostic cues about student understanding. In other

words, when teachers don't have clear evidence of what students understand, they fill in the blanks and often get it wrong.

This insight underscores the importance of checking for understanding as a formative assessment tool. Frequent, probing checks for understanding can supply the cues teachers need to make more accurate inferences about learning. By surfacing what students truly know and don't know, teachers can avoid the blind spots created by their own expertise.

The findings from Tullis and Feder carry key implications for how teachers design and deliver instruction:

Start from Demonstrated, Not Assumed, Understanding

- Planning should begin with evidence, not intuition. Prior knowledge checks, prerequisite quizzes, and initial probing questions can reveal what students actually understand. These help ensure that lesson design builds on solid, visible foundations rather than guesswork.

Design for Conceptual Variation, Not Just Content Coverage

- Tullis and Feder highlight a key paradox: as teachers grow more expert, they often become less attuned to what learners find difficult. Instruction should, therefore, include variation and contrast, using strategies such as contextual interference and interleaving to surface misunderstandings. Hinge questions, which appear later in this book, are especially useful for identifying and addressing misconceptions early.

Include Opportunities for Perspective-Taking

- Teachers should regularly ask themselves: "What might confuse someone seeing this for the first time?" Reviewing past student work and using a diverse range of formative techniques can help maintain empathy for the novice perspective and reveal common stumbling blocks.

Structure Lessons to Surface Misconceptions

- Well-designed tasks make student thinking visible and allow incorrect ideas to emerge productively. This might include low-stakes quizzes with plausible distractors, carefully designed questioning sequences, or classroom dialogue routines that prioritise explanation over correctness. Combined with spaced and interleaved practice, these tools help reveal which ideas are stable and which remain fragile.

In short, the findings from Tullis and Feder suggest the curse of knowledge does not stem from knowing too much; it stems from seeing too little. Without valid cues about student thinking, even experienced teachers may teach past their learners. Checking for understanding, then, becomes a critical corrective, closing the gap between teachers' assumptions and students' learning.

The Dunning-Kruger Effect: When Students Don't Know What They Don't Know

The curse of knowledge reminds us that even as experts, teachers can misjudge what their students understand, especially when there are no valid cues. However, this problem is not exclusive to teachers. Students themselves are often poor judges of their own learning. This brings us to another well-documented phenomenon: the Dunning-Kruger effect. Here, the miscalibration runs in the opposite direction: those with low competence are more likely to overestimate their ability, while those with higher competence are more likely to underestimate it.

At some point in your career, you've likely used, or seen someone use, techniques like red, amber, and green cards, thumbs up/thumbs down, or the classic "Do you understand?" to gauge student competence. On the surface, these methods appear practical and efficient. But they share a critical flaw: they rely on confidence as a proxy for understanding.

The first issue is social. Most students, especially in a full classroom, are unlikely to admit confusion. Imagine asking, "Do you understand?" after you have just explained how the Treaty of Versailles contributed to the outbreak of World War II. How many students would interrupt the flow of the lesson to say no? As Doug Lemov puts it, "There are too many implicit social pressures pushing them [students] to keep the confusion to themselves."[11]

But there's a deeper cognitive problem. Students often don't know what they don't know. In their seminal 1999 study, Kruger and Dunning offered a sobering insight: those who know least are often the least aware of how little they know. Known as the Dunning-Kruger Effect, this bias arises because "the skills that engender competence in a particular domain are often the very same skills necessary to evaluate competence in that domain - one's own or anyone else's."[12]

In their research, individuals who performed poorly on tasks involving grammar, logic, and humour significantly overestimated their ability.

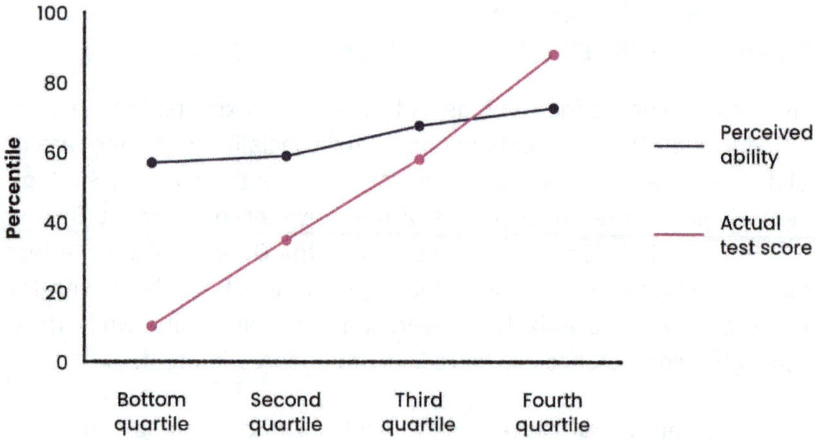

These findings remind us to be cautious: the students who appear most confident or finish a task quickly might, in fact, harbour deep misconceptions. Asking students to rate their confidence and then justify their reasoning takes us a step closer to reliably checking for understanding. However, confidence, justified or not, still provides limited insight into the depth of a student's grasp.

5 Desirable Difficulties

The Paradoxical Nature of Learning

A counterintuitive insight from Bjork is that learning and performance are often at odds: conditions that hinder performance tend to produce the most durable and flexible learning.[13] In contrast, those that promote smooth, error-free performance rarely result in lasting understanding.

How can this be? For many teachers, it's almost seductively easy to equate engagement with progress, confidence with comprehension, and correctness with understanding. When students radiate positive body language or score well on an end-of-lesson quiz, it *feels* like learning has happened. But these signs can be deceptive.

Many teaching techniques that produce smooth performance, such as heavy scaffolding, fluency drills, or repetitive practice on identical problems, often create the illusion of learning without ensuring long-term retention or transfer. What seems like mastery in the moment can quickly evaporate when conditions change or the content is revisited later.

The message here isn't about avoiding scaffolding or deliberately making tasks unachievable. Instead, it's a reminder not to draw premature conclusions about learning based on short-term performance.

There is now overwhelming empirical evidence supporting these claims. In their paper, "The Shuffling of Mathematics Problems Improves Learning," Rohrer and Taylor demonstrated that smooth performance

DOI: 10.4324/9781003657019-8

doesn't always translate into long-term retention.[14] In their study, students learned how to calculate the geometric volume of four different shapes. Learners were divided into two groups:

- One group practised *blocked problems*, working on one shape at a time before moving on.
- The second group practised in a *mixed format*, encountering different shapes in a shuffled sequence.

Immediately after instruction, the group that studied the problems in a blocked format outperformed those who encountered them in a shuffled order. The results flipped when both groups were tested on the same problems one week later. The students who practised in a shuffled format significantly outperformed those in the blocked group, correctly answering three times as many questions. Despite their earlier struggle, these students retained more knowledge and could apply it flexibly.

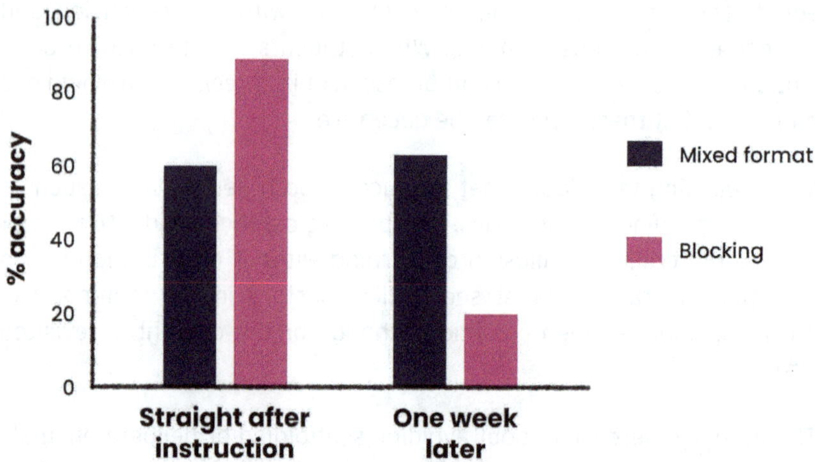

If we only check understanding immediately after instruction, when familiar cues and scaffolds are present, we risk measuring performance, not learning. In these moments, what we are witnessing is often the residue of well-structured practice, not deep understanding.

This example underscores a crucial point: performance during instruction can be an illusion of understanding. When learning feels smooth and effortless, it's tempting to assume mastery. But durable and flexible learning often happens under conditions of **desirable difficulty**, where mistakes are frequent (identified by the teacher and addressed), and retrieval is effortful.

"Desirable difficulties" is a term coined by Elizabeth and Robert Bjork to describe strategically designed impediments that make learning more effortful.[15] Paradoxically, these temporary challenges lead to more durable and flexible learning. The key to understanding desirable difficulties is recognising that while they may momentarily impair performance, they fortify learning by engaging students in deeper cognitive processing.

Not all difficulties are desirable. The word desirable is critical. Asking a group of Year 7 (ages 11–12) students to analyse the ecological impacts of climate change across biomes without first mastering food webs and energy transfer in smaller ecosystems isn't *desirably* difficult; it's just difficult. Overwhelming students with tasks like this will only result in frustration and a lack of motivation.

Desirable difficulties are not about making tasks inherently hard, nor are errors the intended goal; mistakes are a by-product of effortful retrieval and cognitive struggle.[16] The real learning benefits arise when memory traces become more durable through effortful retrieval after a period of forgetting. When errors do occur, they provide teachers with formative information, evidence of gaps in understanding that can be addressed before misconceptions solidify. Incorrect answers are valuable learning opportunities. In these moments, teachers can help students to analyse their mistakes and understand why they made them.

Spaced Practice and the Role of Forgetting in Learning

Contrary to intuition, forgetting is not the enemy of learning. Cognitive science reveals that forgetting plays an essential role in enhancing memory. When students struggle to retrieve information that has partially faded, their brains "engage in a more effortful reconstruction process that actually strengthens the long-term memory trace."[17]

This understanding of forgetting as a mechanism for strengthening memory brings us to the first of our desirable difficulties: spaced practice. The strategic act of revisiting information at spaced intervals leverages the power of forgetting, transforming the cognitive struggle of recall into long-term retention.

Spaced practice, sometimes called distributed practice, involves spreading learning out over time. Rather than reviewing the material in one intensive burst, it intentionally schedules intervals between learning episodes to allow some forgetting, which requires students to engage in more effortful retrieval. This approach offers a more accurate estimate of what has been learned, compared with massed practice (cramming), which can boost short-term performance but stifle long-term retention.

When students revisit material too soon after encountering it, they process it less deeply. The content feels familiar, so fluency increases, but actual understanding may not. As Dunlosky and colleagues point out, this fluency can be deceptive:

> ... students do not have to work very hard to reread notes or retrieve something from memory when they have just completed this same activity, and furthermore, they may be misled by the ease of this second task and think they know the material better than they really do. [18]

Another key benefit of spaced practice is its ability to surface misconceptions that massed practice often masks. When there's enough time for forgetting, teachers can use probing checks, asking students to explain, justify, or apply knowledge in varied contexts to make more reliable inferences about what has truly been retained. These moments also help identify which misunderstandings are proving more stubborn to unpick.

The benefits of spaced practice are not just about the time between learning episodes. A key insight from Benjamin and Tullis is that spacing is effective not simply because learning is distributed over time, but because later sessions trigger the retrieval of earlier episodes, stabilising memory through active reminding.

> When a stimulus or task reminds the learner of a previous episode, the retrieval of that episode enhances memory for its contents.[19]

When checking for understanding is spaced over time, it becomes more than an assessment of what students remember; it becomes a learning event in itself. Each retrieval acts as a reminder cue, prompting the effortful reconstruction of knowledge that enhances long-term memory and consolidates understanding.

Later in this book, you'll read how cold calling can be used for covert retrieval, providing a simple yet effective way to embed spaced practice into your repertoire of classroom routines. For now, let's look at some practical guidance on how to structure and adapt spaced practice within real teaching constraints.

There is extensive research exploring the optimal timing of spaced intervals, much of which focuses on the spacing gap between when students first encounter the material and a later test or assessment. While such studies offer valuable insights, it's easy to get bogged down in the pursuit of precision. In reality, the variables at play in a classroom, including student-to-student variance, make strict adherence to research-derived intervals impractical. Avoid overcomplicating the timing when using spaced practice. Instead, consider these five key recommendations:

1. **Aim for strong initial encoding**

   The quality of initial instruction must establish a memory trace strong enough to withstand delay. If encoding is weak, spacing offers no benefit, as there's simply nothing to retrieve. This underscores the importance of teachers regularly checking for understanding during instruction to gauge how well students grasp the material in real time.

2. **Prioritise effortful retrieval**

   For spaced practice to be effective, students must engage in activities that require meaningful cognitive effort. Tasks such as rereading notes or highlighting text often feel productive, but their passive nature limits long-term retention. Instead, opt for low-stakes quizzes, elaborative questioning, and graphic organisers. These are considered retrieval-rich strategies that help deepen and stabilise memory.

3. **Align spacing with content complexity**

   Conceptually rich or challenging material often requires more retrieval attempts to embed securely in long-term memory. The more complex the content, the more carefully planned the spaced retrieval opportunities should be. This means being intentional about where, when, and how you will revisit the big ideas of your subject. We've already seen how crucial prior knowledge and prerequisite checks are for effective learning; similarly, retrieval events should be purposefully integrated rather than set as random quizzes detached from meaningful learning sequences.

4. **Adjust spacing intervals over time**

   The first retrieval should occur soon after the initial exposure to interrupt forgetting, ensuring the material doesn't fade completely. From there, intervals should gradually lengthen as students demonstrate a greater understanding.

5. **Map spaced practice into the curriculum**

   For spacing to be effective, it must be designed into the curriculum, not added as an occasional activity or end-of-unit recap. When retrieval opportunities are deliberately planned across topics and terms, students encounter prior learning at intervals that make recall effortful yet achievable. This prevents spacing from becoming disjointed or tokenistic, making it more likely that each revisit serves a clear purpose. It also means teachers are intentional about connecting new content to existing knowledge stored and organised within students' schema. Teachers are more likely to engineer retrieval opportunities when the material to be retrieved meaningfully relates to the new learning. This, in turn, broadens understanding, deepens connections, and prepares students to apply knowledge in new contexts.

A well-mapped curriculum shows when and how key ideas return, linking knowledge both within and across units. In curriculum design, it is useful to think about spacing at two complementary levels.

- At the **macro level**, we revisit big disciplinary ideas across multiple years. Each encounter builds complexity and depth, helping students connect learning across time and cumulatively build knowledge.
- At the **micro level**, we build in structured retrieval opportunities within the year, prompting students to recall and apply knowledge from earlier units or terms.

These two levels of spacing are evident in how primary geography curricula revisit and connect key concepts over time.

The following **macro-level** plan involves revisiting big geographical ideas such as place, space, scale, and environment across multiple years so that students encounter them repeatedly in new contexts. Each revisit builds on prior learning, helping students make connections between concepts and see how their understanding deepens over time. For example, the concept of place might be introduced in Year 1 through a study of the local area, revisited in Year 3 through a regional study of the UK, explored again in Year 4 through a European comparison, and then extended in Year 5 through a focus on a North or South American region. Each encounter challenges students to apply earlier knowledge to new scales and contexts, gradually enriching their understanding of place.

Note: *Each concept runs through multiple units within a year. The table shows where each concept is explicitly developed or extended, not every instance where it appears. In practice, students revisit and apply ideas such as place, environment, and interdependence several times a year, through different contexts and enquiries.*

Concept	Year 1	Year 2	Year 3	Year 4	Year 5	Year 6
Place	Explore local area (home, school): identify features. Learn continent and ocean names.	Compare a UK locality with a contrasting non-European place.	Investigate a UK region: identify its physical and human characteristics, and locate it on a map.	Investigate a region in a European country and compare its features with those of a UK region.	Investigate a region in North/South America: compare its features with the UK region.	Broaden place knowledge: link studied places to global patterns.
Space	Use simple maps (e.g., a school plan or a world map); practice locational terms. Identify the UK on a globe.	Use world maps and atlases to locate continents and oceans. Use basic compass points to give directions.	Locate European countries and UK cities on maps. Use a 4- and 8-point compass to navigate.	Locate countries in the Americas using maps. Introduce map keys and symbols; begin using latitude and longitude.	Understand hemispheres, the Equator, Tropics; map global physical zones (e.g. climate belts).	Use latitude and longitude fully (Prime Meridian, time zones); analyse global spatial patterns (e.g. land use).

(Continued)

Concept	Year 1	Year 2	Year 3	Year 4	Year 5	Year 6
Scale	Understand local scale (classroom, home); see the school on a town map.	Compare local vs distant (own village vs faraway village); recognise area sizes (village, town, city).	Recognise regional vs national scale (county vs country); see the UK as part of Europe on a map.	Recognise continental vs global scale (Europe vs world); extend the "zoom lens" beyond Europe.	Relate local and national scales to global (e.g. country vs continent); consider scale in case studies.	Analyse issues at multiple scales (e.g. local river vs entire watershed; local climate vs global).
Interdependence and Connections	Observe local connections (e.g. where food/goods come from locally); discuss the weather's impact on the community.	Identify links between places; understand that seasons and weather vary globally.	Map transport and trade routes in the UK/Europe (roads, rails); understand goods and people movement.	Study trade and migration examples in Europe/Americas (simple import and export case studies).	Explore global links: world trade, the internet, migration, and the role of resources in connecting places.	Analyse global supply chains, climate-change impacts, and sustainable development.

(Continued)

Concept	Year 1	Year 2	Year 3	Year 4	Year 5	Year 6
Physical and Human Processes	Identify weather and seasons; name simple landforms (hill, river, coast) and human places (city, village, farm).	Describe weather patterns; locate hot and cold zones (Equator, poles); explain the weather's effect on people.	Explain UK physical processes (river flow, erosion); outline basic water cycle. Describe local settlement patterns and land use.	Learn about volcanoes, earthquakes, mountains, and the water cycle; link to human impacts.	Study climate zones, biomes, major river systems; human processes (settlements, land use, trade).	Deepen understanding of Earth systems (e.g., global climate) and human systems (e.g., urbanisation).
Environment	Explore local environment (plants, animals, weather); discuss caring for it (e.g. school recycling, planting trees).	Compare environments (urban vs rural, UK vs another country); introduce basic conservation concepts.	Investigate local environmental changes (e.g., new buildings) and learn how to save resources (water, energy) at home.	Study biomes and climate zones; discuss the conservation of habitats and renewable vs non-renewable resources.	Explore global issues: deforestation, pollution, and climate change; learn about sustainable resource use.	Discuss sustainability and human impact, including climate change basics, environmental protection, and the management of resources globally.

Micro-level spacing involves planning deliberate retrieval opportunities within the same year or topic so that key knowledge is revisited at spaced intervals. These structured returns to prior learning strengthen recall, help students make meaningful connections between units, and build confidence through low-stakes challenge. For example, in Year 4 geography, Rivers and Coasts might first be taught in Autumn 1, then revisited in Autumn 2 through links to Mountains and Volcanoes, and again in Summer 1 within the context of Human Impact and Sustainability. Retrieval opportunities might take the form of short quizzes on maps, key vocabulary, or physical processes; mini-enquiry lessons that prompt students to apply earlier learning (for instance, How does a river shape settlement in our European region?); or map-based challenges using OS symbols and grid references. Even brief writing tasks, such as completing causal "because" or "so" explanations, can help consolidate and extend geographical understanding over time. The table on the following page provides an example of how micro-level spacing might be mapped across the year.

Interleaving: The Power of Mixing Things Up

If spacing improves the retrievability of knowledge by making retrieval more effortful over time, interleaving enhances learning by challenging students to discriminate between ideas. Interleaving requires us to consider not just when we revisit material but how we structure that revisit to deepen understanding.

Interleaving refers to mixing different but related topics or problem types during practice, whereas blocking is studying one topic repeatedly before moving on to the next.

In blocked practice, students might complete ten questions on the same concept before moving on to ten questions on the next concept. Think: AAA BBB CCC. This approach can boost short-term performance but often results in weaker long-term retention and limited flexibility.

Interleaving, on the other hand, mixes problem types across a single practice session. Think: ABC BCA CAB. Students must distinguish

Topic	First Taught	First Revisit	Second Revisit	Big Concepts Emphasised
Rivers and Coasts	Autumn 1	Autumn 2 (linked to Mountains and Volcanoes)	Summer 1 (linked to Human Impact and Sustainability)	Place, Physical Processes, Environment
Mountains and Volcanoes	Autumn 2	Spring 1 (linked to European Region Study)	Summer 1	Physical Processes, Scale, Interdependence
European Region Study	Spring 1	Spring 2 (through Water Cycle and Climate)	Summer 2 (linked to Sustainability project)	Place, Space, Interdependence
Water Cycle and Climate	Spring 2	Summer 1 (through Human Impact and Sustainability)	Summer 2	Physical Processes, Environment, Interdependence
Human Impact and Sustainability	Summer 1	Summer 2	Summer 2 culminating project/ assessment	Environment, Sustainability, Interdependence

between problems and concepts. As a result, they process the material more deeply and build more durable, transferable knowledge.

> Mixing exemplars from different categories (i.e., interleaving), compared to learning exemplars from one category at a time (i.e., blocking), tends to enhance inductive learning. [20]

Yet, the benefits of interleaving are not immediately apparent to students. Klimovich and Richter found that students struggled more with interleaved practice and perceived it as less effective than blocking. Students made more errors and felt their learning was less successful during the practice phase. However, when tested later, they were significantly better at retrieving the words they'd practised under interleaved conditions compared to the words practised under blocked conditions.

> Children made more spelling errors during the interleaved compared to the blocked practice phase, perceived interleaved practice as more difficult, and rated their learning process as less successful compared to blocked practice, supporting the assumption that interleaved practice is a desirable difficulty.

Over time, students showed " . . . fewer spelling errors when they practised exemplars in an interleaved than a blocked sequence . . ."

These findings highlight the paradox of desirable difficulties: what feels more challenging at first leads to more durable learning. They also reinforce a central message: we must not confuse performance with learning. Interleaving may appear less effective during instruction, but it reveals its power in long-term retention and transfer.

The Bjorks clarify that interleaving enhances learning because switching between different but related topics requires students to reload information from memory actively:

> . . . interleaving forces learners to reload memories: If required to do A, then B, then C, and then A again, for example, the memory for

how to do A must be reloaded a second time, whereas doing A and then A again does not involve the same kind of reloading.[21]

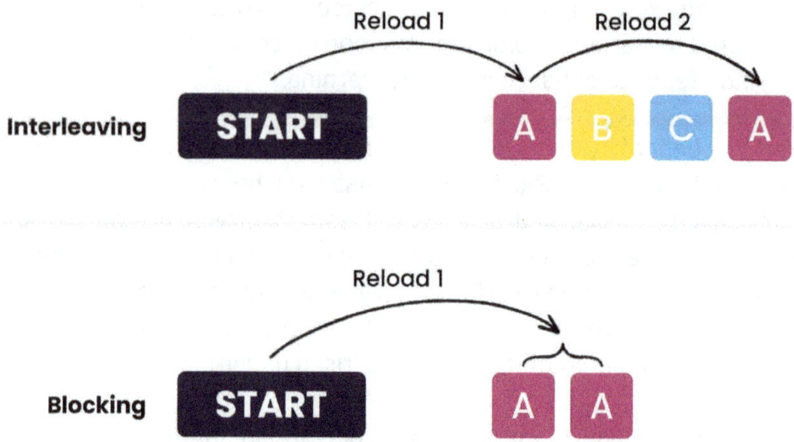

This act of reloading strengthens the memory trace and builds retrieval strength over time.

Moreover, Soderstrom and Bjork note that interleaving promotes discriminative contrast, the ability to spot critical differences between related but different concepts.[9] When students encounter similar ideas side by side (interleaving), they are forced to look more closely, noticing the underlying distinctions rather than relying on surface familiarity.

This principle aligns with Arthur Shimamura's 3Cs of Categorise, Compare and Contrast, which encourage students to organise information by identifying conceptual boundaries.[22] Shimamura's 3Cs can be seen as a deliberate application of discriminative contrast. When students actively compare and contrast related ideas, they are not just rehearsing facts; they are developing conceptual clarity, identifying nuances, and constructing richer schema.

While at first effortful, this process helps students move beyond smooth, in-the-moment performance. Students build more durable and transferable knowledge as they learn not only about specific concepts and ideas but also how they differ.

Despite the cognitive and memory benefits, interleaving isn't always easy to implement in the classroom. It can feel messy, counterintuitive, and often less effective in the moment. But research shows the payoff is worth it.

In a recent study conducted in real science classrooms, Sana and Yan found that students who completed weekly interleaved quizzes outperformed those who took blocked quizzes on a surprise test one month later.[23] Despite taking only 10–12 minutes each week, these low-stakes quizzes produced significant and lasting learning gains.

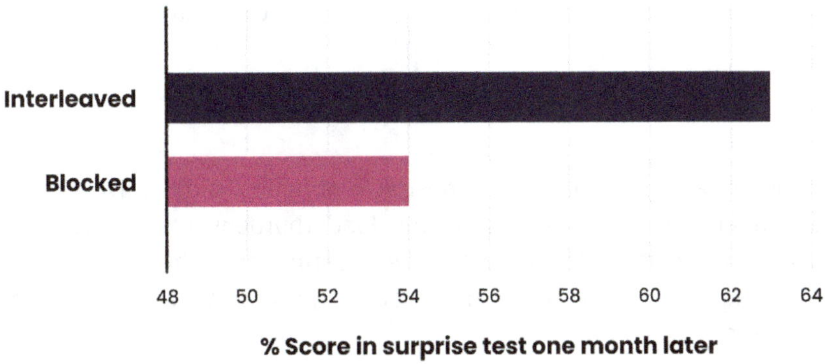

The study shows that interleaving can serve as a low-cost, high-impact tool for formative assessment, helping teachers make better inferences about learning while strengthening memory through effortful retrieval.

As Dunlosky and colleagues point out, a crucial consideration when using interleaving is that it's most effective once students have built an initial understanding:

> In fact, in educational contexts, introducing a new concept or problem type (e.g., how to find the volume of a spheroid) would

naturally begin with initial instruction and blocked practice with that concept or problem type, and most of the studies reported in this section involved an introduction to all tasks before interleaving began.[18]

This reflects a key instructional sequence: block first to build the foundations and manage cognitive load; interleave later to deepen learning and consolidate memory.

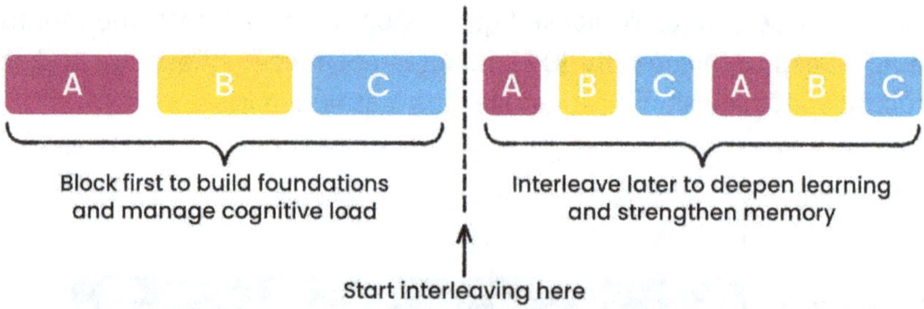

For interleaving to qualify as a desirable difficulty, it must avoid overwhelming students with extraneous load (burdens caused by poor design or unclear instruction) while creating enough intrinsic load (task-relevant effort) to prompt deeper processing and long-term retention.

The real question is: how much initial practice is enough before students can benefit from interleaving? Since interleaving asks students to discriminate between concepts and retrieve them across contexts, teachers need real-time insight into when that shift is appropriate. Blocked practice may build foundations, but checking for understanding reveals when those foundations are strong enough to support the challenge of interleaving. Probing questions, elaboration, and the 3Cs help determine students' readiness to make that leap.

The following examples show how teachers across different phases and subjects can use interleaving to deepen learning, promote discriminative contrast, and boost long-term retention. Each example illustrates how the teacher checks for understanding to determine readiness, then introduces interleaving to stretch and stabilise learning.

EYFS (AGE 4-5) (PHONICS - BLENDING AND SEGMENTING)

The teacher begins by revisiting previously taught sounds (/s/, /m/, /t/) to check that children can accurately identify and articulate each phoneme. Through brisk choral responses and cold calling, she ensures that these foundational sounds are secure before introducing the new sound /p/. She then blends and segments CVC words such as sat, mat, pat, and tap in varied order. This deliberate mixing requires children to retrieve both familiar and new phonemes rather than relying on repetition or sequence. Over time, this interleaving strengthens sound recognition, blending fluency, and phonemic flexibility across all taught sounds.

KS3 MATHEMATICS (AGES 11-14) (GEOMETRY - AREA)

The teacher begins with a short diagnostic task to check that students can accurately recall and apply the area formulas for triangles, parallelograms, trapezia, and circles. Once this foundational knowledge is secure, she introduces an interleaved problem set in which questions alternate among these shapes rather than being grouped by type. Students must first identify which formula applies before calculating. This purposeful mixing broadens conceptual understanding and retrieval fluency, enabling students to discern when and how to apply each method rather than relying on pattern or repetition.

Contextual Interference: Flexible Knowledge Requires Flexible Practice

Like spaced practice, interleaving creates the kind of productive struggle that makes retrieval effortful but ultimately more effective. It sharpens students' ability to distinguish between similar ideas. Our next desirable difficulty, varying the conditions of practice, ensures they can apply those ideas flexibly across different contexts.

At some point in your career, you are likely to encounter students who appear proficient during lessons, only to fall short when applying the same knowledge in a test or unfamiliar context. This discrepancy often stems from the material becoming contextually anchored, too tightly tied to the specific environment or conditions in which it was practised. To remedy this, teachers can use contextual interference, also known as varying the conditions of practice.

Changing variables such as the study environment, question format, learning modality, or stimulus type reduces reliance on familiar cues and improves students' ability to apply knowledge in new situations. While this may initially increase error rates, it leads to a more robust understanding of core principles.

Making the initial learning experience smooth is often necessary to build confidence and manage cognitive load. However, we must remember that success at this stage is a measure of performance, not learning. To generate more valid insights into student learning, teachers must vary practice conditions to elicit the productive struggle needed to determine whether students can retrieve and apply their knowledge flexibly.

In essence, students practising under varied conditions ask themselves: What is the underlying idea here, and how do I apply it now?

Here is a classroom vignette to illustrate how varying the conditions of practice can promote learning.

KS3 GEOGRAPHY (AGES 12-13)

Ms Khan, a Year 8 geography teacher, is introducing a lesson on river meanders. Knowing her students have encountered river systems in KS2 (ages 7-11), she opens with a prerequisite knowledge check to probe their understanding of erosion and deposition patterns. Once confident they have sufficient prerequisite knowledge, Ms Khan begins varying the conditions of practice:

- First, students label plan-view diagrams of meanders to indicate where erosion and deposition occur.
- Next, they annotate oblique aerial photographs, describing how processes change over time and how river cliffs and slip-off slopes form.
- Then, they locate and interpret meander features on an OS map, recognising how meanders are represented in topographic contours and river path markings.

These shifts in format, from schematic diagrams to real-world imagery and cartographic data, require students to retrieve and apply their knowledge in new contexts, deepening their understanding.

After students demonstrate a secure understanding across these formats, Ms Khan takes them further. She introduces a new layer of complexity by asking students to consider how different types of bedrock geology affect meander formation.

Drawing on prior units on coastal erosion and river landscapes, she asks students to:

- Compare meanders formed in soft sedimentary rocks versus those formed in resistant granite.
- Analyse photos of meanders from contrasting global environments, such as the Amazon floodplains vs upland Scottish rivers, and explain differences using prior learning.

This layered variation pushes students to connect new and prior knowledge. Crucially, Ms Khan checks for understanding not by hunting for correct answers, but by listening to student reasoning. Misconceptions, such as confusing erosion and deposition in aerial photographs, become visible and can be addressed immediately.

By varying conditions, Ms Khan avoids cognitive ventriloquism: students arriving at correct answers for the wrong reasons. Instead, she makes thinking more visible and identifies which concepts are stable and which remain fragile. Through diverse stimuli and probing formative checks, she gains more accurate insights and intervenes more precisely.

Varying the practice conditions helps reveal how close students are to genuine learning: the ability to retrieve and apply knowledge in flexible ways. When conditions remain too uniform, performance can be polished while understanding remains fragile. A correct answer might reflect guesswork, mimicry, or recognition of familiar patterns. This is why varying conditions and checking for understanding matter so much: they help teachers overcome the illusion of learning. In the absence of such information generated from checking for understanding and desirable difficulties, it is easy to fall into traps that distort our judgements. Introducing desirable difficulties allows teachers to avoid pitfalls such as the curse of knowledge and relying on students' self-reported confidence levels as a proxy for understanding.

6 Assessment

The Bridge Between What is Taught and What is Learnt

To gain meaningful information, we must go beyond surface impressions. Yet too often, checks for understanding rely on shallow routines: a few questions posed to the class, a handful of volunteers offering (typically correct) answers, and the assumption that everyone else has either reached the same conclusion or learnt the material by listening to their peers.[24]

Tom Sherrington, via Oliver Caviglioli, reports that, based on thousands of classroom observations, teachers' checks for understanding are often too infrequent and insufficiently probing to provide feedback that reliably informs next steps.[25] One explanation for this is that insufficient attention is given to the role of the student as an active partner in the process, as O'Connor and McDermott highlight:

> For example, we are used to understanding communication between teacher and learner as the teacher teaching the learner. Seen like this, it looks like a one-way, linear relationship, defined by role. But we could look at it another way. The teacher could not teach without feedback from the learner, as the teacher only knows what to do next by the learner's response.[26]

Checking for understanding as a way of making formative inferences should be a dynamic and iterative process. It creates feedback loops in which both teacher and student engage in cycles of observation,

DOI: 10.4324/9781003657019-9

inference, probing and instructional adjustment. Or, as Bennett (2011) puts it:

> Thus, each teacher-student interaction becomes an opportunity for posing and refining our conjectures, or hypotheses, about what a student knows and can do, where he or she needs to improve, and what might be done to achieve that change. [27]

In both cases, the message is clear: without valid, fine-grained evidence of student thinking, teachers risk teaching to an illusion. Teaching and learning should be understood as an ongoing iterative loop in which instruction and assessment continually inform one another. Within this loop, the role of the students is pivotal: their responses, explanations, and misconceptions provide the teacher with the necessary insight to determine what to do next.

We've already seen how Tullis and Feder attribute the curse of knowledge to teachers' lack of valid diagnostic cues about students' understanding. Wiliam offers similar insights, suggesting that teachers often make instructional decisions based on evidence that doesn't reliably reflect their students' needs. He describes checking for understanding as *low-hanging fruit*: an accessible lever for improving teacher effectiveness.[28] More frequent and sufficiently probing checks for understanding can lead to better-founded instructional choices and, ultimately, stronger learning outcomes.

To recognise this and to embrace the idea of ongoing feedback loops is to understand checking for understanding as a process of assessment. In essence, whenever teachers check for understanding, they are engaged in assessment. They gather evidence to support inferences about student learning and guide instructional decisions.

Yet, despite its central role in teaching, assessment is often misunderstood. This view is shared by Black and Wiliam, who argue against treating assessment as a distinct activity separate from pedagogy.[29] Rather than seeing assessment as something that occurs after teaching to confirm what students have learned, they position it as inseparable from the act of teaching itself. They argue that assessment occupies such a central position in good teaching because it is too difficult to reliably predict what students will learn, no matter how well we design our lessons, stating:

> If students learned what they were taught, then assessment would be unnecessary; we could simply document the educational experiences of each student, secure in the knowledge that this would describe their capabilities accurately.

In other words, effective teaching involves ongoing assessment, as teachers continuously probe students' thinking, draw inferences, and, where needed, adjust instruction in response. Pedagogy and assessment are not separate processes; they are two sides of the same coin.

Yet this view is often obscured by persistent misconceptions. Assessment is often viewed as merely a tool for measuring and reporting student achievement rather than as a means of supporting learning. Much of this confusion stems from the unhelpful and artificial distinction between formative and summative assessment, a distinction Black and Wiliam themselves describe as counterproductive and unhelpful.[29]

At its core, assessment is the process of drawing inferences (Cronbach, 1971, cited in Wiliam, 2016).[28] Summative and formative assessments are not separate "types" of assessment tasks. Instead, we define them by the kinds of inferences made from them. In other words, what makes an assessment formative or summative is not the task itself but how teachers use the resulting information.

When evidence serves to evaluate a student's current level of achievement or to predict future outcomes, it serves a summative function. These inferences are judgement-oriented and help answer questions such as:

- What level of proficiency has been achieved?
- Are students ready for the next phase in their education?
- What grade or score best represents a student's achievements?

When the same evidence informs instructional decisions and aims to maximise learning, it has a formative purpose. These inferences are action-oriented and support decisions about:

- What have students understood or misunderstood?
- Which instructional approaches are most likely to result in student progress?
- Are students ready to move to the next phase of learning, such as from guided to independent practice?

In the reality of the classroom, such distinctions are rarely clear-cut, as they don't reflect how teachers work. The rigid discontinuity between formative and summative assessment can lead to fragmented practices, inflexible planning, and missed opportunities, such as failing to draw formative inferences from an end-of-topic test; formative inferences that are likely to better inform the teacher or her students about what to do next.

Black and Wiliam argue that rather than treating these forms of assessment as distinct or opposing categories, there should be a productive synergy between them.[29] The same assessment can serve both formative and summative purposes. A mid-topic quiz, for instance, is formative when it informs real-time instructional decisions. That same quiz might later contribute to a report on student progress, fulfilling a summative role. As Wiliam points out, the critical factor is not the assessment itself, but how the resulting information is interpreted and acted upon.[28]

Defining Formative Assessment

So, if formative assessment is not a type of assessment, what is it? There is a long and well-established body of research on formative assessment, with many definitions and frameworks in circulation. Those working in the science of learning have debated its definition and nuances for decades. It is not the aim of this book to settle those discussions, nor to offer a definitive definition. Instead, the scope is intentionally narrow: to clarify the role of checking for understanding within the formative assessment process, and to show how it helps teachers make better, or rather, *better-founded*, responsive decisions.

The following definition from Black and Wiliam captures the many ways others have described formative assessment.

> Practice in a classroom is formative to the extent that evidence about student achievement is elicited, interpreted, and used by teachers, learners, or their peers, to make decisions about the next steps in instruction that are likely to be better, or better founded, than the decisions they would have taken in the absence of the evidence that was elicited.[30]

There is much to unpack in this definition, and it's worth exploring the implications for teachers.

Function Over Form

First, the definition reminds us that formative assessment is not a thing. No assessment is inherently formative. Whether a quiz, discussion, or extended written task serves a formative purpose depends entirely on how the teacher, or her students, use the evidence it yields. When that information is fed back into the teaching and learning process to guide likely improvements, it functions formatively.

Better-founded Decision

Black and Wiliam use the phrase "better-founded" to describe formative assessment. Too often, formative assessment is mistakenly equated with redirection, spotting gaps and reteaching. But its value also lies in confirming that the decision being made is the right one. A check for understanding that demonstrates students understand the content doesn't prompt a course correction; instead, it verifies their readiness to move on. The decision is better-founded because the evidence gathered has helped the teacher or her students make the next-step decision more wisely than they would otherwise.

It's about improving the quality of the decision, even when that decision is to continue as planned. In other words, evidence from a check for understanding may confirm that students are progressing as expected; the teacher now has evidence to justify proceeding.

Probabilistic

Building on this, the definition states that the decisions are "likely to be better or better-founded," signalling a probabilistic benefit rather than an absolute guarantee. Formative assessment increases the odds of success by aligning instructional choices more closely with students' needs, but it is not a panacea that works in every situation. We have already seen how deeply learning depends on prior knowledge. It is simply too complex a process for any single approach to reliably improve success for all students, especially when there are wide variances in starting points.

Thus, we should view formative assessment as a powerful tool that tilts the balance toward better learning, helping to reduce the risk of failure, while still acknowledging the inherent challenges of teaching and learning.

Moments of Contingency

A hallmark of formative assessment is the teacher's (or student's) ability to adjust course based on the information generated from checks for understanding. In practical terms, this means instruction includes built-in decision points, often referred to as hinge points, at which it can shift direction based on students' responses. Dylan Wiliam describes formative assessment as the creation and use of "moments of contingency" in instruction: junctures where the learning episode can pivot depending on what the evidence reveals.[31] For example, when checking for understanding uncovers confusion or a lack of clarity, the teacher revisits the concept using a different approach. These real-time or short-cycle adjustments increase the likelihood that learning remains on track. When input isn't achieving its intended effect, the teacher or learner responds, rather than pressing on and hoping for the best.

Without these moments of contingency, teachers risk skating across the surface of the curriculum. In doing so, they may seduce themselves with a comforting chimaera: the illusion that covering content equates to learning, even if some students get overlooked.

It is also worth noting that while formative assessment is often associated with in-the-moment decisions, it can operate across much longer timeframes. For example, subject leaders will analyse test data to identify gaps and use those insights to shape professional development. Or teachers revise how curriculum content is taught or sequenced based on findings from end-of-topic or end-of-key-stage assessments. In both cases, evidence contributes to improving learning over time, not just in the moment. These examples reveal that formative assessment is not limited to classroom student-teacher interactions; it also supports colleagues' development and long-term curriculum refinement.

Students and Peers as Agents of Formative Assessment

Formative assessment is not something done to students, but rather something students do for themselves and with one another. The definition clearly states that evidence is used by "teachers, learners or their peers," emphasising that anyone involved in the learning process can be an agent of formative assessment.

To provide a conceptual framework for formative assessment and to highlight the role of learners, Leahy, Lyon, Thompson, and Wiliam (2005) developed the now-widely-cited grid.[32]

In doing so, Leahy and colleagues distilled teaching and learning into three key processes, involving three kinds of individuals. The processes

<table>
<tr><th></th><th>Where the learner is going</th><th>Where the learner is right now</th><th>How to get there</th></tr>
<tr><td>Teacher</td><td rowspan="3">Clarifying, sharing, and understanding learning intentions</td><td>Eliciting evidence of learning</td><td>Providing feedback that moves learning forward</td></tr>
<tr><td>Peer</td><td colspan="2">Activating learners as learning resources for one another</td></tr>
<tr><td>Learner</td><td colspan="2">Activating learners as owners of their own learning</td></tr>
</table>

include identifying where learners are in their learning, clarifying where they are going, and determining the most effective means of getting there. The three individuals are the teacher, the learner, and their peers.

While the central focus of this book aligns most closely with determining "where the learner is now" and includes the roles of teacher, peer, and learner, it would be remiss not to briefly acknowledge the importance of learning intentions and feedback as key components of the broader formative assessment process.

The Role of Subject Knowledge in Formative Assessment

Given the strong consensus that formative assessment improves student achievement, recent discussions have shifted toward how best to support teachers in implementing it effectively, sparking an important question: Is formative assessment domain-general, applicable across all subjects, or domain-specific, shaped by the unique demands of particular disciplines? Dylan Wiliam argues that formative assessment is irreducibly both.[33]

Certain formative assessment principles and techniques are ubiquitous across subjects. These include practices such as sharing and clarifying learning intentions, eliciting evidence of student thinking, and providing feedback. Such strategies are widely applicable. For instance, checking every student's understanding, rather than relying solely on volunteers, is a technique that transcends subjects and should be a staple of all classrooms.

Collecting responses from all students using hinge questions, mini whiteboards, or exit tickets is a general method that can enhance instructional decision-making across most subjects. As Wiliam notes, "evidence from all students in the group about their current level of understanding of the material being taught is likely to result in better instructional decisions," a principle that "can be applied to any group teaching situation."[33] In other words, teachers do not need deep subject expertise to benefit from involving every student in the learning process.

However, domain-general approaches can only take you so far. Generic techniques, while helpful, can sometimes feel abstract or disconnected from the everyday realities of a particular subject. One of the aims of this book is to go beyond a surface-level list of strategies and instead explore the principles that make checking for understanding effective. When techniques are deployed without an understanding of the principles that made them effective in the first place, they can do more harm than good.[8] That is why we should consider formative assessment as both domain-general and domain-specific.

Every subject has its own distinctive knowledge, skills, and ways of reasoning. Effective formative assessment must reflect these nuances. A domain-specific approach means tailoring both the assessment itself and the interpretation of the evidence it yields to the unique demands of your subject.

A maths teacher, for example, needs to recognise common misconceptions, such as confusing area and perimeter, and design questions that specifically reveal those misunderstandings. An English teacher, on the other hand, might probe a student's ability to interpret character motivations or use textual evidence in analytical writing: tasks that are very different to those found in maths.

As Bennett notes, "a teacher who has weak cognitive-domain understanding is less likely to know what questions to ask of students, what to look for in their performance, what inferences to make from that performance about student knowledge, and what actions to take to adjust instruction."[27] In short, knowing what to ask and what to look for in a student's response depends on deep knowledge of the subject itself.

Crucially, effective formative assessment looks different in different subjects. What works well in one discipline may not translate neatly to another. In science, formative assessment often centres on identifying and challenging alternative conceptions (e.g., the idea that heavier objects fall faster). Science and maths teachers frequently use diagnostic questions and problem-solving tasks to uncover errors in reasoning.

By contrast, in English, teachers may use discussions, textual analysis, or essay drafting to assess understanding. Here, formative assessment focuses less on correctness and more on interpretation, coherence, and argumentation. As Wiliam notes, "good formative assessment in science looks different to good formative assessment in English Language Arts."[33]

Even within the same subject, formative assessment varies. In a grammar-focused English lesson, checks for understanding might resemble those in maths, with right or wrong answers to rule-based questions. But in a literature discussion, assessment will be more dialogic, probing how students interpret ideas and support their views.

There are real benefits to respecting the uniqueness of individual subjects. As Christine Counsell reminds us, "You can't Rosenshine your way out of a poor curriculum." Effective formative assessment must be rooted in the subject's distinctive content and structures.

That said, an overly siloed, subject-specific approach has its limitations. If every department in a school reinvents formative assessment on its own terms, it can lead to fragmented practice. Teachers may find it difficult to learn from colleagues in other subjects due to a lack of shared language and framework. Students may also experience confusion when each teacher uses entirely different routines and terminology for essentially the same process. A strictly domain-specific model can also make it harder for a school to scale formative assessment effectively, as it may demand separate training and expertise for each subject. This risks isolating colleagues and missing the efficiencies that come from a shared model and vocabulary.

Rather than treating domain-general and domain-specific approaches as mutually exclusive, it is more productive to view them as mutually reinforcing. In practice, this means grounding assessment in core principles while layering on the subject-specific adaptations that make those principles meaningful in context. Wiliam argues for finding the right balance: teachers should use well-established formative assessment strategies while drawing on deep subject knowledge to ask precise questions and interpret the responses they receive.[33]

Understanding the interplay between domain-general and domain-specific approaches can significantly enhance teachers' design and implementation of formative assessment. Here are some practical implications for striking the right balance:

1. **Start with core principles** - Begin with well-established, widely applicable principles of formative assessment. For example, using mini whiteboards to assess each student's understanding is a simple yet powerful strategy that works across most subjects and serves as a baseline for effective practice.
2. **Adapt to subject matter** - Translate generic techniques into forms that reflect the demands of your discipline. The evidence you gather should align with what success looks like in your subject. Deep subject knowledge is essential not only for asking the right questions but also for interpreting the insights those questions reveal.
3. **Collaborate across and within subjects** - Draw on collaboration at multiple levels. Working across subjects can expose you to new

ideas and strategies you might not have considered. Within your subject team, develop shared formative assessment approaches and identify common misconceptions or recurring difficulties students face. Subject colleagues can pool their expertise to co-create high-quality questions and tasks that address the core of disciplinary thinking.

Bringing domain-general and domain-specific perspectives together enables schools to develop a cohesive approach that supports consistency while honouring the distinctive nature of each subject. A shared understanding across the school, combined with specialised knowledge within departments, can help ensure that formative assessment is both scalable and effective.

Section 2: Checking for Understanding and the Science of Learning Concluding Principles for Practice

1. **Do not treat performance as evidence of learning.**

   What students can do during or immediately after instruction is often an unreliable indicator of what they have learned, as learning does not occur in one-off lessons. Smooth, fluent performance, especially when tasks are scaffolded, often reflects temporary conditions rather than durable understanding. Checks for understanding must therefore be designed to look beyond in-the-moment success and avoid making premature assumptions about long-term learning.

2. **Treat errors as more informative than correct answers.**

   Mistakes, misconceptions, and hesitation provide clearer insight into student thinking than polished responses. Effective checking for understanding is less about confirming correctness and more about surfacing misunderstandings that would otherwise remain hidden.

3. **Build desirable difficulty into checks for understanding: deliberately and conditionally.**

   Effortful retrieval, spacing, interleaving, and varied practice improve long-term retention and transfer, even though they impair immediate performance. However, these difficulties are only desirable once sufficient initial understanding is in place. Checking for understanding indicates when students are ready for that challenge.

4. **Vary conditions to test whether knowledge is flexible, not just familiar.**

   When understanding is secure, students should be able to retrieve and apply knowledge across different formats, contexts, and representations. If checks for understanding always keep conditions the same, students may succeed by recognising surface patterns rather than by drawing on underlying concepts. Deliberately varying conditions helps teachers distinguish genuine understanding from the illusion of learning.

5. **Use checking for understanding to make better-founded decisions.**

   Formative assessment does not eliminate uncertainty. It improves the *quality* of instructional decisions by grounding them in evidence rather than assumptions. The goal is not certainty, but wiser next steps, whether that means proceeding, revisiting, or adapting instruction.

Section 2: Checking for Understanding and the Science of Learning References

1. Wiliam, D. (2018) "Foreword." In: H. Fletcher-Wood (ed.) *Responsive teaching: cognitive science and formative assessment in practice*. Abingdon: Routledge, pp. xv-xvii.
2. Shulman, L.S. (2004) *The wisdom of practice: Essays on teaching, learning, and learning to teach*. San Francisco: Jossey-Bass.

3. Mccrea, P. (2023) Developing expert teaching: A practical guide to designing effective professional development, for others and ourselves. Independently published.

4. Coe, R. (2015) "From evidence to great teaching," paper presented at the ASCL Annual Conference, London, 20 March.

5. Nuthall, G. (2007) *The hidden lives of learners*. Wellington: NZCER Press.

6. Hendrick, C. (2025) "Cognitive ventriloquism: Why students give the right answers for the wrong reasons." The Learning Dispatch. Available at: https://carlhendrick.substack.com/p/cognitive-ventriloquism-why-students (Accessed: 5 May 2025.)

7. Didau, D. (2025). "How do I know all students are mastering the skills I want them to learn?" The Learning Spy. Available at: https://daviddidau.substack.com/p/how-do-i-know-all-students-are-mastering (Accessed 7 May 2025.)

8. Fletcher-Wood, H. (2018). *Responsive teaching: Cognitive science and formative assessment in practice*. London: Routledge.

9. Soderstrom, N.C. and Bjork, R.A. (2015). "Learning versus performance: An integrative review," *Perspectives on Psychological Science*, 10(2), pp. 176–199. https://doi.org/10.1177/1745691615569000.

10. Tullis, J.G. and Feder, B. (2023). "The 'curse of knowledge' when predicting others' knowledge," *Memory & Cognition*, 51(5), pp. 1214–1234. https://doi.org/10.3758/s13421-022-01382-3.

11. Lemov, D. (2021) *Teach like a champion 3.0: 63 techniques that put students on the path to college*, 3rd ed. Hoboken, NJ: Jossey-Bass.

12. Kruger, J. and Dunning, D. (1999) "Unskilled and unaware of it: How difficulties in recognizing one's own incompetence lead to inflated self-assessments," *Journal of Personality and Social Psychology*, 77(6), pp. 1121–1134.

13. Bjork, R.A. (1994) "Memory and metamemory considerations in the training of human beings." In: J. Metcalfe and A. Shimamura (eds) *Metacognition: Knowing about knowing*. MIT Press, pp. 185–205.

14. Rohrer, D. and Taylor, K. (2007) "The shuffling of mathematics problems improves learning," *Instructional Science*, 35(6), pp. 481–498. doi:10.1007/s11251-007-9015-8.

15. Kirschner, P.A. and Hendrick, C. (2020) *How learning happens: Seminal works in educational psychology and what they mean in practice*. Abingdon: Routledge.

16. Neelen, M. and Kirschner, P.A. (2023) Demystifying desirable difficulties 2: What they're NOT. 3-Star Learning Experiences. Available at: https://3starlearningexperiences.wordpress.com/2023/02/28/demystifying-desirable-difficulties-2-what-theyre-not/ (Accessed: 7 May 2025.)

17. Hendrick, C. (2025) Making retrieval practice actually work. The Learning Dispatch. Available at: https://carlhendrick.substack.com/p/making-retrieval-practice-actually (Accessed 18 May 2025.)

18. Dunlosky, J., Rawson, K.A., Marsh, E.J., Nathan, M.J., and Willingham, D.T. (2013) "Improving students' learning with effective learning techniques: Promising directions from cognitive and educational psychology," *Psychological Science in the Public Interest*, 14(1), pp. 4–58.

19. Benjamin, A.S. and Tullis, J.G. (2010) "What makes distributed practice effective?" *Cognitive Psychology*, 61(3), pp. 228–247. https://doi.org/10.1016/j.cogpsych.2010.05.004.

20. Klimovich, A. and Richter, T. (2025) "Interleaving as a desirable difficulty in elementary spelling education: Effects on performance, retention, and transfer," *Learning and Instruction*, 84, 101773. https://doi.org/10.1016/j.learninstruc.2023.101773.

21. Bjork, R.A. and Bjork, E.L. (2011) "Making things hard on yourself, but in a good way: Creating desirable difficulties to enhance learning." In: M.A. Gernsbacher, R.W. Pew, L.M. Hough, and J.R. Pomerantz (eds) *Psychology and the real world: Essays illustrating fundamental contributions to society*. New York: Worth Publishers, pp. 56–64.

22. Shimamura, A.P. (2018) *MARGE: A whole-brain learning approach for students and teachers*. North Charleston, SC: CreateSpace Independent Publishing Platform.

23. Sana, F. and Yan, V. X. (2024) "The effects of interleaved retrieval practice in high school science classrooms," *Psychological Science*, 35(2), pp. 247–257. https://doi.org/10.1177/09567976231219982.

24. Rosenshine, B. (2012) "Principles of instruction: Research-based strategies that all teachers should know," *American Educator*, 36(1), pp. 12–19.

25. Caviglioli, O. (2025) Walkthrus npoint no.5: Thinking in loops. [LinkedIn post], 11 June. Available at: https://www.linkedin.com/posts/oliver-caviglioli-25386a15_walkthrus5-onpoint-no-5-thinking-in-loops-activity-7241069257055252480-i3nv (Accessed: 14 June 2025.)

26. O'Connor, J. and McDermott, I. (1997) *The art of systems thinking: Essential skills for creativity and Problem solving*. London: Thorsons.

27. Bennett, R.E. (2011) "Formative assessment: A critical review," *Assessment in Education: Principles, Policy & Practice*, 18(1), pp. 5–25. DOI: 10.1080/0969594X.2010.513678.

28. Wiliam, D. (2016) Leadership for teacher learning: Creating a culture where all teachers improve so that all students succeed. West Palm Beach, FL: Learning Sciences International.

29. Black, P. and Wiliam, D. (2018) "Classroom assessment and pedagogy," *Assessment in Education: Principles, Policy & Practice*, 25(6), pp. 551–575. DOI: 10.1080/0969594X.2018.1441807.

30. Black, P. and Wiliam, D. (2009) "Developing the theory of formative assessment," *Educational Assessment, Evaluation and Accountability*, 21(1), pp. 5–31. https://doi.org/10.1007/s11092-008-9068-5.

31. Wiliam, D. (2011) *What works in formative assessment*. UCL Institute of Education. [pdf] Available at: chrome-extension://efaidnbmnnnibpcajpcglclefindmkaj/https://discovery.ucl.ac.uk/id/eprint/1507217/1/Wiliam2011What2.pdf (Accessed: 21 July 2025.)

32. Leahy, S., Lyon, C., Thompson, M., and Wiliam, D. (2005) "Classroom assessment: minute-by-minute and day-by-day," *Educational Leadership*, 63(3), pp. 18–24.

33. Wiliam, D. (2019) Why formative assessment is always both domain-general and domain-specific and what matters is the balance between the two. In H.L. Andrade, R.E. Bennett, and G.J. Cizek (eds) *Handbook of formative assessment in the disciplines*. New York: Routledge, pp. 243–262.

SECTION 3

Checking for Understanding in Action

7 Ratio
Involve All Students All of the Time

At the core of effective teaching, checking for understanding serves two broad and essential purposes.

- First, it provides diagnostic information that helps teachers identify where students stand relative to the intended learning outcomes, enabling them to make more informed decisions about what to do next.
- Second, and a less well-recognised benefit, is that frequent checking and probing of students' understanding provides them with opportunities to become more familiar with the content. By regularly answering questions, students rehearse and become more fluent with the material. They consolidate fleeting memories into secure knowledge.

Dan Willingham reminds us that "Memory is the residue of thought."[1] In other words, humans learn what they think about. No thinking, no learning. Every cold call, mini whiteboard routine, hinge question and exit ticket is another opportunity for students to think, practise, and make meaning.

The following chapters examine the high-leverage practices effective teachers use when checking for understanding. Before reading these, let's consider a set of guiding principles that maximise how well these checks reveal student thinking, promote meaningful cognitive effort, and involve all students all of the time.

DOI: 10.4324/9781003657019-11

Doug Lemov's concept of ratio provides a valuable lens for understanding these principles.[2]

The term ratio describes the proportion of students in a class who are thinking, how often this occurs, and how challenging the thinking is. In *Teach Like a Champion*, Lemov uses a graphic to represent ratio like this:

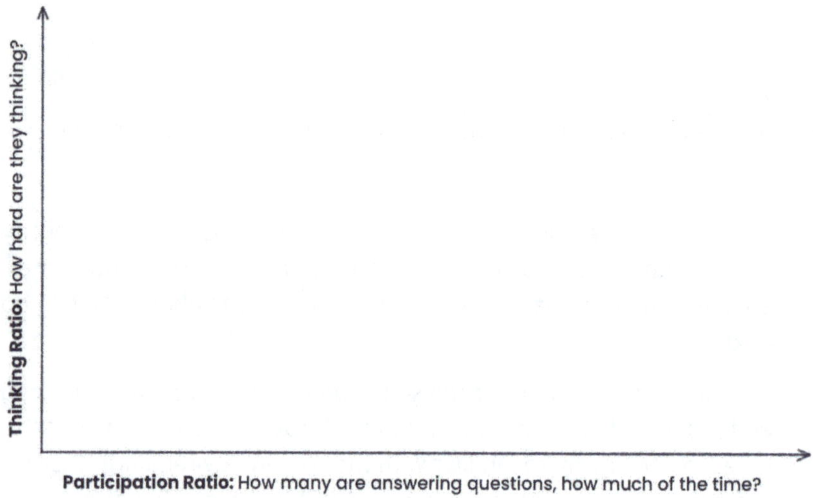

Participation Ratio

Participation ratio reflects how many students are thinking and for how much of the lesson. In the following chapters, whole-class response approaches, such as mini whiteboards and hinge questions, along with techniques like cold calling and wait time, demonstrate how teachers can dramatically increase the participation ratio.

It is all too common for teachers, who feel pressured to keep the lesson going, to ask only a handful of questions, call on the same few students who usually have the correct answer, and use this to represent the whole class's understanding. Conversely, in high-stakes environments, such as an amateur rock climbing wall, the instructor examines all participants' harnesses before giving them the all-clear to ascend. Why should learning be any different?

In his seminal paper, "Principles of Instruction," Barak Rosenshine asserts that the most effective teachers ask many questions and routinely check the answers of all students.[3] In other words, they maintain a high participation ratio during lessons. Against a backdrop in which inclusion has become one of the most prominent issues in recent education discourse, such insights, provocative as this may seem, prompt us to consider whether the principles of classroom inclusion differ in any substantive way from those long associated with effective teaching. Later in this book, you will read how formative assessment, and by extension, checking for understanding, shares its intellectual roots with pioneering studies in special education.

An underlying principle of the four checking-for-understanding techniques explored in the following chapters is that, when done well, they involve all students all the time.

Think Ratio

Think ratio is a measure of how hard students are thinking about the content. In other words, is there sufficient desirable difficulty for encoding to take place?

Consider the following two scenarios. A teacher poses a question, only to be met with blank, bewildered faces. The room falls into an awkward silence. Doug Lemov refers to these moments as "crickets," so quiet that you can almost hear them chirping.[4] In these moments, participation is low because the teacher hasn't posed the question in a way that prompts all students to think. The think ratio is also extremely low. The off-the-cuff question didn't prepare students to rehearse a response. It didn't require all students to think and prepare an answer.

Next, consider this all-too-familiar scenario where students instinctively shout out the first thing that comes to mind, or the teacher poses a question directly to an individual student. "Billy, what is 8 x 9?" The participation ratio is low because students either shout out or know in advance who will answer, leaving them no time to consider their response. Similarly, the think ratio is low, as impulsive answers are typically of lower quality than those given after thoughtful consideration.

As you read in the previous chapter, domain-specific knowledge is crucial for teachers to craft checks for understanding that reveal students' thinking. Creating questions that elicit the kind of desirable difficulty needed to boost the think ratio is not easy. The message here is to dedicate faculty time to collaborate on such work. Explore what makes a question challenging in the context of your subject. Identify common misconceptions and carefully craft questions to determine whether students hold them.

For now, to help you along the way, let's unpack a common error teachers might make when trying to raise the challenge of their questions. In the pursuit of challenge, many reference Bloom's Taxonomy, albeit through a distorted lens. You've likely seen the Bloom's pyramid.

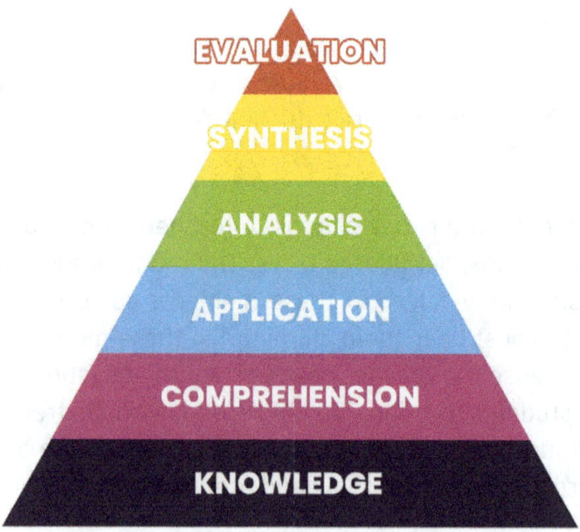

Erroneously visualised, the pyramid positions knowledge at the bottom with "high order'" thinking at the top. This misleading visualisation has led many leaders and teachers to undervalue "low-tariff" recall questions. What makes this problematic is that, viewed as a pyramid, teachers instinctively rush to get their students to reach the apex, overlooking the foundational importance of knowledge in student learning.

Ironically, Benjamin Bloom never included this pyramid diagram in his original work.[5] Colleagues of Bloom, who knew his work well, have since insisted that his work stressed that factual knowledge and recall provide the essential foundation for all higher-order thinking. Bloom argued, consistent with cognitive science, that critical thinking builds upon facts stored in long-term memory rather than information simply present in the environment. Properly interpreted, Bloom's taxonomy should not be seen as a ladder to rush up, but as Dylan Wiliam points out, a structure showing that advanced thinking depends on secure knowledge.[6]

A further issue with Bloom's Taxonomy is that the command words can be misleading. In his insightful blog, Challenge Beyond Bloom's, Adam Boxer demonstrates that increasing challenge is not as simple as choosing different command words or levels from Bloom's framework.[7] To illustrate this point, consider this example, adapted from Adam's work.

> Compare the features of rural settlements with those of urban settlements.
>
> Recall the features that rural settlements have in common with urban settlements and the features that are different.

Compare is typically associated with the "analyse" level (level 4) in Bloom's hierarchy, while recall sits at level 1 under "remember." Yet despite this apparent difference in difficulty, the teacher would almost certainly receive the same answer to both questions.

The misconceptions about Bloom's Taxonomy highlight why some teachers struggle when trying to increase cognitive demand. We should think of challenge in terms of students' existing knowledge, the cognitive processes a task elicits, and how teachers structure opportunities for retrieval and application. Moving beyond categorical notions of "higher" and "lower" questions requires us to consider the mechanisms through which meaningful challenge is created. The intrinsic difficulty of the material, the timing of a question, and the level of support (i.e., grouping problems and asking blocks of similar questions versus mixing it up) are all levers teachers can use to adjust the challenge.

In Chapter 3, we saw how rote learning can be a spark for meaningful learning because it bolsters the foundations, facts, ideas, and concepts that underpin each domain. In a more nuanced version of the ratio graphic (see next page), Doug Lemov and InnerDrive describe an area on the graph called shallow land: a space where questions may not demand maximal cognitive effort but serve a useful temporary purpose by building confidence through early success.[4] These small wins can be what students need to feel prepared to tackle more challenging questions or feel safe to share their thinking during cold calls.

Designed by InnerDrive and Doug Lemov.

Even so, as Lemov and InnerDrive point out, the long-term goal is for students to think hard.

When considering how to boost challenge in the classroom, it is worth reminding ourselves that not all content carries the same level of cognitive demand. Some content is inherently more challenging, and this matters. As seen in Chapter 5, Desirable Difficulties, conceptually rich and demanding material requires more retrieval attempts. This requires us to be deliberate about where, when, and how the more challenging content is first introduced and revisited. Spaced practice offers a way to regulate how hard students think.

Closely linked to this idea is Rob Coe's poor proxies for learning. Coe explains that teachers can make premature assumptions about learning. One such way is when students provide the correct answer for the wrong reasons. A question answered immediately after instruction might elicit an accurate response. The same question asked the next day or a week later is more likely to render an incorrect response. The timing of our questions can influence the cognitive demand.

Students can also provide correct answers for the wrong reasons simply by spotting a pattern. If the problems look too similar, once students solve the first one, they can often get the rest correct without truly understanding the idea. We can overcome this by using interleaving and adding a bit of helpful "mixing up," as explained in Chapter 5.

Optimising the think ratio can be supported by drawing on Rosenshine's Principle 7: Obtain a high success rate. Rosenshine's work provides a simple yet effective heuristic for striking a balance between challenge and success. His work suggests that when students answer approximately 80% of the questions correctly, they are both achieving and experiencing enough difficulty to encode the content. Higher success rates indicate that the material may be insufficiently challenging, thereby reducing the think ratio. Conversely, lower success rates often indicate that the content was not taught effectively. The 80% guideline is not an exact science, but it provides a helpful reference point when calibrating the level of challenge in your classroom.

Before exploring the four checking-for-understanding techniques in detail, the following decision matrix offers a high-level overview of when each technique is most useful and how they can increase the participation and the think ratio at different points in the instructional sequence. The guidance in the table is not prescriptive. Rather, it highlights design considerations that help teachers raise the quality of thinking and participation when using each approach. Effective checking for understanding depends on selecting and combining techniques in ways that generate high-quality evidence when it is most needed.

	When to Use	Maximise Participation
CC	Most effective after think time and a shared stimulus (image, text) to ensure students have something to think with. When you want to surface reasoning, misconceptions, or partial understanding. As a follow-up to other techniques.	Use question - pause - student name sequence to signal the expectation that all students should be thinking before responses are sampled. Signal that all voices matter. Give students advance notice that they will be asked questions.
MWB	When you need to sample every student's thinking. During guided practice to determine when students are ready to work independently. When checking, students have the prerequisite knowledge required for new content.	100% response requirement: all students have an MWB, a pen, and a rubber. The teacher scans all boards, not just a sample. Norms ensure all boards go up simultaneously, and students do not copy answers.
HQ	When the next instructional step depends on an understanding of a concept. When you need a rapid go/no-go decision. After initial teaching but before independent practice.	All students respond simultaneously (MWB, ABCD cards, digital). All students must commit to an answer before instruction continues.
ET	When you want to identify who is still unsure or has misconceptions at the end of a lesson. Sample and respond when planning the next lesson. When you want delayed retrieval.	Every student responds independently. Students can see how the exit ticket informs the next lesson, increasing buy-in. Participation is universal, but independent participation is key.

CC — Cold Call | **MWB** — Mini Whiteboards | **HQ** — Hinge Questions | **ET** — Exit Tickets

Maximise Thinking	Additional Guidance
Provide wait time (3–5s factual; 15–30s complex). Unbundled questioning makes listening accountable. Probing follow-ups ("Why", "How do you know?"). Sustains attention and retrieval because any student may be asked to respond.	Cold calling is not random. Plan who you will call on. Some students will need scaffolds to get going with Cold Calling, e.g., plan their answer on a MWB first. Cold Calling requires psychological safety and error-normalisation.
Writing reduces impulsive guessing. Develop routines to ensure students' responses are their own. By requiring all students to commit to an answer before responses are shared.	Most powerful when routines are automatic. Avoid talking while students write to reduce cognitive load. Treat boards as diagnostic, not performative. Responses must be brief and legible to preserve diagnostic value.
Carefully designed options require discrimination, not recall. Ensure all options are plausible. Ensure all options align with common misconceptions.	They require an investment of time to create, but you gain the time back in the lesson. Plan follow-up moves for what to do when students select the misconceptions/plausible distractors. Hinge questions must assess one idea/concept at a time.
Ensure it assesses the core content of the lesson. Target the main concept that everything else in the lesson relies on. Vary the format by using closed and open questions.	Best when short and sharply focused. Most valuable when reviewed promptly and acted on to inform the next lesson. Exit tickets are not to be marked exhaustively. Plan how you will sample them for efficiency.

8 Cold Calling

Take a moment to read these two examples. As you do, consider the following:

- Which classroom feels more inviting?
- What is the teacher doing to foster a culture of psychological safety that encourages all students to *have a go*?
- In which classroom are most students likely to be actively participating in thinking?

Classroom One	Classroom Two
Mr Johnson stands at the front of the room, arms folded, hopeful someone will give him the right answer. "Who can tell me what erosion is?"	Ms Patel steps forward. "Let's take a moment to think about how you would explain erosion. I will ask a few of you to share in a moment." She pauses, scanning the room, ensuring she smiles and makes eye contact.
Emily raises her hand immediately. "It is when rocks get worn away!"	"I am really interested to know what you are thinking, Michael."
"Yes, well done, Emily." He nods. "And who remembers one type of erosion?"	Michael is not 100% sure but feels comfortable giving it a go. "Is it when water breaks rocks?"

(*Continued*)

DOI: 10.4324/9781003657019-12

Classroom One	Classroom Two
Sarah hesitates, then raises her hand. "Um . . . abrasion?"	Ms Patel nods. "That is a great start. Is erosion just about rocks breaking? Safia, can you build on Michael's idea?"
"Correct, Sarah!" Mr Johnson praises. "And another one?"	Safia thinks. "It is when the sea or a river breaks up rocks and then carries them away?"
Silence.	"Excellent! Michael, how does that add to what you were thinking?"
Liam looks down at his book, avoiding eye contact. He thinks he might know the answer, but he is not confident. If he gets it wrong, everyone will hear. Instead, he just waits; someone else will answer.	Michael nods. "So erosion is when water breaks rocks and moves them somewhere else?"
Jake finally speaks. "Hydraulic action?"	"Exactly!" Ms Patel smiles. "Now, let's think about the different ways this happens. Can you give me one type of erosion, Shafiq?"
"Yes, good!" Mr Johnson says, quickly moving on.	Shafiq smiles. "Hydraulic action?"
	"Yes! Can you explain how that works (pause), Zoe?"
	Zoe frowns. "I . . . I am not sure."
	"That is okay," Ms Patel reassures her. "Let's think it through together. Turn and talk to your partners to see if you can explain how hydraulic action works."

There are stark differences between the two examples. The questioning approaches in the first classroom are common: a few students contributing, usually with the correct answers, whilst the rest of the class passively observes from the sidelines. But why settle for them when you could create an environment where all students feel safe and confident to have a go, even if their answers aren't quite right or are still forming?

The Transformative Power of Cold Calling

Doug Lemov, the originator of cold calling, defines it as "an invitation to a student to join the conversation."[2]

The routine use of cold calling has the potential to transform lesson effectiveness. But, like any technique, its impact depends on how teachers use it. To get the most from it, it helps to understand its benefits, the conditions for success, the principles guiding its use, and the potential pitfalls. Equally important is knowing how to integrate it with other strategies to maximise its effect.

Cold calling can be transformative, but it is often misunderstood. Misconceptions lead some to reject it outright or, worse, to use it in ways that undermine its benefits.

Three of the most common myths include:

- Cold calling is random.
- Cold calling is a tool to catch students who are not paying attention.
- Cold calling means no hands-up.

This chapter will unpack these misconceptions, how to attenuate common pitfalls, and how to maximise the impact of your cold calls.

Why Cold Calling Should Be Your Go-to Questioning Strategy

Done well, cold calling creates an inclusive classroom where every student's voice matters. It raises participation rates, provides teachers with valuable insight into students' understanding, builds retrieval practice into lessons, and helps manage lesson pace. Let's explore how.

Misconception One: Cold Calling is Random

As you will read, cold calling might appear random, but it is NOT.

To students and even classroom visitors, cold calling may seem random, but in reality, it is anything but. It is easy to conflate cold calling with using random name generators or "lollypop" sticks to call on students. Cold calling is not the same. Instead, the teacher is intentional about who they invite to contribute. It is this intentionality that signals to a child, "your voice matters." By thoughtfully selecting who to call on, teachers create an environment where every student feels that their input adds value. "Ava, your ideas always add depth to our discussions. What's your take on this?"

What could be more inclusive than inviting a student to share their thoughts, especially one who may be unsure of the importance of their voice in the classroom?[2] "Isabella, I'd love to hear your first thoughts, even if they're still forming. What's coming to mind?" These interactions are warm, inviting, and non-threatening. More importantly, they build confidence and increase students' willingness to contribute.

Recent research highlights the power of cold calling in levelling the playing field, particularly in addressing participation disparities and gender equity. Dallimore and colleagues investigated whether cold calling reduces gender gaps in participation and whether it influences students' comfort in discussions.[8] Their findings were striking: in classrooms where cold calling was used frequently, female students, who traditionally participated less, answered as many volunteer questions as their male peers. In contrast, in low cold calling environments, male students dominated the discourse. The researchers concluded that when teachers cold call more often, they foster an environment where all students feel both expected and encouraged to contribute.

Boosting Participation

> "Let's all take a quiet moment to process this example, then I'll be asking a few questions to hear what you're thinking."

Cold calling can significantly increase student participation and the amount of time students spend actively thinking during a lesson. In this example, the teacher signals to students that questions are coming and that they should be ready to share their thinking. This simple move draws attention, sharpens focus, and encourages broader engagement with the material.

Less frequently discussed is the fact that cold calling works best when students have something to think with: a stimulus. When students have a photograph, diagram, or short piece of text to attend to, they are far more likely to be thinking. "Take a moment to study this photograph, and then I am going to ask you some questions." Used in this way, cold calling does not set students up to fail. Instead, it increases the likelihood that students can generate ideas and contribute meaningfully when invited.

These moves are crucial because, as Peps Mccrea puts it, "Attention is the currency of the classroom, the gatekeeper of learning - because what our students attend to is ultimately what they learn."[9] By securing students' attention upfront, the teacher increases the likelihood that all students are thinking attentively, knowing they might be asked to contribute.

To ensure all students engage in thinking, effective cold calling follows a clear sequence: the teacher poses a question, pauses, and then selects a student to respond. This structure is essential, as it encourages every student to consider an answer.

> "What do you notice about the relationship between the two angles in this diagram?" (Pause) "Amira?"

If a teacher accepts answers only from students who raise their hands, those who choose not to volunteer may disengage, not because they lack something to contribute, but because the teacher has signalled that their participation is optional. Over time, this can reinforce a damaging habit: "I don't have to think if I don't raise my hand."

Worse still, for students who lack confidence, being repeatedly bypassed may confirm the belief that their contributions are neither valued nor expected. The result is predictable: the gap widens between the most vocal students and those who remain silent.

This does not mean students should never be allowed to volunteer by raising their hands. More on that later.

Now consider a different approach: "Amira, what do you notice about the relationship between the two angles in this diagram?" In this approach, the remaining students are unlikely to have had time or reason to respond, as the cold call is directed solely at Amira. In both cases, the result is low participation, with only one or two students doing the cognitive work. It is also worth noting that such a routine results in student responses that are superficial at best, as they have not had time to rehearse meaningful ones. Both examples highlight the power of the question, pause, and student name sequence in ensuring that all students think and are ready to contribute.

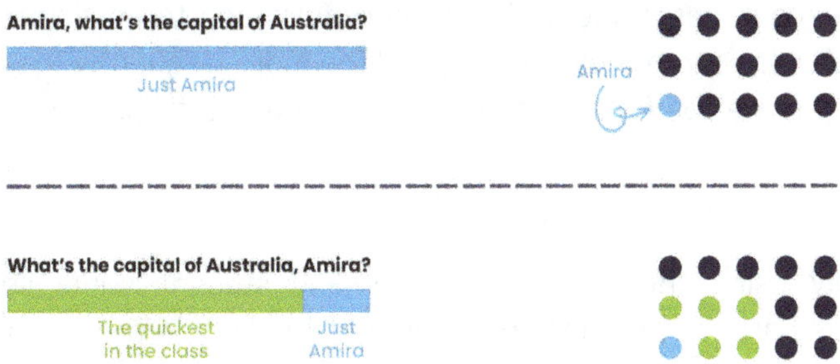

Graphic created by InnerDrive

The length of the pause, often referred to as wait time, is explored later in the chapter.

There is robust research supporting the use of cold calling to increase student participation. In 2013, Dallimore and colleagues investigated its impact on voluntary participation and students' comfort in class discussions.[10] Their findings were clear: in classrooms where cold calling was used frequently, more students contributed voluntarily compared to those in low cold calling environments. Over time, the number of voluntary participants increased, and crucially, cold calling encouraged those who might otherwise be reluctant to engage.

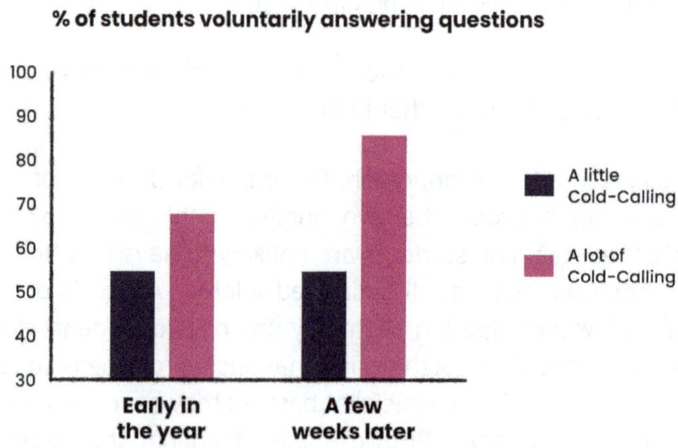

Contrary to concerns that it might cause discomfort, the study found no evidence that students felt uneasy. In fact, the opposite was true: "Cold-calling encourages students to prepare more and to participate more frequently; the more they prepare, and the more frequently they participate, the more comfortable they become when participating."

What Are They Thinking?

Routinely using the question, pause, and student name sequence increases participation and the quality of thinking in the room. In this way, cold calling becomes a powerful tool for checking for understanding. When teachers create an environment where students feel safe, comfortable, and confident to contribute, Cold calling becomes normalised: "Cold calling is just a normal part of what we do every lesson, and I know my input is valued."

This has two key benefits. First, students develop the psychological safety needed to share their thinking publicly. Second, the teacher gains access to a wider range of responses, providing a more accurate picture of student understanding and reliable information about what to do next.

As discussed earlier in this book, the wrong way to check for understanding is to rely on responses from a handful of volunteers who are likely to have the correct answer and to assume the rest of the class is equally secure in their understanding.[11] By only sampling these students, the teacher risks missing gaps in understanding across the wider group. Cold calling prevents this by providing a more strategic and intentional sampling of students' thinking.

Teachers who use cold calling are intentional about who they invite to share responses. They might select a student they are supporting to help build their confidence. They may call on a student who struggled with a concept in a previous lesson, giving them the opportunity for extra practice. In an inclusive classroom, all students are called on, not to make them uncomfortable or to catch them out, but to give the teacher the insights they need about who needs more support.

Cold Calling: A Shortcut to Retrieval

When students retrieve information after a period of partial forgetting, their brains work hard to reconstruct it, thereby improving retention. In this sense, instead of viewing forgetting as the enemy of learning, we might consider how it helps learning.

Timed right, retrieval practice interrupts forgetting (at the right moment) and reinforces learning by forcing students to reconstruct what has begun to fade.[12] Given its powerful impact, why limit retrieval practice to a do now activity at the start of a lesson?

Cognitive science has shown that when students connect new information to prior learning, they build more meaningful schemas, deepening understanding and improving retention. Failing to weave retrieval opportunities throughout a lesson is a missed opportunity.

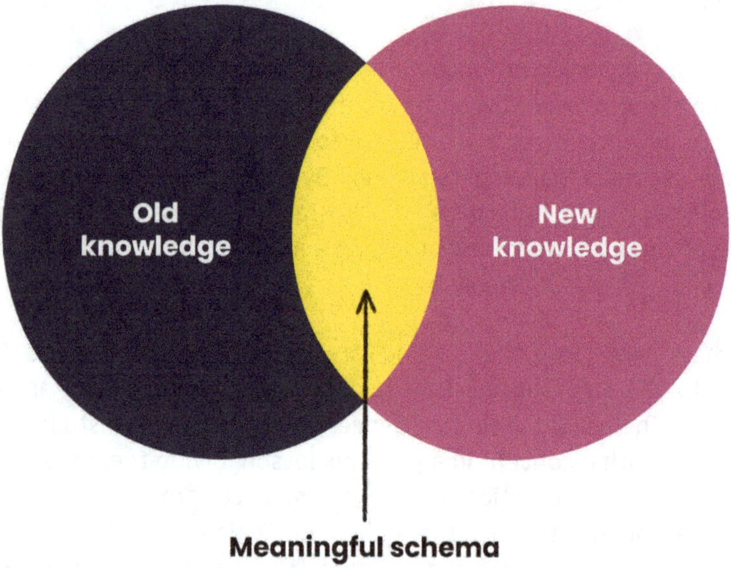

An efficient and effective way to embed retrieval practice throughout a lesson is through cold calling. Making retrieval a routine part of lesson flow via cold calls increases the frequency with which students recall prior learning. It also presents an opportunity to build confidence. By starting with lower-tariff questions and gradually increasing the level of challenge, students experience success, boosting their willingness to participate more meaningfully. Every time students successfully retrieve an answer during a cold call, they consolidate their memory of the concept. But the benefits extend beyond recall; each successful retrieval also provides a moment of achievement, a "small win" that builds confidence and increases their willingness to participate. Over time, these moments accumulate, reinforcing motivation and making students more likely to engage in future discussions.

This form of retrieval practice is known as *covert retrieval practice*, where students formulate responses in their heads rather than producing a written answer. In a 2022 study, Sumeracki and Castillo found that covert retrieval was just as effective as overt retrieval (where students write down their responses).[13] Both were significantly more effective than no retrieval at all.

Another benefit of retrieval through cold calling is that *students learn what they do*.[14] If students regularly recall prior learning through cold call questioning, they are more likely to adopt similar self-questioning strategies when studying independently, helping them strengthen their long-term retention.

Cold Calling Manages Lesson Pace

It's common for teachers to feel pressured to get a response from their students, whether that means accepting shouted-out answers or relying on the same few students raising their hands. Hearing a correct answer provides false reassurance that the teaching was effective. But in some cases, it also reinforces a false assumption that if a student cannot answer, they weren't listening.

This dynamic creates an awkward pause after a question is asked, as the teacher waits for a hand to go up, almost begging someone to answer, even if it's the same student who answered the last few questions. These moments add up. Over time, they steal valuable thinking time: minutes in a lesson, hours across the school year.

Later in this chapter, we'll explore wait time, the practice of giving students time to think before calling on them. But it's important not to conflate the wasted time described in the preceding example with wait time. The issue here is that in many classrooms, most students feel no expectation to think or prepare a response. They know that the hand-raisers will do the heavy lifting. Their attention isn't being directed to the content, and the classroom culture doesn't signal that everyone's voice matters. Worse still, when no one responds, the teacher often ends up answering the question themselves, further reinforcing the habit of passivity.

Cold calling remedies this by inviting all students to contribute. When students know they may be called on regardless of whether they've raised their hand, they are far more likely to engage with the question. The result? Less time is wasted waiting for volunteers, allowing students more time to think.

Cold Calling Done Right

There is a right way and a wrong way to use cold calling. Its success depends on the classroom culture we create. When used effectively, cold calling is warm and inviting, fosters success, and builds student confidence. The way it is delivered through tone, body language, and active listening signals to students that their contributions are valued.

Invitation, Not Interrogation

> "I know you all have great ideas on this. Take a second to think it through, and I'll ask a few of you to share."
>
> "What strategy do you think works best for solving this type of problem? I'd love to hear what you are thinking." (Pause) "Liam?"

Notice how warm and non-threatening this invitation to contribute is. The teacher signals that questions are coming, ensuring students are not suddenly thrust into the spotlight. The language is welcoming. The phrase "I'd love to hear what you are thinking" reassures students that the teacher is not expecting a perfect or complete answer, just a sense of where they are in their thinking.

Research suggests there are two ways teachers use cold calling: warm and supportive or intimidating and confrontational. The second approach is a lethal mutation and undermines both the purpose and benefits of cold calling. When used in this way, it erodes student confidence and discourages participation.

Misconception Two: Cold Calling is a Tool to Catch Students Who Are Not Paying Attention

Cold calling is **NOT** a tool to catch students off guard. While it is an excellent technique for increasing the number of students who are thinking, it should never be used to expose or embarrass students.

A 2022 study by Morek and colleagues examined how effective teachers engage silent students.[15] Their findings highlight why a warm and supportive approach is so important. Teachers who use cold calling in this way create inclusive discussions where all students, especially those who are usually quiet, feel encouraged to participate. These teachers use positive body language, maintain eye contact, and offer positive reinforcement. The result? A psychologically safe space for thought-sharing. Morek and colleagues concluded that this approach reduces anxiety, promotes high participation, and fosters a sense of belonging.

By contrast, some teachers misuse cold calling to catch students unprepared, using abrupt tones, unsupportive gestures, and focusing on errors rather than effort. Morek and colleagues found that this confrontational approach increases student anxiety, leading to feelings of incompetence and reluctance to participate.

How teachers respond to mistakes plays a significant role in shaping students' confidence. Doty and colleagues found that error framing, reducing students' fear of mistakes by normalising them as part of the learning process, helps alleviate anxiety when students are cold called.[16]

One way to do this is by front-loading information about the level of challenge to signal that perseverance is important in the face of challenging questions:

> "This is a challenge, but I know you're ready for it. Let's break it down together . . ."

Another technique is normalising uncertainty, which frames questions in a way that reassures students they are not expected to have a fully formed answer:

> "This is a big question, and we don't expect a perfect answer yet. What's one idea that might help us move forward?"

One of the simplest yet most effective teacher responses to "I don't know" is to move into paired talk. Giving students time to discuss their thinking before revisiting the cold call allows them to formulate ideas with peer support. If uncertainty still lingers, this is valuable feedback: it suggests students need further instruction, not that they should be put on the spot.

The key is not to make a big deal out of mistakes or uncertainty. Instead, remind students that forgetting is learning in disguise because revisiting content enhances memory. When errors are treated as a normal part of learning, students feel more at ease and more willing to contribute.

The Role of Body Language, Listening, and Tone

> "There might be more than one way to think about this. Let's see where your ideas take us." (Pause) "How could we test if our answer is correct?" (Pause)

Making cold calling a positive and natural part of your lessons requires a nurturing tone and positive body language. An abrupt, aggressive, or condescending tone can discourage students from contributing, creating an environment where anxiety overrides thinking. In contrast, a warm, encouraging, and welcoming tone does the opposite. Paired with open and positive body language, it fosters a classroom culture in which students feel safe taking risks in the service of learning.

Tofade and colleagues researched best practices for effective questioning.[17] Their findings highlight the importance of tone, body language, and eye contact in shaping student participation. Behaviours such as turning away while a student speaks, interrupting them mid-response, or grimacing at an answer can feel alienating and should be avoided. Instead, teachers who use positive body language by smiling, nodding, and maintaining an open, welcoming posture create a more supportive and inclusive environment.

Breaking eye contact while a student speaks can signal disinterest or disapproval, discouraging further participation. Maintaining eye contact, on the other hand, conveys confidence in the student and value in their contribution. However, a word of caution: some students, particularly those with autism or high anxiety, may prefer not to have direct eye contact. In these cases, meeting students halfway by fostering a warm environment without insisting on eye contact can help them feel included and at ease.

Making cold calling feel conversational helps put students at ease. When students speak, teachers should lean in, demonstrate active listening through positive body language, and respond thoughtfully to what they share.

Listening elevates cold calling in several key ways:

- It signals to students that their voice matters.
- It frames learning as a dialogue, shifting the classroom from a one-way flow of information to a collaborative space.
- It creates a safe environment that encourages students to speak up.
- It recognises effort in the pursuit of knowledge, reinforcing that thinking, even when incomplete, is valued.

Here are some follow-up cues to build on cold call responses.

Validating Their Effort

"That's a really thoughtful way to approach it, Liam. I can see your thinking there."

Building on Their Idea

"Nice point, Ethan! You're onto something important. Let's explore that a little more."

Encouraging Further Thinking

"Great insight, Isabella! How could we connect that to what we learned earlier?"

Highlighting Growth and Confidence

"Alex, I can tell you've been thinking deeply about this. That was a great contribution."

Normalising Partial Answers and Encouraging Risk-taking

"That's a great start, Leo! You're on the right track. Let's build on that."

Connecting Their Answer to the Class Discussion

"Chloe, that was a really insightful point. Let's use that to help us tackle the next part."

Building Motivation Through Success

Of all the things teachers can do to create the right conditions for students to thrive during cold calling, ensuring student success is arguably the most impactful. Success builds self-efficacy, confidence, and motivation, leading to greater participation and a willingness to engage with more challenging work.

In their seminal book, *How Learning Happens*, Kirschner and Hendrick debunk a common myth about motivation.[18] There is a widespread belief that if we want students to learn, we must first engage and motivate them. The research does not support this. Motivation does not directly cause better learning and performance, nor is there a simple two-way relationship in which motivation fuels learning and learning, in turn, fuels motivation.

Kirschner and Hendrick conclude, "When we experience success, no matter how small that success is, it feeds our motivation to continue."

Success is fundamental in developing students' motivation.

Ensuring student success does not mean diluting the level of challenge. Instead, we should focus on widening points of access to challenging questions by structuring them so that they set students up for success before increasing difficulty. Also, students are more likely to feel successful when they have something to think with. Directing students to attend to a photo, diagram or passage of text will likely help them to generate ideas and prepare a response.

We can also draw on Rosenshine's Principles of Instruction. He notes that the most effective teachers obtain a high success rate (Principle 7) by moving through learning in small steps and providing sufficient practice before advancing.[3] We can apply the same principle to our cold call questions. Instead of posing a single, complex question upfront, we can "unbundle" it into a series of smaller, more accessible steps, distributing them across multiple students.[2]

This technique, highlighted in Doug Lemov's *Teach Like a Champion 3.0*, yields multiple benefits:

- More students experience success, which in turn increases motivation.

- Thinking and engagement improve as students must listen to build on their peers' responses.
- A sense of belonging develops as problem-solving becomes a shared, community effort.

Unbundling is a simple yet powerful approach to structuring cold calling that fosters maximum participation, deeper thinking, and student success. Here are some examples that illustrate the spirit of this technique.

PRIMARY EXAMPLE: YEAR 4 (AGES 8-9) SCIENCE

Ms Davis: What is it called when water from rivers, lakes, or the sea turns into water vapour, Leo?

Leo: Evaporation.

Ms Davis: Good! And what causes water to evaporate, Sophia?

Sophia: Heat from the Sun.

Ms Davis: Yes! So, Oliver, when water evaporates, does it stay visible or become invisible?

Oliver: It becomes invisible.

Ms Davis: That's right. Now, when the water vapour rises, what happens as it cools, Ethan?

Ethan: It turns back into tiny water droplets.

Ms Davis: Great! What do we call this process, Ava?

Ava: Condensation.

Ms Davis: Yes! And where do we see condensation happening in the sky, Lucas?

Lucas: In clouds.

Ms Davis: Excellent. Now, Zoe, how does temperature affect evaporation?

Zoe: If it's hotter, water evaporates faster.

Ms Davis: That's correct! So, would a puddle dry faster on a hot day or a cold day, Henry?

Henry: A hot day.

Ms Davis: Brilliant! Now we understand how evaporation and condensation work in the water cycle. Can we explain the whole sequence from the beginning?

SECONDARY EXAMPLE: YEAR 9 (AGES 13–14) GEOGRAPHY

Mr Khan: What are the two tectonic plates doing at a destructive plate margin, Maya?

Maya: One plate is moving under the other.

Mr Khan: Good. What's the name of this process, Daniel?

Daniel: Subduction.

Mr Khan: Yes! Now, Isla, what type of plate is subducting beneath the other?

Isla: The oceanic plate is subducting beneath the continental plate.

Mr Khan: Well done. And why does the oceanic plate subduct rather than the continental plate, Alex?

Alex: Because the oceanic plate is denser.

Mr Khan: Yes, exactly! Now, what happens to the oceanic plate as it is forced down into the mantle, Jack?

Jack: It melts.

Mr Khan: And what does that create, Ruby?

Ruby: Magma.

Mr Khan: Good! Now, what happens when there's too much magma, Ethan?

Ethan: It rises through cracks in the crust.

Mr Khan: Right! And what happens when the pressure becomes too great, Chloe?

Chloe: The magma erupts out as a volcano.

Mr Khan: Excellent! Now, can we put all of that together to explain how volcanoes form at destructive plate margins?

Make Cold Calling the Fabric of Your Classroom

When fully embedded, cold calling signals that it's time to think, that students' contributions matter and are valued, and that it's safe to make mistakes.

To achieve this, Doug Lemov recommends making cold calling transparent by explaining to students why and how it will be used at the start of a new year or term.[2] If cold calling is already integrated into your school or trust, students are likely to view it as a standard part of classroom life. Still, occasional reminders can reinforce its purpose. You might use a speech like this to explain cold calling to students.

> In my lessons, I will use cold calling to invite you to contribute, share your answers, opinions, and thoughts. This means I may ask you a question even if you haven't raised your hand. Not to catch you out, but to encourage you to think and engage with the lesson. More importantly, I do this because your voice matters, and I genuinely want to hear what you have to say.
>
> You never need to feel nervous about making mistakes, forgetting something, or not having a complete answer. These are all normal in learning, and they actually help strengthen our memory and understanding. I want you to feel confident in sharing your thoughts, knowing that every contribution helps us all learn and improve.
>
> You will often see me smiling when I ask you a question. This is my way of encouraging you to keep going! Learning is a journey, and I am here to support you every step of the way.

> To ensure everyone has a fair chance to participate, we won't accept shouting out, and we'll try to avoid raising hands. Instead, I'll check in with as many of you as possible so that everyone feels included and valued in our learning.
>
> By working together in this way, we can create a classroom where everyone's contributions help us all grow.

Another way to improve cold calling and make it feel natural for students is simply to use it more often. In classrooms where cold calling is routine and woven into the fabric of every lesson, students participate more, volunteer contributions more freely, and feel less anxiety about being called on.[10]

Remember, the wrong way to check for understanding is to ask only a few questions, call on only a handful of volunteers, and assume it's safe to move on.

To improve at cold calling and to make students feel at ease, teachers should use it more frequently.

As mentioned earlier in this section, planning questions and follow-ups are crucial, especially when cold calling, given its fast-paced, dynamic nature. Thinking through questions in advance reduces the burden on a teacher's working memory, allowing them to focus on managing the classroom and responding to students in real time. Planned questions and expected answers ensure clarity, preventing confusion that might cloud students' thinking.

If teachers want to use cold calling to yield a more representative sample of the class's thinking, they will likely benefit from planning who they will call on. Cold calls are intentional: teachers might select students based on insights from the last lesson, homework, an exit ticket, or real-time observations. Many of these decisions can be made in advance, allowing teachers to adapt their cold calls more fluidly in response to what happens in the lesson.

Misconception Three: Cold Calling Means No Hands Up

Cold calling DOES NOT mean students can't raise their hands.

Dictating that students cannot raise their hands risks undermining one of cold calling's key purposes: creating psychological safety so students feel comfortable volunteering and contributing publicly. Strictly banning hand-raising may deter students from offering their thoughts in the future.

Instead, remind students that you might cold call them even when they don't raise their hand. Think of hand-raising this way: if many students volunteer to answer, it signals that they feel safe, confident, and motivated to share their thinking.

Wait Time, Scaffolds, and Probing

Some students will need careful nurturing to build confidence in cold calling. When viewed through the lens of inclusion, Cold calling should be about bringing students into classroom conversations rather than excluding them altogether. Teachers create conditions in which all students feel comfortable having a go.

To support this, some students may need scaffolds when being cold called, allowing them to experience success and, in turn, develop motivation and confidence. It is our responsibility as teachers to create these conditions and guide them through this process.

Wait Time: Giving Students Space to Think

Research shows that the average time between a teacher posing a question and calling on a student to respond is just 0.7 to 2 seconds.[19,20] This short wait time leads to three key problems:

1. **Shallower responses**: Students provide less rich, reflective, or developed responses. It signals that speed is valued over thoughtful contributions.
2. **Increased anxiety**: The pressure to respond immediately can heighten student anxiety, making participation feel stressful.[17]

3. **Teachers answering their own questions**: With little pause after asking a question, teachers often fill the silence themselves, encouraging students to "wait it out" rather than engage in critical thinking.

Wait time, or think time, is the deliberate pause between posing a question and selecting a student to respond. For factual or short-answer questions, 3-5 seconds is typically enough. For more complex or open-ended questions, 15-30 seconds may be necessary. At first, this pause might feel awkward, but as students and teachers experience the benefits, it quickly becomes second nature.

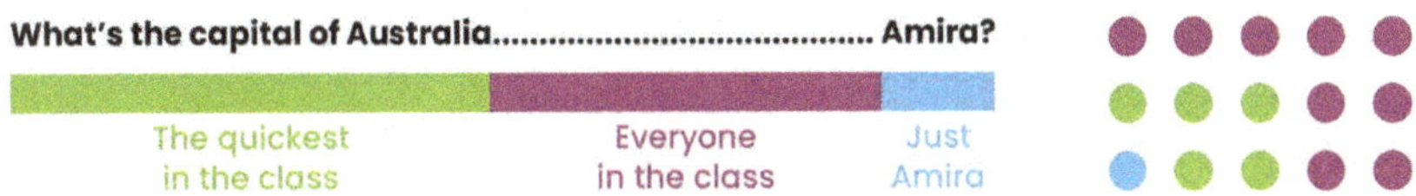

Graphic created by InnerDrive

When first extending your wait times, it can be helpful to explain why you're doing it:

> "This one might take a little extra thinking time, and that's okay . . ." (Pause) "What do you notice about this pattern?"

You might also narrate during wait time to encourage students to think and prepare their response:

> "I'm seeing a lot of thoughtful expressions. I can tell you're really working through this. I'm hoping someone can connect this idea to something we discussed yesterday."

However, as students adjust, it's important to step back and allow time for silent thinking. Too much narration can disrupt students' thinking and prevent them from focusing on formulating a response.

Incorporating deliberate thinking time before calling on students has a powerful impact on student learning. It raises the think ratio, as students rehearse richer, more thoughtful responses and have the opportunity to develop and articulate their thinking more fully. It also increases participation, giving all students time to formulate a response rather than leaving only the quickest thinkers to dominate discussions.

Research suggests that longer wait times reduce the number of "I don't know" responses, encouraging more students to attempt an answer rather than default to avoidance.[17] Additionally, it fosters greater student-to-student interaction. If an initial response needs further development, a longer pause makes the teacher more likely to have other volunteers ready to contribute. Perhaps most significantly, increased wait time has been shown to reduce student anxiety during cold calling.[19] With more time to think, students feel less pressure to come up with an immediate answer, making participation feel less intimidating and more manageable.

Scaffolding Cold Calling

A common and understandable consideration when using cold calling is how best to support shy or reluctant students. Of course, some students will feel more confident in these situations. But for those who are not, how will they ever gain the self-belief to speak in front of their peers if teachers do not give opportunities to do so?

There are many ways teachers can creatively support shy and introverted students during cold calling to help build their confidence. The goal is to gradually lead students to a place where they no longer feel hesitant to contribute. If we don't encourage these students to participate, they will struggle to develop the confidence and resilience needed to engage meaningfully. The key is to bring them along step by step.

Pair Share and Group Work as a Scaffold

A simple yet effective strategy is to combine cold calling with pair share or small-group discussions. In this approach, students have time to think, distribute responsibility, and test their ideas with their peers before sharing them with the class. Research suggests that this *dress rehearsal* effect helps reduce anxiety, making cold calling feel less daunting.[17] When students have a chance to articulate their thoughts in a low-stakes setting first, they are more likely to participate confidently in whole-class discussions.

Mini Whiteboards as a Sandbox for Ideas

Another approach is to use mini whiteboards so students can write down their responses before speaking. Mini whiteboards offer multiple benefits (covered in depth in the next chapter), but in this context, they serve as a sandbox for students' thinking: an extension of their working memory. A teacher can scan the room, identify a shy student's response, and read it aloud to the class:

> "Michael had a great response, listen to this . . ."

This moment of positive reinforcement boosts confidence and may encourage the student to participate voluntarily in future cold calls. Additionally, writing responses down can lead to higher-quality answers, as students are not wrestling with content while simultaneously managing the anxiety of being called on, and are less likely to respond with the first thing that comes to mind.

Warm Calling

Building on the mini whiteboard strategy, teachers can use **warm calling**, a gentle prompt signalling they want the student to share an answer with the rest of the class. This approach helps remove the element of surprise while reinforcing that their contributions are valued:

> "David, that's a wonderful answer on your whiteboard. I'd love for you to share it with the class."

By signalling that David's response is worth sharing, the teacher acknowledges his effort while reducing any anxiety he may have initially felt. Warm calling helps hesitant students step into participation with greater confidence.

Grouped Cold Calls

Another effective technique is to group cold calls by identifying 3-4 students who will contribute in sequence. It might look like this:

> "What do you notice about how Macbeth is portrayed in Act 5 compared to Act 1? I'll start with you, Lily, then Billy, then Lauren. Everyone else needs to listen so you can contribute too."

This method allows students to prepare their answers in advance while feeling a sense of shared responsibility. Knowing they are part of a sequence makes the experience feel less isolating and helps ensure that all students actively listen so they can build on the discussion.

Scaffolded Sentence Starters

For students who struggle to articulate their ideas, providing structured sentence starters can make cold calling feel more manageable. When faced with an open-ended question, some students may hesitate, not because they don't have an answer, but because they're unsure how to begin expressing it. This hesitation can lead to unnecessary anxiety and avoidance.

By offering simple, structured prompts, teachers can help students ease into participation while reducing the cognitive load of formulating a response from scratch. Examples include:

- "One thing I noticed was . . ."
- "I think this connects to . . ."
- "Based on what we learned earlier, I'd say . . ."
- "I'm not completely sure, but one idea I have is . . ."

These sentence starters serve multiple purposes. First, they provide a clear way into an answer, helping students organise their thinking. Second, they signal that responses don't have to be perfect; what matters is engaging with the question. Finally, they give students a safety net, ensuring that even if they aren't fully confident in their response, they have a structured way to begin contributing.

Over time, as students become more comfortable formulating responses, the reliance on sentence starters will naturally decrease. However, for those who need extra support, having these scaffolds readily available can turn hesitant speakers into confident participants, ensuring that cold calling remains an inclusive and effective classroom strategy.

Crucially, the metaphor of scaffolding signals that support should be temporary and gradually withdrawn. If it is not, students risk becoming over-dependent on it. Scaffolds may be necessary to build early success and motivation during cold calling, but as students' confidence and competence develop, that support should be deliberately faded.

Probing for Depth

According to Rosenshine, great teaching hinges on asking the kinds of questions that probe students' thinking.[3] These questions push students to articulate the reasoning behind their responses, requiring them to process material at a much deeper level. In doing so, they deepen both their understanding and memory of the content.

Remember: students learn what they do.[14] This means that the cognitive work they engage in is what gets encoded into long-term memory. If we want students to develop a deep understanding, it's not enough for them to simply recall facts or answers. They need to grasp the underlying *why* and *how*: how a concept can be applied, how it connects to prior learning, and how it links to broader ideas.

To achieve this, we need questioning strategies that draw out and expand students' thinking, ensuring they engage in the kind of hard thinking that leads to lasting learning.

One such approach is the use of probing questions, which Tom Sherrington describes as the hallmark of great teaching.[21] The idea is that every teacher-student interaction becomes a short dialogue: an exchange of three to four follow-up questions designed to deepen or widen the student's initial response.

Executing this effectively requires strong subject knowledge. Many of these follow-up questions will be responsive and in the moment, making them difficult to plan in advance. This means teachers must listen carefully to students' answers and adapt their questioning accordingly.

Probing questions are a powerful yet simple tool for increasing the cognitive effort students exert. By consistently pushing students to explain, justify, and connect their thinking, teachers ensure that learning moves beyond surface-level recall.

Here are some examples based on Tom Sherrington's concept of probing questions.

- Can you expand on that idea?
- What evidence supports your answer?
- How does this connect to what we learned earlier?
- Can you think of a counterargument or an alternative perspective?
- What would happen if we changed one part of the problem?
- Can you explain that in your own words?
- How did you arrive at that conclusion?
- What might be the implications of this idea?
- Can you justify your reasoning?
- What assumptions are we making here?
- How does this link to a real-world example?

- Can you break that down step by step?
- What would you say to someone who disagrees with you?
- Is there another way to think about this?
- What makes this idea important?

Another technique is ABC: agree, build, or challenge. This strategy works similarly to unbundling, as each response is contingent on the previous answer. Students must listen carefully to their peers and decide whether they want to agree, build on the idea, or challenge it with a different perspective. Whatever they decide, they must be able to explain their reasoning.

This approach is particularly effective for helping students identify misconceptions and errors. The key is that the teacher does not reveal the correct answer too soon. Instead, they guide students toward clarity by allowing them to work collaboratively to refine their thinking.

Here, tone and body language are crucial. The teacher should remain neutral and non-dismissive, ensuring that students feel comfortable exploring ideas, even if they are incorrect. At the same time, students should be expected to think deeply and work collectively to reach their best possible conclusions.

Here are some examples to give you a sense of how it works.

YEAR 5 (AGES 9–10) MATHS: ORDERS OF OPERATION

Mr Khan: Here's a number sentence: 16 + 4 × 2 =? What do you think the answer is . . . Sam?

Sam: 40.

Mr Khan: Mmm, interesting. Do you agree, want to build, or challenge that . . . Ben?

Ben: I challenge! I think Sam added 16 and 4 first, but I think multiplication should come first.

Mr Khan: Hmm, so you're saying Sam might have done the operations in the wrong order? Do you agree, want to build, or challenge that . . . Maya?

Maya: I agree with Ben. We should do 4 × 2 first, which is 8, then add 16. That makes 24.

Mr Khan: Okay, so we now have two different answers, 40 and 24. Can you explain why we do multiplication first . . . Olivia?

Olivia: Because in maths, multiplication happens before addition unless there are brackets.

Mr Khan: Yes! That's called the order of operations. Sam, let's go back to you. Do you see where you went wrong?

Sam: Oh! I added first, but I should have multiplied first. The answer is 24.

Mr Khan: Excellent! Now, what if I wrote it like this instead: (16 + 4) × 2 =? Would that change the answer? Let's think about it . . .

YEAR 8 (AGES 12–13) ENGLISH: A MIDSUMMER NIGHT'S DREAM

Ms Reynolds: In *A Midsummer Night's Dream*, love often causes problems. Why do you think that is, Luke?

Luke: Because people fall in love with the wrong person.

Ms Reynolds: Mmm, interesting. Do you agree, want to build, or challenge that . . . Zara?

Zara: I agree, but I think magic plays a big role too. The love potion makes people fall in love with the wrong person.

Ms Reynolds: Hmm, so love itself isn't the problem, but the magic makes it chaotic? Do you agree, want to build, or challenge that . . . Sam?

Sam: I want to challenge it. Even before the magic, Hermia and Lysander have problems because her father doesn't want them to be together.

Ms Reynolds: Ah, so love creates conflict even without magic. Do you want to build on that . . . Jake?

Jake: Yes! Egeus wants Hermia to marry Demetrius instead, creating a conflict between her and her father because of her love.

Ms Reynolds: That's a strong point. Does love create problems only between lovers, or does it also affect families and friendships . . . Ava?

Ava: I think it affects families, too, like with Hermia and Egeus, but also friendships, because Helena and Hermia fall out over the love potion mix-up.

Ms Reynolds: Mmm, so love is quite disruptive in different ways. Final question: Does the play suggest that love is a positive or negative force? Let's hear some thoughts.

The Seven Deadly Sins of Cold Calling

This chapter provides a comprehensive guide to getting cold calling right, highlighting common pitfalls along the way. When used effectively, cold calling boosts participation, deepens thinking, and fosters a culture of high expectations. However, when misused, it can erode student confidence, discourage participation, and create unnecessary anxiety.

The following is a summary of common pitfalls and how to avoid them, ensuring that cold calling remains an inclusive and effective tool for checking for understanding.

1. **Turning cold calling into a "Gotcha" moment**
    - **The problem:** Some teachers use cold calling to catch students off guard and punish them for not paying attention. This leads to fear-based participation rather than genuine engagement.
    - **The remedy:** Frame cold calling as an invitation, not an interrogation. Give students advance notice and always keep cold calls

warm and supportive. Provide a resource for students to consider: a photo, diagram, or passage of text.

2. **Not giving enough wait time**
   - **The problem**: Rushing students to answer immediately increases anxiety and results in shallow responses.
   - **The remedy:** Extend the wait time to give students a moment to think. If necessary, narrate the silence: "Take a few seconds to think. I'll wait."
3. **Moving too quickly through questions**
   - **The problem:** Some teachers ask a cold call question, receive an answer, and immediately move on. This discourages deeper thinking and signals that quick responses are more valued than thoughtful ones.
   - **The remedy:** Use probing follow-ups to stretch thinking. Instead of moving on, ask: "What makes you say that?" or "Can you expand on that idea?"
4. **Cold calling without scaffolding**
   - **The problem:** Shy or reluctant students may feel overwhelmed if called on without proper support.
   - **The remedy:** Use scaffolds such as warm calling, mini whiteboards, or pair share to help students build confidence before speaking.
5. **Over-reliance on the same few students**
   - **The problem:** Teachers may unintentionally call on the same confident students, reinforcing participation gaps.
   - **The remedy:** Plan your cold calls in advance to ensure a balance between confident volunteers and reluctant speakers.
6. **Eliminating hands-up participation entirely**
   - **The problem:** While cold calling is designed to engage all students, banning hand-raising altogether can backfire by discouraging students who want to volunteer.

- **The Remedy**: Strike a balance. Cold calling should complement, not replace, voluntary participation. Explain to students: "I may cold call you even if your hand isn't up, but if lots of hands go up, that's great! It shows confidence."

7. **Failing to normalise mistakes**
   - **The problem:** If students fear getting an answer wrong, they will disengage from cold calling.
   - **The remedy**: Use error framing to demonstrate that mistakes are an integral part of the learning process. Reinforce that thinking, even when incomplete, is valuable. "That's a great attempt! Let's build on it together."

Cold Calling Spotlight – Alex Fairlamb

Alex is a Trust Teaching and Learning Coach and an education consultant. She is a Fellow of the Chartered College of Teaching and an Honorary Fellow of the Historical Association. Alex is the co-author of the best-selling The Scaffolding Effect *and co-editor of* What Is History Teaching, Now?.

Cold calling is an invaluable tool for checking understanding and one I believe offers many benefits. Cold calling:

- Demonstrates that we have high expectations of everyone; there is no one that we believe cannot offer a formative answer, opinion or idea.
- Creates conditions for all students to think hard.
- Ensures 100% participation.
- Generates feedback that supports responsive teaching, informing whether strategies such as additional scaffolding are needed.

Moreover, what makes it incredibly powerful is that, over time, it makes classrooms more equitable by fostering an ethos and culture in which every voice is valued. For these reasons, cold calling is used as a core strategy in our school from EYFS to Year 13.

Our decision to implement cold calling came as part of our focus on assessment and feedback, which was the golden thread of our CPD programme for two academic years. We created a bank of ten core feedback strategies, one of which is questioning, and this is where cold calling sits as a technique. To implement cold calling, alongside the other ten strategies, we set up a half-termly focus on one core strategy throughout the year. Following whole school PD where the ten strategies were launched, our PD cycle consisted of:

- **Deimplementing**: removing techniques which may have previously been used as part of cold calling but should not be used, such as moving away from the random selection of students to call upon for feedback to strategically selecting students. This has led to the removal of things such as lollysticks and random name generators.
- **Whole school development and nudges**: a focus per half term with a core training manual which included the steps to implementation, along with blogs, podcasts, and videos of the technique in action. The weekly T&L bulletin would also include tips to raise awareness of the technique and support the development of mental models. The sequenced and chunked nature of our PD programme meant that even when we began to focus on another feedback technique, we would retrieve our knowledge of cold call and revisit areas that needed tweaking, such as ensuring that names were being used after the question and wait time, and that staff were letting students know that cold calling would be used. We also ensured that, when we introduced cold calling, we introduced "no opt out" (except in PSHE). The purpose of threading "no opt out" alongside it was to ensure that we were promoting the sense of "giving it a go" in an environment where it is safe to fail, to demonstrate our high expectations that everyone is expected to participate, and prevents (over time, usually in later year groups) students thinking that they can simply state that they don't know.

- **Departmental/phase**: each subject and phase curated over time a "Sharing Good Practice" booklet that brought together examples of how that strategy and technique should look. This provided the opportunity to create subject-specific examples to support subject/ phase PD and also provide a crib sheet for novice staff or those new to the school (to support induction). This is important so that the subject and age/stage are recognised, and teachers have examples of these powerful feedback strategies being used within contexts that they genuinely work in.
- **Quality assurance:** this included SLT and subject/phase learning walks to see strategies in action with the ethos of looking at, not looking for (Didau); in essence, if we happened to be focusing on cold calling that half term, don't throw it in to demonstrate compliance when we walk through the door! Instead, if we see it as a natural part of the lesson, that's fine. However, if cold calling wasn't an appropriate strategy at that time in the classroom, we would consider other feedback strategies. We intended that, therefore, cold calling would be used when meaningful to do so and that it would be used responsively, rather than as part of a rigid lesson checklist. Moreover, lesson observations which have pupil voice in them, included open questions about how the teacher checks for understanding: "How does your teacher gather information about what you know? What does it look like? What happens if you don't know it yet?"

YEAR 4 EXAMPLE: ROMAN BRITAIN

Teacher: We're going to look very carefully at two pictures. One of a Stone Age Village, the other of a Roman town. I want you to think about the differences that you can spot between the two images. There are three. I'm going to give you 30 seconds. I will then cold call to get your suggestions. Remember, there's no opt-out, so give it a go!

[Turn and talk lasts 30 seconds, and the teacher calls for attention.]

Teacher: What differences can you spot between the Stone Age village and the Roman town . . . . Suha?

Suha: I'm not certain . . .

Teacher: Don't worry, Suha. I'm going to go to two other people, and then I'll come back to you. Use this additional thinking time to look again. Now, what did you spot . . . . . . Rayan?

[The teacher would then return to Suha after cold calling two further students, either gather a final difference, or, if Suha was still stuck, ask her to build on the two responses her peers had given before asking another student for the final difference.]

Our subsequent CPD golden threads have been "attention" (looking at attention, 100% participation, and everyone thinking hard) and "adaptive teaching and scaffolding." This means we can develop our cold calling mental models, as we now have a stronger understanding of how to use cold calling powerfully and how scaffolds, such as turn-and-talk and mini whiteboards, can create conditions for high participation and everyone thinking hard. We must embed cold calling from EYFS through to Year 13 so that it becomes the norm across all classrooms, driving our students' motivation and building a sense of belonging.

9 Mini Whiteboards

Imagine a typical classroom of 30 students. Over a 60-minute lesson, the teacher poses 10 questions and calls on 3-4 students each time. By the end of the lesson, the teacher receives 30-40 answers. Now imagine the same lesson with one key difference: instead of calling on a few, the teacher requires every student to respond on a mini whiteboard. In the same amount of time, the teacher receives 300 responses. With every student answering, the teacher's judgements about what the class knows, misunderstands, or is ready for become more accurate, representative, and actionable.

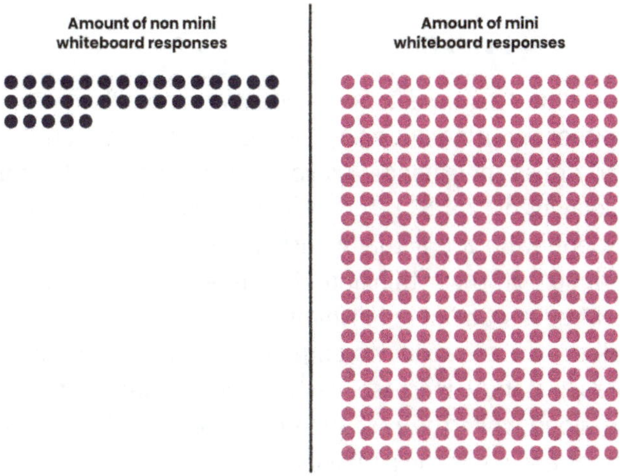

DOI: 10.4324/9781003657019-13

You will recall from earlier chapters in this book that Barak Rosenshine asserts that the most effective teachers ask many questions and routinely check the understanding of all students.[3] He notes that in less effective classrooms, teachers pose only a few questions, call on the same volunteers (who usually provide correct answers), and assume this reflects the whole class. Mini whiteboards are an efficient way to sample each student's thinking simultaneously.

Used effectively, mini whiteboards help reveal what students are thinking. They help reveal every student's thinking, rather than just the confident few. Sceptics may say they are onerous. But as Craig Barton puts it:

> If you are not going to use mini-whiteboards, how are you going to get an accurate sense of the effort and understanding of every student?[22]

This chapter will demonstrate how the pedagogical affordances of using mini whiteboards far exceed any minor drawbacks.

Why Use Mini Whiteboards?

They Boost Participation

It is not uncommon to see a few students monopolise classroom dialogue by either shouting out or by the teacher calling on them because they eagerly raise their hands. As you will recall from Chapter 7, Doug Lemov's concept of "ratio" refers to two aspects of learning: the number of students who are actually participating (the participation ratio) and the rigour of their thinking (the level of desirable difficulty).[2] A significant advantage of mini whiteboards, compared to the dynamics just described, is their ability to engage every student in thinking. Mini whiteboards instantly increase participation. Instead of one student answering aloud while the rest tune out, every student must attempt the questions and show their thinking.

Such an all-student-response mechanism secures students' attention, keeping them accountable whilst reducing passivity. This is important for two reasons:

- Their use creates universal participation. This means all students get to practice using the facts, ideas, and concepts they are learning. Using mini whiteboards is a low-stakes way for all students to rehearse, elaborate, and consolidate what they are learning.
- They provide an instant snapshot of understanding across the class. This offers teachers an efficient way to spot common patterns, see who has understood, and identify who is unsure.

They Promote Responsive Teaching

Rather than speculating about what students are thinking, mini whiteboards make the invisible visible. The immediate feedback they provide enables teachers to diagnose and address misconceptions quickly.

The benefits of mini whiteboards are far-reaching. Mini whiteboards help teachers to spot misconceptions, such as a reversed letter or a misspelt sound pattern, during phonics lessons.[23] Integrating writing and reading in phonics strengthens memory. When children write a new letter or word while saying the sounds aloud, they double the chance of encoding it. In this way, the mini whiteboard reinforces the link between grapheme and phoneme. It also provides a live check for understanding.

In English, contrary to what many teachers likely assume, mini whiteboards can be used in a variety of ways. When introducing new vocabulary, for example, the teacher can display examples and non-examples and ask students to indicate whether the word has been used correctly in context by holding up a tick or a cross on their whiteboard. Teachers might also ask students to practise producing sophisticated sentences by presenting a simple example on the board and directing them to rewrite it using more academic language.

In maths or science, mini whiteboards can help reveal common calculation errors or mistaken reasoning patterns. They allow teachers to address these with the group. Importantly, the whole class snapshot from a mini whiteboard routine helps the teacher decide what to do next. If 80% or more of the class provides the desirable response, the teacher can confidently move on and offer support for the few who are still unsure. If 40-80% of the class can answer correctly, this suggests there is still some confusion and uncertainty. The best course of action is to add clarity by providing contrasting examples or models and then check again. When fewer than 40% of the class can answer the question correctly, it is a case of reteaching the material.

The decision to move on or reteach is more valid because it rests on a larger, more representative sample of students' thinking than traditional question techniques allow.

What is 0.006 ÷ 0.02?

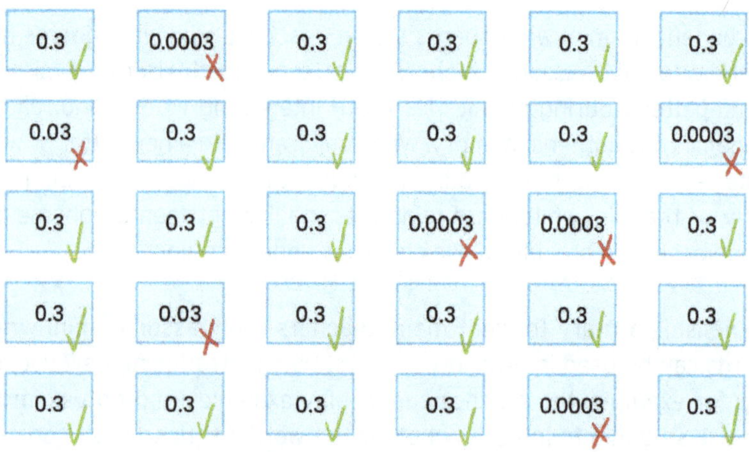

They Are Low Stakes

Even quieter or more reluctant students join in with mini whiteboards, since writing an answer to display is less daunting than speaking aloud.

Their impermanence makes them feel low-stakes. The erasable surface frees students from worrying about mistakes or messy work. In this way, mini whiteboards create a safe sandbox for thinking, allowing students to experiment with answers, knowing errors won't be permanent or harshly judged.

Later in this chapter, concerns such as the lack of written evidence in students' books when using mini whiteboards are addressed. For now, consider this: David Didau observes that if we prioritise permanence, we must also prioritise quality.[24] He suggests that having students write incorrect answers in their exercise books without correction is counter-productive. Instead, mini whiteboards let students practise and refine their responses before recording a more permanent version.

They Are Versatile

Mini whiteboards are versatile tools that enrich almost any subject. In maths, they are ideal for working out problems, sketching shapes and graphs, or completing a quick hinge question to check whether students understand a concept such as negative numbers.

Similarly, in science lessons, mini whiteboards facilitate quick diagram drawing (cells, circuits, chemical structures) and labelling for retrieval practice, or summarising experimental results.

In English or history, mini whiteboards might serve different purposes: students can brainstorm ideas, write short analytical sentences, or record key points from a text or source, which the teacher can then scan and share as model responses.

In language learning, teachers use mini whiteboards for vocabulary and grammar practice. For example, students might translate sentences or conjugate verbs.

Mini whiteboards also help complement other pedagogical approaches. We have already seen how they can support cold calling in the last chapter. They can also elevate think-pair-share. This technique becomes more rigorous when each student first records their ideas on a mini whiteboard (think). Then, students discuss with a partner (pair) and potentially refine their answer. Finally, the teacher calls on a few students to share. The initial think stage, facilitated by the mini whiteboard, increases the likelihood that all students have something valuable to contribute during their pair work. It also means they get two attempts to rehearse their answer before potentially being called on to share it with the rest of the class.

Benefits of the Mini Whiteboard

The research base for mini whiteboards comes mainly from studies on *response cards*: small, erasable boards used by every student to present an answer simultaneously. Since response cards function in the same way as mini whiteboards, the benefits discussed here apply entirely. For clarity, this chapter will continue to use the term mini whiteboards.

Numerous studies and meta-analyses show significant gains in participation, achievement, and on-task behaviour when all students use mini whiteboards rather than traditional hand-raising.

A foundational study by Gardner et al. (1994) compared students answering questions on mini whiteboards and hand-raising in 5th-grade (UK Year 6) science lessons.[25] The results were striking. The frequency of responses was 14 times greater during lessons using mini whiteboards than during hand-raising lessons. This increased participation resulted in improved achievement. All 22 students in the class scored higher on follow-up quizzes and tests after mini whiteboard lessons compared to hand-raising lessons. By increasing participation, the entire class demonstrated improved content retention, as shown by follow-up tests conducted the next day and again two weeks later.

Building on these results, similar findings have been observed across subjects and age groups. For example, Christle and Schuser's (2003) study in a 4th-grade (UK Year 5) maths class similarly found that using mini whiteboards boosted learning and on-task behaviour.[26] In their

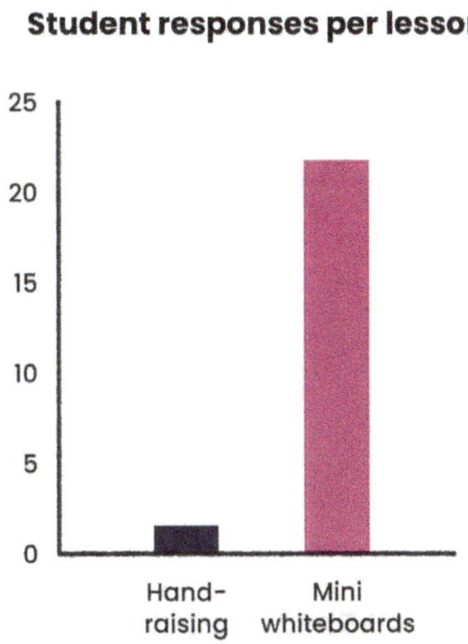

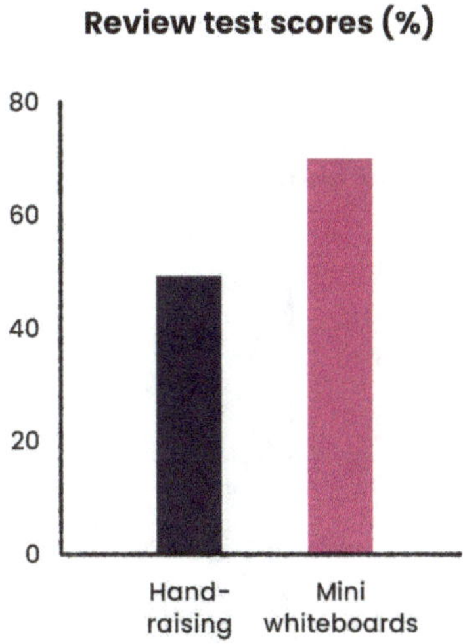

study, student participation was significantly higher during the mini whiteboard condition than during hand-raising. Significantly, weekly quiz scores improved when using mini whiteboards. An additional observable benefit was reduced disruptive behaviour as students spent more time thinking and responding to questions. This study suggests that mini whiteboards not only improve participation but also translate this increased engagement into a better grasp of the material and a more focused learning environment.

Beyond individual studies, meta-analyses examining multiple mini whiteboard studies also demonstrate their efficacy across multiple outcomes. Building on Randolph's (2007)[27] meta-analysis of 18 studies, Marsh and colleagues (2023)[28] reviewed 15 additional studies (totalling 33) from 2005–2019, offering a comprehensive synthesis of the research. Both meta-analyses found large, statistically significant positive effect sizes for using mini whiteboards over traditional hand-raising across multiple outcomes. The meta-analyses show that mini whiteboards significantly improve test and quiz scores and class participation rates. They also indicate that students exhibit less off-task, disruptive behaviour. Reassuringly, these benefits were replicated in different age groups and subjects. Notably, the updated meta-analysis concludes that mini white-boards particularly benefit students with special educational needs.

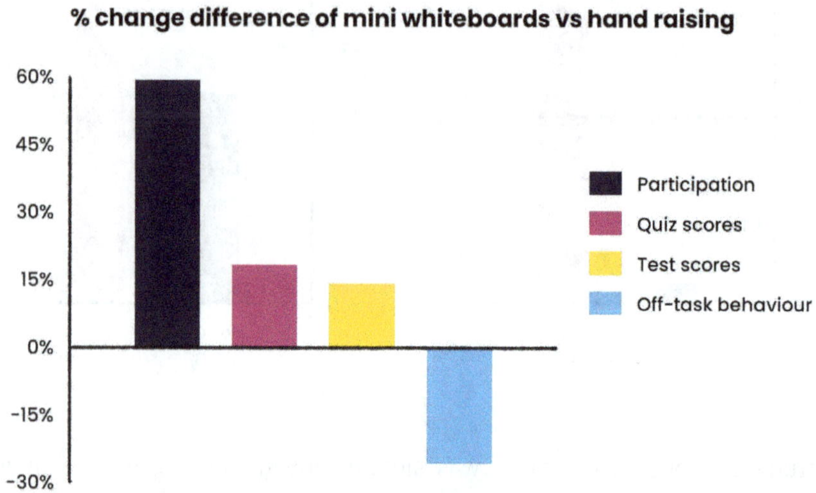

Research consistently demonstrates the effectiveness of mini white-boards. They markedly increase participation rates, which in turn foster better learning and behaviour. These effects have been replicated across age groups, subjects, and in both mainstream and special education settings. The evidence affirms that mini whiteboards represent a low-cost, high-impact tool for formative assessment.

So, if mini whiteboards are the *number one bit of classroom kit*, why don't all teachers use them?[29] In their meta-analysis, Marsh et al. attribute teacher reluctance to their dissatisfaction with distributing and collecting the mini whiteboards. They also suggest that some teachers do not perceive students' low response rates as problematic and, therefore, are less likely to invest the time and effort to learn and implement a tool to boost participation. The key to overcoming such perceptions lies in this question: ***Would I rather spend one minute handing out whiteboards, or an entire lesson unsure of what most of my students are thinking?***

Most teachers who use mini whiteboards find that seeing all students' thinking more than compensates for the time it takes to distribute them. Nonetheless, practical barriers do exist. The following sections examine how to implement them effectively in practice and address the obstacles that sometimes deter teachers from using them.

Routines

Plan Questions and Formats in Advance

> Questions that provide a window into students' thinking are not easy to generate, but they are crucially important if we are to improve the quality of students' learning. (Wiliam, 2011)[30]

Like all the strategies in this book, the success of using mini whiteboards begins before entering the classroom. Questions that reveal students' thinking are challenging to create, but vitally important if we are to keep learning on track. Wiliam suggests that in schools where teachers spend a lot of time marking individual books, the time would be better spent creating questions that would tell them what students understood in the lesson. He goes on to point out that doing so allows teachers to deal with misconceptions and knowledge gaps in the moment rather than writing the same repetitive feedback comment in each book.

In the context of mini whiteboards, this is important. Some teachers, when first using mini whiteboards, mistakenly pose complex questions on the fly that require an extended written response that won't fit legibly on the board, or vague questions that don't yield actionable feedback. More proficient users tend to map out key questions they intend to ask. For example, a prerequisite knowledge check before introducing a new concept, a hinge question (next chapter) midway, and a deeper application question before independent practice. Wiliam suggests that teacher collaboration is key to building a stock of good questions.

It is also essential to plan ahead of the lesson and decide on the format for student responses. For short written responses, insist that students fill their boards with their answer in big writing. If you are using them for a hinge or multiple-choice question, direct students to write the letter or number. If a maths problem, specify the form, e.g. "Draw the graph of . . ." Planning these details avoids confusion and improves your ability to scan and sample answers in the moment. It is essential to clarify the format with your students so they know what you expect of them.

The Setup

Some teachers argue that mini whiteboards consume valuable learning time. However, as seen in the cold calling chapter, teachers can spend considerable time filling gaps during questioning because they have not adopted a routine that requires all students to prepare an answer. Mini whiteboards address this by prompting all students to prepare answers. Nonetheless, it pays to have routines to promote a smooth execution and reduce lost learning time.

Plan how you will distribute: Determine the method and timing for students to collect their mini whiteboards. There is no absolute method. Consider where you will store your mini whiteboards, pens, and erasers, either in individual plastic folders or in baskets at the end of rows. Do students collect them upon entry, or does one student per row/table distribute them? Base these choices on your classroom layout. The goal is to streamline the routine to minimise wasted learning time. After planning, rehearse and refine the process as needed. Expect routines to become faster within a week or two of practice.

Plan how you will maintain whiteboard pens: They tend to dry out, especially when used frequently. Maintaining reliable supplies supports continuous student participation and prevents avoidable disruptions. Some schools include a whiteboard pen and a rubber in their equipment policy. If this applies to your school, you will know whether this is an embedded part of your school culture and whether it means students always have a pen ready when required. It is sensible to always have extra pens and erasers on hand to avoid hiccups.

Another solution to the problem is to invoke Craig Barton's Pen Trilogy.[31] He suggests that a faulty pen might seem like a minor issue, but in his experience observing hundreds of teachers, this small detail can derail a check for understanding. The remedy involves three steps: first, have students check that their pen works before posing a question; second, train students to put the lid on the top of the pen when using it; and third, train students to put the lid back on the pen when not in use. These tips extend the pen's lifespan and reduce distractions, such as students doodling or pen lids going missing.

Respond and Show

To maximise the effectiveness of mini whiteboards, establish routines for how students should respond and present their answers.

Front-load the means of participation: Some students instinctively answer questions before the teacher finishes asking or giving instructions. Eager students might shout out, grab their pens and start writing, or tell their partner the answer. Adam Boxer suggests that to address this, teachers need to front-load the means of participation.[32] In other words, inform students first that they will write their answers on mini whiteboards before posing the question. For example, "Right, class, in silence, we are going to answer this question on our mini whiteboards. Get your boards and pens ready. What is the difference between . . . ?" By explicitly telling students how they will participate before sharing the question, you make your expectations clear and reduce the likelihood of distractions.

Instruct students to write big: A common pitfall is students writing answers that are too small to read. Instruct them to write their answers in large, clear letters. Show them an example and a non-example for reference. Doing so will make your sampling and response interpretation much more efficient.

Use routines to reduce the risk of copying: Having students write their answers in large print can create a new problem: students copy one another's answers, reducing the integrity of your check for understanding. There are a few ways to mitigate this problem. First, explain to your students the purpose of using mini whiteboards. Remind them that you are not recording their answers and that it isn't a test. Communicate your desire to understand each individual's thoughts, allowing you to celebrate novel ideas and support them when their answers aren't quite correct or fully formed. Also, fostering a culture in which students feel safe making mistakes reduces the incentive to copy.

You might also use a routine that encourages students to conceal their responses from their peers. Have students hover their boards face down once they've finished. Doing so reduces copying and gives you a visual cue that they are ready to reveal their answers.

If you suspect copying, use cold calling to probe individual thinking and reveal how students arrived at their answers. Students will be less likely to copy in the future as they know you might ask them to elaborate on their responses.

Control how and when students reveal their responses: Specify how and when students will present their mini whiteboards. Without guidance, students may reveal answers too soon, which can encourage them to copy one another. Use a simple countdown: "3-2-1 and show me your boards." Insist students keep boards up as long as necessary to process responses.

Scan and Feedback

The primary purpose of reviewing students' mini whiteboard responses is to quickly assess the whole class's understanding. To avoid being overwhelmed by processing 30–32 boards at once, establish routines for efficiently sampling and reviewing answers.

Manage the volume of information: When it is time to view answers, your goal is to scan the room. Stand where you can see all the boards at once. Ensure to be seen scanning by looking at each whiteboard. Scanning every board signals to students that their effort is valued and that you intend to read each response, even if you can't. There will be occasions when it would take too long to read every response verbatim, especially when the question requires a more extended response. In these moments, still be seen scanning, but pay particular interest to responses from specific students. For example, check the answers of students least likely to know. If they have a correct answer, you can assume that everyone else got it right, too. Conversely, if higher-attaining students are struggling, this likely implies the rest are too.

Another way to manage the volume of responses is to do so systematically, instructing students on each row or table to lower their boards in turn. You could sample the back row, absorb their answers, ask them to lower their boards, and repeat this process for the row in front. And so on.

Make inferences and act: As you scan, make a mental note of outliers. If more than 20% of your class has a misconception, address it with the whole class. "I see a few of you answered . . . Let's clarify why that might seem right, but . . ." Suppose the question requires a more open-ended response or is a problem with more than one solution. In that case, this provides an excellent opportunity to analyse different responses under a visualiser.

Act on the information from scanning. If 80% or more answer correctly, proceed and quickly address the remaining 20% of errors. If confusion is widespread, stop and reteach before moving on. The 80:20 split is a rough guide; below 80%, pause to clarify or risk leaving students behind.

Probe student responses: Mini whiteboards provide a rich supply of feedback. Leverage them fully. You can do this by using follow-up cold calls to probe students' thinking. "I see some of us got 58. How did you get 58 (pause), James?" The bottom line is that it pays to slow down and respond to feedback, whether that means discussing the trickiest questions, explaining or clarifying a point, or noting individuals to support.

Preempt and plan for misunderstanding: The primary reason for using mini whiteboards is to check all students' understanding so that you can make better-informed decisions. The most effective teachers will anticipate and plan for what happens when students give incorrect answers. You can't prepare for every eventuality, but you can plan for what happens if students don't have secure prior knowledge.

An effective way to do this is to use mini whiteboards to assess prerequisite knowledge before introducing new content. When planning to introduce new content, identify the prior knowledge students need to have a secure grasp of to access the new learning. Use mini whiteboards to surface the reliability and strength of this knowledge. If students can't reliably retrieve this information, it is essential to invest time in teaching it to avoid building new knowledge on unstable foundations.

In addition to improving prerequisite checks, using mini whiteboards streamlines the process compared to students completing the questions in their exercise books. The teacher quickly gains a clear snapshot of class readiness, avoiding the time-consuming process of circulating and deciphering students' handwriting in their exercise books. This efficiency means more time is available for what matters most: reteaching and reinforcing foundational concepts.

The mini whiteboard exercise book comparison serves as a natural segue into the next section on concerns and obstacles to using mini whiteboards.

Addressing Potential Challenges

What About a Lack of Work in Exercise Books?

If you're concerned that using mini whiteboards might mean there's less written evidence of learning in students' books, allow Dylan Wiliam to allay your fears:

> The best formative assessment processes often leave no written evidence; just a smarter decision by the teacher about what to do next . . .[33]

The work students produce on mini whiteboards is ephemeral. For some, especially in schools with rigid book scrutiny policies, this can be concerning. However, take a moment to reflect on the purpose of the permanent record in exercise books. If the purpose is to generate information for formative purposes, is it really necessary to keep every rough attempt on paper?

David Didau points out that students often fill their books with incomplete answers that, outside the lesson context, don't demonstrate much.[24] For example, writing answers to a retrieval quiz that make no sense later without the question. He goes on to suggest that in English, exercise books often contain low-level comprehension tasks that students usually answer poorly, making many errors.

If teachers fail to mark and correct every piece of work meticulously, students' books memorialise misconceptions, errors, and sloppy work. By contrast, students use mini whiteboards to draft, think, and practise in a way that teachers can instantly check and correct. Learning happens here, and arguably to an even greater extent.

Of course, students should be writing in exercise books, and no one is saying they should always write on mini whiteboards. There are no false dichotomies here. A sensible way to think about this is to use mini whiteboards for practising, rehearsing, and checking for understanding. Then have students solve problems or write in their books once understanding is secure and misconceptions are resolved. In this way, students' books become a valid showcase of their best thinking and progress, providing enduring evidence of learning and development.

Won't Students Misuse Them?

Some teachers and leaders are reluctant to use mini whiteboards, especially with "tricky classes," because they fear students might misuse them. The findings of Marsh and colleagues (2023) should dampen such concerns.[28] They found that using a clearly defined set of routines and expectations results in mini whiteboards doing the opposite. Mini whiteboards reduce off-task behaviour.

Nonetheless, developing such routines takes time and patience. This chapter contains many routines to help you reduce the risk of students misusing mini whiteboards. It would be unrealistic to implement them all at once. A routine needs repeated practise and reinforcement to become automatic. In *Atomic Habits*, James Clear calls the valley of latent potential a place where your initial effort does not yield visible results.[34] The valley of latent potential can be frustrating. Some people abandon an approach before they see results. To overcome this, keep practising the routine with students. Practise should involve refining and updating the routine as necessary. Consistently reinforce it in line with your school's behaviour and expectations policy.

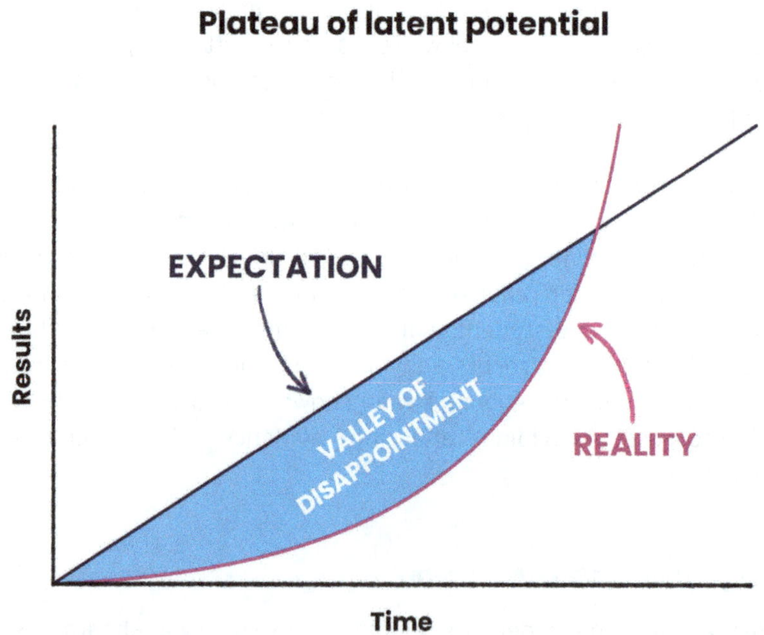

The success of the routine is contingent on its consistent application. Teach the behaviour you expect by setting unambiguous guidelines and following these through when students fall short. By running the routines covered earlier in this chapter, off-task behaviour is likely to be significantly reduced. Ultimately, consistent, patient application of these routines empowers you to harness the benefits of mini whiteboards, creating a more participatory and productive classroom environment.

What Do I Do About Reluctant Users?

Another potential obstacle is students' reluctance to use a mini whiteboard. Some feel self-conscious about peers seeing their answers; others fail to see their value, especially if they equate a lot of written work with learning.

Both concerns are best addressed by establishing a culture in which students understand that making their thinking visible on a mini whiteboard provides immediate feedback, encourages discussion, and helps clarify their ideas. Those who worry about getting answers wrong benefit from knowing that mistakes are expected and safe in your classroom. For those who believe that learning is measured by the amount of writing in their exercise books, present mini whiteboard work as a valuable tool for drafting and refining their thinking, a practical way to plan and experiment with ideas before committing them to paper.

How Do I Stop Students from Rubbing Out Their Work Too Soon?

The transient nature of mini whiteboard work is double-edged. Some students instinctively erase their work after presenting it. The frustration here is that you miss an opportunity to leverage the information on students' boards. You might want to examine an answer more closely, celebrate a novel idea, or explore a problem with more than one solution. So when students erase their boards too soon, it can be frustrating. To solve this issue, instruct students not to rub out their work. It is best to do this while they hold their whiteboards aloft and call on a few students to repeat the instruction to confirm that everyone understood it.

What Do I Do About Questions that Require an Extended Response?

Mini whiteboards are, by nature, small. They work great for short answers: a word, a phrase, a number, or a quick sketch or sentence. They shine when the question requires a concise response. But don't be put off using them for lengthier responses. One tip for longer responses is to systematically sample students who you predict might struggle with the question or are least likely to know the answer. This helps you check for understanding where it's most uncertain and guides your decision-making, especially when reading every board in detail isn't feasible. If these students are on the right course, you can be confident the rest are too.

Another method described by Craig Barton has students work in pairs and exchange their mini whiteboards.[11] Then, ask questions like, "Who disagrees with their partner's answer?" or "Who used a different strategy to solve the problem than their partner?" The teacher can then place selected whiteboards under the visualiser and ask follow-up questions to explore their thinking.

What Are the Alternatives to Mini Whiteboards?

There are alternative all-student response mechanisms for checking for understanding. Choral responses, hand signals, or pre-printed response cards for voting during multiple-choice questions all allow teachers to sample whole-class responses. Each of these gathers information from everyone at once. However, mini whiteboards provide far more flexibility. Students can write words, draw diagrams, and solve mathematical problems. While choral response, hand signals, and multiple-choice questions are valuable techniques in a teacher's toolkit, they do not offer the richness of information provided by a well-run mini whiteboard routine.

Mini whiteboards thus combine the breadth of all-student responding with the depth of response that many other methods can't capture.

They provide students with an external workspace to externalise their thinking. Furthermore, it is not just low-tech options that mini whiteboards outperform.

Research on polling apps and electronic clickers shows outcomes similar to those of mini whiteboards (or response cards): increased participation and improved retention. For instance, a 2020 study by Schulz and colleagues comparing high-tech clickers to mini whiteboards found no significant difference in effectiveness.[35] Both increased participation, improved performance, and reduced disruptive behaviour.

Moreover, the accuracy of students' responses was similar in both conditions. In other words, the critical factor is whole-class participation, not the technology used. Mini whiteboards offer the same benefits as costly alternatives, but at a fraction of the price. They also allow for open-ended responses, not just multiple-choice or numeric answers. While some systems and apps include analytics that may be popular in settings like large university lectures, in most classrooms, mini whiteboards provide comparable gains in participation and learning without the need for electronic devices.

Mini Whiteboards Spotlight: Jamie Clark (English)

Jamie Clark is the author of the best-selling One-Pagers series. His role focuses on driving excellence in everyday classroom teaching. He works closely with teachers and school leaders to embed high-impact, evidence-informed strategies that support effective instruction. His work centres on developing a professional growth culture where staff continually sharpen their practice, engage with research-informed ideas, and work collaboratively to improve outcomes for all students.

Without regular checks for understanding, teaching quickly becomes a guessing game, making it impossible to respond effectively to what students have or haven't learnt. Having a reliable method to systematically check everyone "gets it" ensures you can adapt your teaching in the moment and keep the whole class on track.

Mini-whiteboards (MWBs) are cheap, portable, and exceptionally effective for precisely this purpose. They are a cornerstone of our school's core practices listed below, helping to guide instruction and establish a shared language of excellent teaching across our classrooms:

Practice 1: Purposeful Greeting and Entering
Practice 2: Explaining the Learning Objective
Practice 3: Signalling to Gain Students' Attention
Practice 4: Inclusive Questioning with Cold Calling
Practice 5: Using Mini Whiteboards to Check for Understanding
Practice 6: Circulating and Giving Actionable Feedback

MWBs help us to establish a brisk, purposeful lesson pace, and create a low-pressure feedback loop, enabling teachers to check understanding and adapt their teaching in the moment. Not only that, we recognise their power to:

Increase Thinking Ratio: They engage 100% of students in low-stakes, hard thinking.
Diagnose Misconceptions: They catch misunderstandings before they become embedded.
Promote Retrieval Practice: They promote retrieval practice to help consolidate knowledge.

Our Professional Growth Program plays a vital role in embedding our core practices into our day-to-day lessons. Each strategy is supported by a set of baseline steps that provide teachers with a clear starting point before adapting the practice to suit their subject and context. For MWBs, our baseline steps are:

MWB Baseline Steps

Step 1: Pose a "MWBs friendly" question (multiple-choice, true or false, one keyword, etc.)
Step 2: Provide adequate wait time so students have time to think and form a response.
Step 3: Remind students to write in large handwriting so it''s quick and easy to read.

Step 4: Ask students to flip and hover their board to signal they're ready to share.
Step 5: Choose a familiar signal for students to show their answers ("3, 2, 1 . . . show me!").

At the start of the year, teachers explicitly teach and rehearse routines with their classes. This serves two key functions: to make the learning environment predictable and to ensure students aren't using cognitive bandwidth on classroom procedures, so they can devote it to learning.

For teachers, team meetings provide quarantined time for them to plan, rehearse, and adapt these strategies with colleagues. For example, when using MWBs, we have focused heavily on front-loading instructions ("In a moment, I want you to . . .") whilst using question formats that support healthy MWBs checks. Drawing upon a shared bank of question types helps us select questions that effectively make thinking visible at different points in the lesson:

MWB Question Types

Before instruction: You might open with a baseline question ("Write one example of a reversible change") or a quick recognition check ("Which option correctly defines evaporation?") to activate prior knowledge and surface gaps early.

During instruction: You might implement misconception checks ("True or false: Every force causes motion"), first application prompts ("Draw a simple food chain"), or analytical questions ("What would happen if the power source was removed?") to test understanding in real time.

After instruction: You might use procedural checks ("What's the first step in solving this equation?"), compare and contrast prompts, or a simple self-assessment ("Rate your understanding 1-4 and write one question you still have") to consolidate learning and reveal next steps.

Note: These question types are inspired by Carl Hendrick and Haili Hughes' webinar How Teaching and Learning Happens - Checking for Understanding.[36]

Many teachers use MWBs to collect data, but don't always act on it, treating the process as a mechanical routine rather than a live decision-making process. Brock Fleay is one of our brilliant science teachers and also contributes to our instructional coaching team. Over the past year, he has refined his approach with MWBs, embedding systematic checks for understanding as a habitual and reliable feature of his teaching.

CASE STUDY: BROCK FLEAY YEAR 7 SCIENCE

Here is a short script taken from my observation notes of Brock teaching his Year 7 science class. As you can see, his MWB check is sharp, his feedback is precise, and his instructional decision-making is super responsive:

OBSERVATION NOTES YEAR 7 SCIENCE: SYMBIOTIC RELATIONSHIPS

Brock: Remember, pens down. Thinking first . . . Question 1: What type of relationship is shown in the image on the screen? Is it A, B, C or D?

[Brock waited a few seconds so that students could think.]

Brock: OK . . . Write down your answer. You;ve got 10 seconds.

[Students wrote their answers clearly on their MWBs.]

Brock: Flip and hover when you're finished so I can see you're ready to share . . . OK, 3, 2, 1 - show me!

[Brock scanned the room and quickly spotted a common error: several students had chosen C when the correct answer was B.]

Brock: "I can see some of us have chosen C. The correct answer is B, Mutualism.

[He briefly re-explained the concept to address the misconception.]

Brock: Mutualism is when both organisms in a relationship benefit. In this example, both the clownfish and the sea anemone gain something that helps them survive.

[Brock set up a quick paired talk rehearsal so students could explain the idea in their own words.]

Brock: When I say go, I want you to turn to your partner and explain why the clownfish and sea anemone benefit from having a symbiotic relationship . . . 3, 2, 1 - go!

[Students explained to their partners while Brock circulated the room, listening in and checking for accuracy, prompting where needed.]

Brock: And back to me in 3, 2, 1 . . . Thank you. I'm going to check a few answers to make sure we're all on track.

[Brock sampled a range of responses by cold calling students before moving on.]

Brock's use of MWBs isn't just about quizzing and collecting responses; it actively shapes his next steps by identifying misconceptions immediately, adjusting his explanations, and ensuring every student's schema is accurate. His quick paired-talk task here was spot on for helping students repair any faulty thinking and rehearse a correct explanation before moving on with the lesson.

MWBs are essential tools for every teacher's toolkit. When implemented deliberately and consistently, they become a powerful engine for responsive teaching. They help us check everyone and adapt instruction with precision. As our staff continue to rehearse, refine, and embed this core practice, we strengthen not only individual lessons but our whole-school culture of effective, evidence-informed practice.

Mini Whiteboards Spotlight: Adam Lamb (MFL)

Adam's work centres on school improvement across secondary academies in a range of contexts. He works with schools in Carlisle, Somerset, and Kent. A linguist by background, Adam has a particular interest in communication. Much of his work focuses on supporting heads of department to champion their subjects, while also helping senior leaders and principals ask the right questions to support modern foreign languages provision effectively.

Mini whiteboards are a versatile and essential part of my teaching toolkit. They are non-negotiable in my classroom for several key reasons:

- **Increasing student participation** by enabling guided practice.
- **Facilitating hinge questions** to assess understanding at key points in a lesson.
- **Providing quick, formative checks** of students' grasp of isolated concepts.
- **Supporting student talk and planning**, especially in collaborative tasks.
- Enabling rapid reteaching and intervention during practice activities.

When used effectively, mini whiteboards allow teachers to check every student's understanding simultaneously, not just a select few. Their adaptability has made them a staple in many classrooms, particularly in modern foreign languages (MFL), where real-time feedback is crucial.

Reintroducing Mini Whiteboards Through Policy Change

During a recent review of our school's feedback policy, I saw an opportunity to reintroduce mini whiteboards into our practice. Although they had once been central to my teaching, their use had declined in my previous school, where we had become overly reliant on cold calling and exercise book marking to assess progress.

To prepare for their reintroduction, I first reembedded them in my own classroom. I revisited the many ways they can be used, not just to gather data on student progress, but to shape learning in the moment actively.

Routines and Rituals: Making Mini Whiteboards Work

Establishing clear routines is essential for the successful use of mini whiteboards. Here are some practical tips:

- **Entry and exit routines**: Decide how boards will be distributed and collected. For example, keep them stacked in the middle of the table, with the first student responsible for distributing and collecting them. Consistency is key.
- **Pens**: I used to hand out pens during the silent Do Now and collect them during independent practice to prevent loss. Others prefer keeping them in a pot on each table; find what works for you.
- **"3, 2, 1 - Show me"**: A simultaneous reveal prevents copying. I train students to hold boards at different heights depending on their row: front row flat on the table, middle row at chest height, and back row above their heads, which ensures I can see all responses clearly.
- **"Click your lids and pens down**: A simple but vital routine to preserve pen life!

When paired with careful reverse planning, mini whiteboards help shift cognitive load onto students. In MFL, this is particularly effective for grammar instruction. Here's how I use them to build mastery, using the **near future tense in Spanish** as an example.

USING MINI WHITEBOARDS IN THE MFL CLASSROOM

1) Explanation and modelling

   I begin by clearly explaining the grammar point, e.g., the near future tense, which expresses what someone *is going to do*. I model the structure: conjugate *ir* in the present, add *a*, then an infinitive.

2) **Cold call check**

   I cold-call students to check they understand the steps:

   a) *Voy* (I go)

b) *a* (to)

c) *comer* (to eat)

3) **Hinge questioning**

I display a sentence in English and ask students to choose the correct Spanish translation from three options, writing the letter on their whiteboards:

"I am going to eat"

a) *voy comer*

b) *voy a comer*

c) *voy a como*

Option **b** is correct. Option **a** is missing an *a*, and **c** incorrectly conjugates the second verb. After the reveal, I cold-call students to explain the errors, reinforce understanding, and address misconceptions. It gives language teachers a very quick way to diagnose whether students have a correct mental model of what the grammar concept should look like.

4) **Productive practice**

Next, and increasing the cognitive load slightly, I ask students to translate short phrases onto their whiteboards, e.g.,

"He is going to swim" → *Va a nadar*

I provide any necessary vocabulary so the focus remains on applying the grammar rather than recalling words. This keeps the cognitive load manageable and allows for immediate feedback.

OTHER USES IN THE MFL CLASSROOM

- **Essay planning**: At A Level, students can use whiteboards to map out essay ideas, allowing for easy reordering and quick feedback before writing. This helps ease some of the anxiety of putting pen to paper.

- **Speaking preparation**: During thinking time, students can jot down prompts or sentence starters to support their verbal responses, boosting confidence and fluency by keeping them in front of them.
- **On-the-spot reteaching**: During independent work, I carry a whiteboard marker to correct misconceptions or provide hints quickly. I often write vocabulary for students to copy, ensuring accuracy without interrupting the lesson flow.

While mini whiteboards offer numerous benefits, it's important to remember they are just a tool. Their effectiveness depends entirely on thoughtful planning and purposeful use. Simply handing them out won't improve learning. Instead, their use, as with any activity in the classroom, should be guided by the question: "Why this, and why now?" When integrated with intention, mini whiteboards become a powerful means of gathering whole-class feedback, supporting student thinking, and driving responsive teaching.

Mini Whiteboards Spotlight: Elliot Morgan (Coaching and Implementation)

Elliot Morgan's work centres on school improvement, with a particular emphasis on curriculum design and implementation. He works closely with schools to implement coherent, knowledge-rich curricula and to support their effective enactment in classrooms. This includes helping leaders and teachers strengthen teaching and learning practices and ensure that pupils build secure, cumulative knowledge over time.

My role involves observing a large amount of teaching across the 400 schools I support with curriculum implementation. That breadth of classroom experience gives me a useful vantage point: I see the patterns, habits, and misconceptions that shape how mini whiteboards (MWBs) are used, and I also see the difference they make when they are used well.

As a profession, we often rely on "poor proxies" for understanding.[37] Hands up, a few cold-call responses, or a general feel for the room can all give us the illusion that learning is secure. MWBs are one of the most reliable ways to tackle this issue; they help us move beyond those limited signals and towards genuine insight into what pupils are thinking.

At their most effective, MWBs transform checking for understanding from a passive to an active process (depending on how they are used). Rather than a handful of pupils contributing, everyone participates: every pupil writes, every pupil shows, and therefore, every pupil is accountable for thinking.

Yet discussion of MWBs often reduces them to a mere "strategy" or "technique" – this creates the misconception that they are powerful in and of themselves. I emphasise to teachers that their value lies in the principles behind them, not simply in the act of using them. Having pupils write something on a whiteboard does not guarantee that we have assessed well. It is the intention (securing reliable information about pupil thinking) and the disciplined habits that sit around MWB use that matter. When we see MWBs not as a gimmick or an add-on, but as a practical way of enacting the core principles of responsive teaching, their use becomes far more purposeful and effective. As with anything in education, MWBs only work when the principles underpinning them are understood and consistently applied. I refer to three principles to support their use.

The first principle is the pursuit of reliable information. MWBs give us a whole-class sample in real time, but only if we actually look. A common pitfall is insufficient sampling: a quick glance at two or three boards with the correct answer, followed by the assumption that the whole class must then be secure. Instead, we must scan methodically and systematically – one row, table or group at a time. When doing this, we should be looking for patterns rather than perfection. What I mean by that is that I am mostly looking for who has the wrong answer, and considering how they may have got there, rather than the sea of pupils who may have it right. This short scan often reveals far more variation than expected and becomes the basis for any responsive next steps. Crucially, spending ten or twenty more seconds now to gain a clear understanding saves far more time later; it prevents us from launching into independent work on a shaky foundation and therefore reduces the need for reteaching. I always refer to this as "slowing down to speed up."

The second principle is clarity: clarity in what pupils should write and clarity in what teachers need to see. When pupils put too much information on their boards, or when the prompt is too vague ("*Show me everything you know about X*"), MWBs stop being diagnostic. It is difficult to obtain the reliable information needed to guide our next actions. It is important to support teachers to plan tightly focused prompts – e.g. circle the verb. However, the prompt should not focus just on the quantity of what pupils write, but on the quality of insight their responses will provide the teacher. With "circle the verb," incorrect answers may reveal misunderstandings about word class.

The third principle is follow-through. Checking pupil responses is only useful if it shapes what happens next. A common pattern is that MWBs are used effectively, yet the information they generate is not always translated into instructional action. After scanning, the teacher must decide whether to correct together. Do I reteach to a group or the whole class? Or is the class secure enough to move on? This depends on how many pupils got it right and which misconceptions emerged. MWBs can offer us high-certainty feedback, but it is our responsive follow-through that turns that certainty into improved pupil understanding.

While I would argue that these principles matter more than any particular routine, routines still matter. It is wise to establish clear routines around the use of MWBs, including distributing and collecting them, signalling how and when pupils should show their answers, knowing when to put pens down, etc. Whatever routines we use, they must be quick and automatic so that the cognitive load rests with the learning, not the logistics.

When MWBs are used well, their use tends to share consistent features:

- rapid and consistent routines (ensuring participation from every pupil);
- thoughtfully planned prompts (designed to reveal exactly the thinking we need to check);
- systematic scanning (providing a valid whole-class sample);
- strong follow-through (where teaching adapts immediately to what we have seen).

MWBs are sometimes dismissed as a faff, but this usually reflects surface-level appreciation of their power. When thoughtfully applied, they are one of the simplest, yet most powerful tools in the responsive teacher's arsenal and one of the surest ways we can move from guesswork to certainty about what pupils have actually understood.

10 Hinge Questions

Quick question.

Do you use multiple-choice questions in your teaching?

A. No, students can just guess the right answer.

B. No, I teach English/history/another "discursive" subject, and they won't work there.

C. No, multiple-choice questions aren't suitable for sophisticated or challenging thinking.

D. Yes, but mainly for low-stakes quizzes or recall.

If you chose A, B, or C, you are not alone.

If you chose D, you may still be underusing them.

And if you're already thinking, "This question is badly designed," good. That's the point.

Multiple-choice questions are often unfairly maligned. Many teachers avoid using them for the reasons outlined in the opening example: students can easily guess or recognise the correct answer, they erroneously believe they are not valuable for subjects like English or history, or they do not allow for the assessment of sophisticated material. Some

DOI: 10.4324/9781003657019-14

teachers might tentatively use them, but do so with unease, fearful that the format rests awkwardly alongside ambitions for deep understanding, rich discussion, and disciplinary thinking.

This chapter demonstrates that these concerns, while understandable, are misguided.

To situate this argument, let's explore a non-example and an example.

What is the capital of Brazil?

A. London

B. Brasília

C. Paris

Clearly, this is a poor question. Most students aged 6–7 would know that London is the capital of England and Paris is the capital of France. Even if they didn't, they would likely recognise that, both orthographically and phonetically, Brazil and Brasília share the same root form.

What is the capital of Brazil?

A. Rio de Janeiro

B. Brasília

C. São Paulo

The question remains the same, but the options make it less likely that those answering would arrive at the correct answer for the wrong reasons. In other words, the answer is difficult to guess. What makes this a much better example is that all three options are now plausible. All three are Brazilian cities. What's more, until 1960, Rio de Janeiro was Brazil's capital. Many young people, and even adults, hold this misconception. São Paulo is plausible because it is Brazil's most populous city.

Ergo, when carefully crafted, a multiple-choice format for diagnostic and hinge-point questions can be an efficient way to reveal

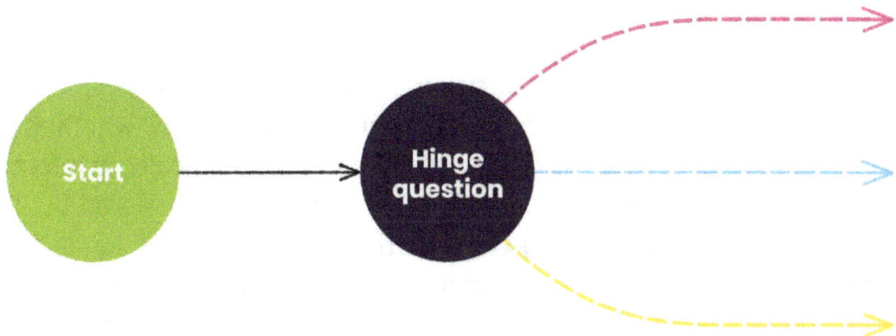

misconceptions, helping teachers make better-informed decisions about what to do next.

Although this book uses the term hinge questions, the focus of this chapter extends beyond that label. A hinge-point question is a diagnostic question posed at a critical juncture in an instructional sequence, where the next move depends on students' understanding. In that sense, hinge questions are a subset of a wider idea: effective diagnostic questions.

The principles you'll encounter in this chapter apply not only to hinge points within an instructional sequence, but also to diagnostic questions used for range-finding at the start of the sequence, where the purpose is to ascertain students' prior knowledge and likely misconceptions.

Hinge questions can play a crucial role in helping teachers make better instructional decisions under real classroom constraints. Teachers routinely face moments where a lesson could branch in different directions. Yet the evidence they rely on is sometimes fragile: volunteered responses from the most vocal students or students' self-reported confidence. Hinge questions replace these thin signals with evidence that is intentionally engineered to support a decision. Students indicate their response using a whole-class participation mechanism. Teachers might have students write their chosen option on a mini whiteboard or use pre-printed voting cards.

In Wylie and Wiliam's terms, hinge questions reflect a decision-pull approach to assessment.[38] In other words, rather than generating data hoping it will be helpful later, decision-pull assessment begins with the decisions teachers already routinely make, most notably whether a class is ready to progress, and designs questions specifically to inform those decisions. A single, well-crafted hinge question, answered by all students, provides just enough information to guide instruction in the moment. Hinge questions do not aim for exhaustive diagnosis or perfect measurements; instead, they prioritise classroom utility and immediacy. They allow teachers to quickly respond to students' understanding and adjust their teaching in the moment.

The multiple-choice format of hinge questions improves interpretability and immediacy. It limits the range of possible responses, which is important when you consider that a central message of this book is that teachers should aim to check the understanding of all students. When 30 students all answer simultaneously, hinge questions mean teachers are not faced with 30 unique responses they must attempt to interpret. Instead, by limiting responses to a small, pre-structured set of possibilities, hinge questions allow teachers to scan patterns, spot misconceptions, and act, all within seconds.

Crucially, all options in a hinge question are carefully planned, each aligning with a specific common misconception. As a result, teachers get to see more than *who* is wrong; they can also see *why* they are wrong. This means the information a teacher requires to make the next instructional decision is embedded in the question itself. When an option dominates, the teacher can immediately infer the underlying misconception and will know what kind of correction, clarification, or re-teaching is required.

Designing Effective Hinge Questions

Across the work of Christine Wylie, Dylan Wiliam, Daisy Christodoulou, and Craig Barton, a set of design principles emerges.[38,39,40] This chapter will explore each in depth, but it is helpful to see them together first.

The Five Design Principles

1. **Targets one concept only.** The question isolates a single idea that is crucial for progress. If a student answers incorrectly, it is clear which concept they still do not understand.
2. **Is unambiguous.** The question and its answer options are written so that it is clear what kind of thinking is being elicited and how responses should be interpreted.
3. **Includes plausible distractors.** Each incorrect option represents a specific, common misconception or partial understanding, rather than a random or obviously incorrect answer.
4. **Suppresses false positives.** It should be almost impossible for students to arrive at the correct answer while still possessing a misconception.
5. **Fast to answer and quick to interpret.** The question does not disrupt the flow of an instructional sequence and allows a teacher to interpret and act on responses within seconds.

Effective hinge questions make it possible for different ways of thinking to lead to different answers. When that condition is satisfied, the teacher can examine the distribution of responses and determine what to do next.

Principle 1: Target One Concept Only

If a question requires students to draw on multiple ideas or complete several steps, an incorrect answer makes it more difficult and time-consuming to determine what went wrong. The diagnostic affordance diminishes. Consider what happens when a question simultaneously tests the understanding of a concept, recall of a procedure, and the accuracy of, let's say, arithmetic or algebraic manipulation. If a student answers incorrectly, the teacher is left guessing where things went wrong. The error might be conceptual, procedural, or just a careless slip. Without significant probing, the response is not interpretable. Consequently, the teacher cannot confidently determine which intervention is required.

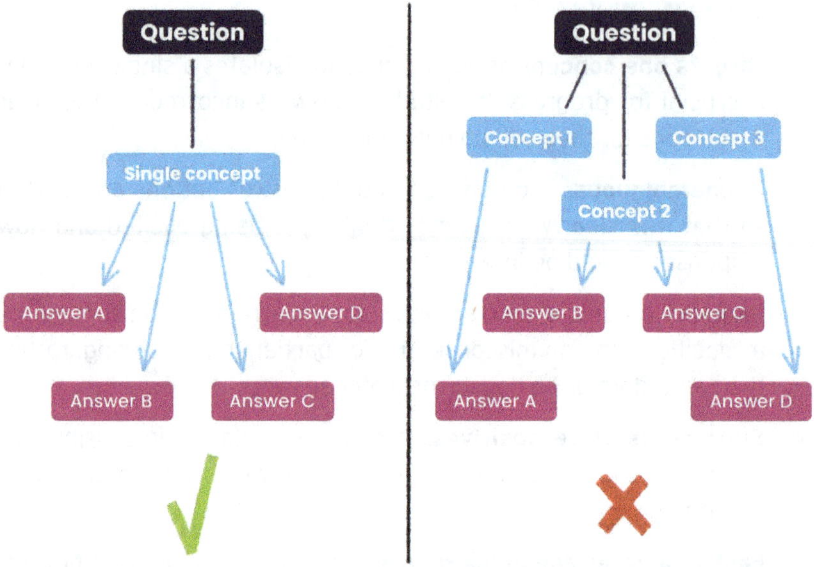

It is common for teachers to privilege complex, open-ended questions, such as those in essays. These types of tasks, whilst vitally important, are ill-suited to rapid instructional decision-making.

Inspired by an example from Daisy Christodoulou's *Making Good Progress?*, the following example illustrates how a question that would typically require an essay-style response can be easily adapted into a hinge question that is very precise and targets a single aspect of the topic.[39] Open-ended tasks and essay writing are important and can tell us how well students are doing. But they aren't efficient for identifying what students need to work on next.

> **What most clearly distinguishes a constitutional monarchy from an absolute monarchy?**

Such an example could be set as an open-ended question requiring an essay-style response. As Christodoulou points out, these types of questions give a general sense of students' knowledge, but they require the teacher to put in far more effort to infer which specific ideas students need to work on. In other words, the decision "what do I do next?" cannot be made in seconds.

The same question can be reframed as a diagnostic multiple-choice item:

> **What most clearly distinguishes a constitutional monarchy from an absolute monarchy?**
>
> A. The monarch is the head of the armed forces.
>
> B. Citizens have limited political freedoms.
>
> C. The monarch's powers are constrained by law.
>
> D. Political opposition is discouraged.

Each option contains a plausible distractor. A student selecting A or B is likely drawing on surface-level features of monarchies or authoritarian systems. These options signal an imprecise understanding of what distinguishes constitutional monarchies from other forms of government.

Option D is a revealing distractor. Students may associate monarchy with limited opposition or repression. Selecting this option indicates a tendency to conflate constitutional monarchy with broader ideas about authority rather than focusing on constitutional structure.

The correct option, C, identifies the defining principle: the monarch's authority is constrained by law, typically through a constitution and parliamentary system.

The diagnostic affordance of this question means the teacher can infer, immediately and without further questioning, why a student's reasoning is wrong. From a quick scan, a teacher can infer whether students are:

- relying on vague associations of power and control;
- confusing different political systems;
- reasoning in terms of constitutional constraints.

Multiple-choice questions might not feel as impressive as broad ones. But their specificity means teachers can answer one crucial question: "If a student answers incorrectly, will I know exactly what they still don't understand, and therefore what to do next?"

Principle 2: No Ambiguity

A core feature of effective hinge questions is that they enable teachers to interpret students' responses quickly. For this to happen, clarity in both the question and potential options is essential. Ambiguity undermines this clarity and, in so doing, strips the question of its diagnostic properties.

A hinge question fails when a teacher cannot reliably interpret what a student's response signifies. In their guidance for constructing high-quality multiple-choice questions, Case and Swanson (2002) assert that ambiguity arises when question stems fail to specify the task clearly or when answer options are not comparable.[41] In such instances, students may select a different answer not because they understand the material

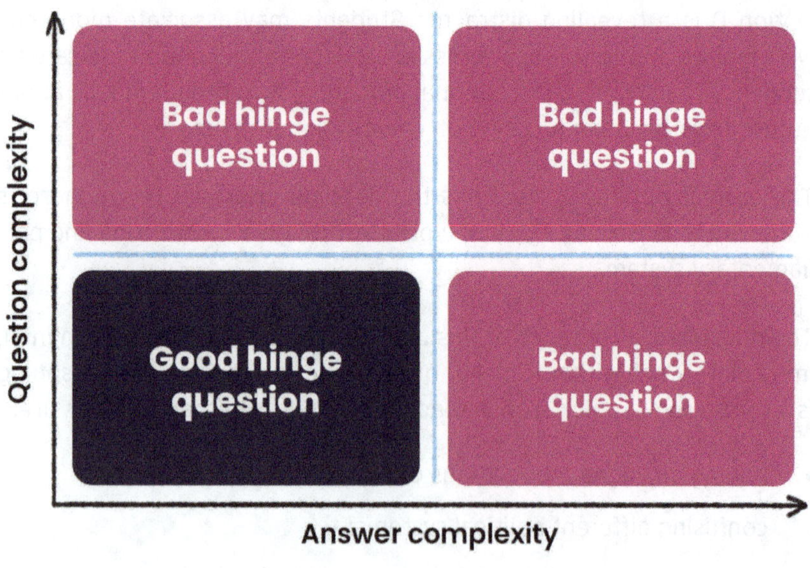

differently, but because they are responding to a different interpretation of the question itself.

Building on the work of Case and Swanson, in practice, ambiguity might arise in one of the following ways:

- Unclear constraints in the question stem: students don't know what type of answer is being sought (e.g. simplified, best, most accurate, from a historian's perspective).
- Answer options that differ along multiple dimensions: options vary simultaneously in accuracy, completeness, and relevance.
- Responses that can be defended for different reasons: a student may select an option for a technically valid reason, but it may not be the reason the teacher is attempting to diagnose.

In all three scenarios, the teacher doesn't know whether a student's choice indicates a misconception, an understandable alternative interpretation, or a misunderstanding of the task. When this occurs, the teacher can no longer make a valid inference to inform what to do next.

It is also worth noting that reducing ambiguity is not a case of simply insisting on one correct answer. Some diagnostic questions are intentionally designed with multiple correct responses. In such questions, clarity comes from making the question stem explicit, e.g. "Select all statements that are true."

The principle of no ambiguity is evident in this science example, courtesy of Claire Badger.

> **Which particles move when a molten ionic compound conducts electricity? Select all that apply.**
>
> A. Electrons
>
> B. Negative ions

C. Positive ions

D. Protons

The correct answers are B (negative ions) and C (positive ions). There is no ambiguity here.

All options are plausible as they are all charged particles that play a role in atomic structure and bonding.

Students are likely to pick electrons, as there is a common misconception that electrons are solely responsible for electrical conductivity, since delocalised electrons move when metals (and graphite) conduct electricity.

As electrons are negatively charged, students may think that only negative ions move when molten ionic compounds conduct electricity, whereas both negative and positive ions move (but in opposite directions).

Protons are positively charged particles that are found in the nucleus of atoms. They are not involved in bonding. However, students may be confused about the role of protons, as they are the particles transferred during acid-base reactions.

Reducing ambiguity can be achieved by asking yourself this question when designing hinge questions: "If two students choose different options, do I know what is different about their thinking?"

Principle 3: Distractors Must Be Plausible

It may sound counterintuitive, but in hinge questions, the incorrect options matter more than the correct answer/s. Hinge questions should reveal to a teacher what to do next. As a result, they involve a deliberate inversion of priorities. When a student selects an incorrect option, and when those options align closely with common misconceptions, the response can reveal far more about a student's thinking than a correct answer would.

It is through selecting these incorrect options that misconceptions, partial understanding and fragility become visible.

The plausibility of the distractors requires an up-front investment of cognitive effort by the teacher. The teacher must anticipate the most probable misconceptions students are likely to make and decide what action would best help resolve these.

The preparatory work liberates a teacher's working memory during the lesson. Rather than attempting to infer misconceptions in real time from 30 different responses, the teacher has already done the intellectual groundwork. Crucially, this allows the teacher to move with speed and precision. Because each incorrect option links to a specific misconception, the teacher can immediately infer how students are reasoning. Each possible option should mean a teacher does not need to ask follow-up questions to clarify students' thinking, allowing them to pivot seamlessly at a hinge point to decide whether to pause for re-teaching, address a specific error with a few students, or move on with confidence.

What Makes a Distractor Diagnostic?

When the possible options are obviously wrong, off-topic, or absurdly different in form, the diagnostic affordance of the hinge question diminishes. Implausible or "silly" options, such as the Brazilian capital

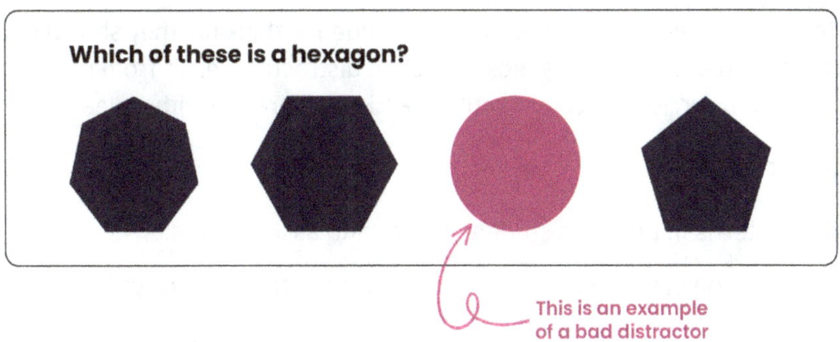

example at the start of this chapter, allow students to dismiss options without thinking. Students could arrive at the correct response for the wrong reasons, creating the very false positive that hinge questions are designed to avoid.

For options to function diagnostically, they must reflect a specific, predictable way of thinking that students are known to adopt when they have not yet grasped a concept.

Effective distractors tend to share three characteristics:

- **They are chosen more frequently by novices than by experts.** If proficient and less-proficient students are equally likely to select a distractor, it does not discriminate between levels of understanding. Such options reduce the question's diagnostic properties.[42]
- **They are close enough to the correct answer to be tempting.** The distractor options represent an almost-right idea applied in the wrong context or with a subtle misunderstanding. This proximity requires students to think carefully.
- **They align with known misconceptions or partial understanding.** Each distractor should embody a hypothesis about student thinking. In other words, a teacher should be able to articulate, in advance, what a student is thinking and how they are thinking if they choose a particular option. When a pattern in a selected option emerges, the teacher knows what went wrong, why students are likely to think this way, and how to remedy it.

Because distractors are hypotheses of students' thinking, they should not be created arbitrarily. The most effective distractors result from ongoing reflection, curriculum conversations, and collaboration with colleagues.

They come from:

- patterns in previous students' work and assessments;
- common errors teachers observe during a topic delivery;

- examiners' reports and curriculum guidance;
- misconceptions during checks for understanding;
- and near-miss answers that students give confidently.

Over time, teachers recognise patterns. Writing hinge questions should be a collaborative endeavour built on professional generosity and subject expertise.

A final implication of this principle is that fewer options are likely to be better than more. Crafting three plausible distractors is genuinely difficult. Attempting to write 4–5 distractors can result in some options being weaker, diluting the question's diagnostic effectiveness. The aim should be to maximise the interpretability of the response. A question with 2–3 strong, well-thought-out, plausible distractors that are all taken seriously by students will almost always elicit more valid evidence than a question with five options, two of which are disregarded.

The following geography example illustrates the principle that distractors must be plausible.

> **Which of these factors has contributed most to global warming in the last century?**
>
> A. The burning of fossil fuels
>
> B. Deforestation
>
> C. The hole in the ozone layer

Each option in this question is plausible and rooted in ideas students might have encountered or misinterpreted. The correct answer is A; the burning of fossil fuels has contributed most to global warming in the past century. Option B is indeed a cause of global warming. A student selecting B shows partial understanding. They recognise deforestation is a cause, but have yet to grasp the concept of scale. Option C is a common misconception among young people and even some adults. Many mistakenly think the ozone hole causes global warming. In reality, the ozone hole has minimal effect on global temperature. It primarily lets in more UV radiation, not heat.

All three options sound plausible in some way and reveal how students are reasoning.

When writing hinge questions, ask: "If students choose different incorrect options, do those choices point me towards different misconceptions that I know how to address?"

Principle 4: Suppress False Positives

Dylan Wiliam argues that the effective design of hinge questions rests on a fundamental asymmetry in teaching.[30] When teachers judge students' understanding, not all assumptions are equal.

When teachers assume students do not know something when they do, the consequences are minimal:

- The teacher might unnecessarily re-explain a concept.
- Students may experience a brief redundancy.

At worst, students receive extra practice. This is a low-cost error.

By contrast, when a teacher assumes students know something when they actually do not, the consequences are more significant:

- The lesson moves on prematurely, leaving many students behind.
- Gaps widen as new material rests on a flawed understanding.

This is a high-cost error, and the effects compound over time.

Seen this way, the purpose of a hinge question is to shield against one of the most damaging instructional mistakes of all: moving on too soon.

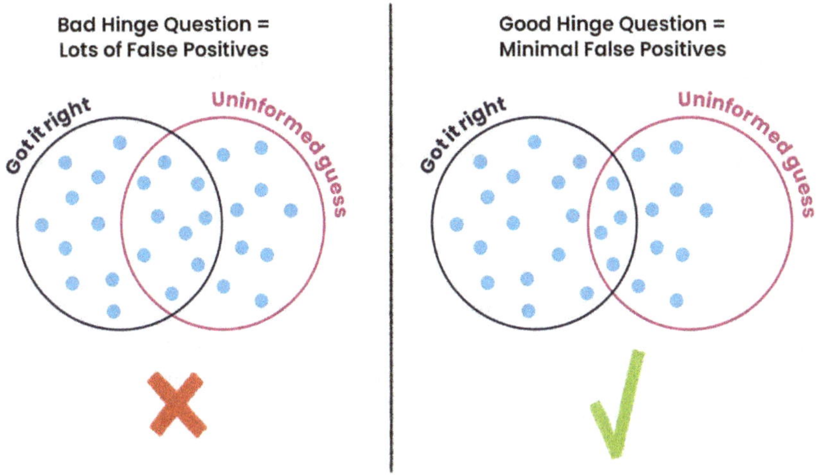

This is why William insists that an effective hinge question must make it almost impossible for a student to get the correct answer while still holding a misconception.[30]

Suppressing false positives is about designing questions that respect this asymmetry. When students select the correct option, it should indicate a secure understanding.

In many ways, this principle draws together several strands already explored in this chapter.

Suppressing false positives depends on:

- **Specificity**. Questions target a single concept and reduce the number of alternative pathways to the correct answer.
- **Clarity**. The question stem and options are unambiguous.
- **Plausible distractors**. Wrong answers actively appeal to students holding particular misconceptions.

False positives tend to arise when:

- Questions contain implausible and "silly" distractors that can be easily eliminated.
- The correct answer is longer, more precise, or stylistically distinct.
- The question inadvertently cues the answer through language or layout.

In such instances, students may appear secure while retaining a brittle understanding of the concept. The evidence the question elicits is misleading. Suppressing false positives protects the integrity of the inference the teacher is about to make.

When effectively addressing false positives, teachers create more trustworthy hinge questions that tell them:

- students who are correct are genuinely secure;
- students who are incorrect are incorrect for interpretable reasons;
- and the balance of responses provides a reliable signal about what to do next.

This is what allows hinge questions to function as genuine pivot moments in a lesson. The teacher can move on confidently, knowing the class is ready, or intervene decisively, knowing they have reliable evidence to support their decision.

The following maths example illustrates these principles in action.

Expand: $3a(4b-5)$

A. $-3a+b$

B. $12ab-15a$

C. $7ab-2a$

D. $12ab^2-15a$

Students Selecting A. −3a+b

These students are attempting to simplify by combining unlike terms. They may be treating the expression $12ab-15a$ as though the terms can be merged by separating coefficients and variables.

The term $12ab$ contains two variables, a and b, whereas $-15a$ contains only the variable a. Because the variables are not the same, these terms cannot be added or subtracted. Only terms with the same variables raised to the same powers can be combined.

Selecting this option allows the teacher to diagnose a common algebraic misconception: the belief that expressions should always be simplified into fewer terms, even when the terms are not like terms. Importantly, this error occurs after correct expansion, indicating that the student understands the distributive law but does not yet have a secure grasp of term structure.

Students Selecting B. 12ab−15a

This is the correct answer. Students choosing B have correctly applied the distributive law by multiplying both terms inside the bracket by $3a$ and have not attempted to combine unlike terms.

Crucially, this correct option is also interpretable: there is no common misconception that would accidentally lead to $12ab-15a$. Students who select B are therefore highly likely to have understood both the expansion and the structure of the resulting expression. In other words, it is almost impossible for students to select this response for the wrong reasons.

Students Selecting C. 7ab−2a

Option C diagnoses additive thinking across a bracket. Students selecting this answer appear to have added coefficients (e.g. $3+4=7$, $5-3=2$) or combined numbers across the bracket without respecting the multiplicative structure of the expression.

This distractor reflects a common misconception in algebra: treating brackets as signals to "do something" to the numbers inside, without a secure understanding of multiplication as repeated scaling. Selecting C indicates that the student has not yet internalised the distributive law.

Students Selecting D. $12ab^2-15a$

Students choosing D have correctly multiplied the coefficients but have incorrectly handled indices, increasing the power of *b* during multiplication. This suggests confusion between multiplication and exponentiation, or an overgeneralisation of index rules (for example, believing that multiplication always increases powers).

This distractor allows the teacher to distinguish between students who understand the distributive structure but misunderstand index laws and those whose difficulty lies elsewhere.

Principle 5: Fast to Answer and Quick to Interpret

Hinge questions should be fast for students to answer and even quicker for teachers to interpret. This principle is the practical consequence of the preceding four.

A question that targets one concept, is unambiguous, uses plausible distractors, and suppresses false positives should also be one that students can answer swiftly and that teachers can decode at a glance.

Dylan Wiliam suggests that a hinge question should typically take no more than one minute to answer and no more than 30 seconds for the

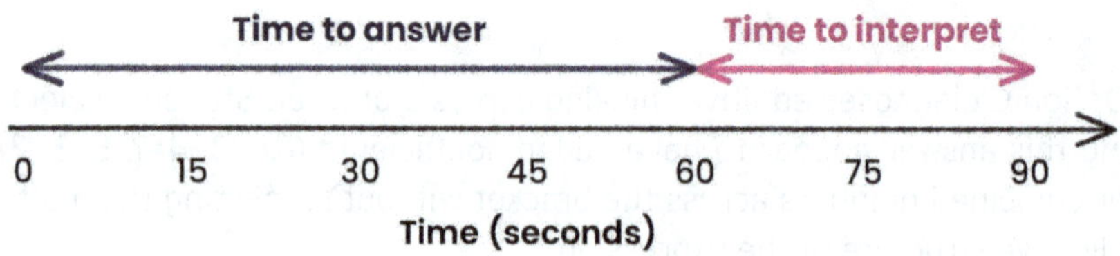

teacher to interpret.[30] Don't think of this as an arbitrary limit. It reflects the purpose of the question: to act as a pivot, not a pause.

If a teacher has to study responses carefully, ask follow-up questions to clarify, or reconstruct students' thinking after the fact, valuable time for responsive teaching might be lost. When the preceding four principles are satisfied, common problems, such as disrupted lesson momentum or increased teacher cognitive load at the very moment a decision is required, are largely avoided.

It is important to stress that "fast" does not mean "easy." Adhering to the principles outlined in this chapter can preserve the desirable difficulty that teachers aspire to achieve, whilst ensuring efficiency.

Principle 5 reminds us that hinge questions are a diagnostic tool that, when used effectively, help teachers decide whether to stay on course or pivot in real time. A useful final check, then, is this: "Can this question be answered quickly, interpreted immediately, and acted on decisively, without breaking the flow of the lesson?"

Hinge Follow-up Moves

Hinge questions should reduce uncertainty when the teacher must decide how to proceed. Their value lies in demystifying the next steps. As discussed later in this book, adaptive teaching results from teachers using elicited evidence to adjust instruction. In practice, it helps for teachers to have a small, rehearsed repertoire of follow-up moves. The following might provide a useful heuristic to shape your thinking.

Most Students Correct: Move On and Bank Time

When most students select the correct option, the hinge question has served its purpose. The teacher can move on with confidence, knowing that understanding is secure enough to support what comes next. The teacher can bank some time and devote it to working with the few who didn't get the answer right. The key move here is restraint. Over-teaching at this point risks dulling momentum and undermining the hinge question's efficiency.

Split Responses: Surface and Compare Thinking

When responses are split between the correct answer and one or more distractors, the hinge can provide a productive moment for the teacher to capitalise on student uncertainty. Teachers often instinctively praise students for correct answers and correct them when they've gone wrong. But D'Mello and colleagues show that when students experience manageable confusion, triggered by contradictions or competing ideas, and are then supported in resolving it, they demonstrate deeper processing and stronger learning gains than when no such disequilibrium occurs.[43]

The message here is not to rush to reveal the answer. To make the most of student uncertainty, you might:

- Ask students to explain why someone might have chosen a particular option.
- Use a brief turn-and-talk discussion focused on justifying choices.
- Use cold calling to have students articulate the reasoning behind different responses.
- Use a combination of these moves and then invite students to have a second vote to see if their thinking shifts in response.

So long as the distractors map carefully onto specific misconceptions, the discussions should remain focused.

Many Students Incorrect: Re-model and Re-check

When a substantial proportion of the class selects incorrect options, the hinge signals that it is not safe to move on. The appropriate response here is to re-explain and re-model the concept, directly addressing the misconceptions revealed by the answers. Crucially, a follow-up diagnostic check is needed. Without this, the teacher has no way of knowing whether the re-teaching has worked.

The following hinge question illustrates how this might apply in a discursive subject such as history.

Industrial Revolution . . .

A. was a period in which new machines quickly improved living and working conditions for most people in Britain.

B. made life worse for everyone, creating poverty and hardship across the whole country.

C. was mainly an economic change, with little effect on people's everyday lives.

D. was a major period of change that affected people differently, improving opportunities for some while creating serious problems for others.

The correct answer is D.

The Industrial Revolution did not affect everyone equally. Its impact varied by class, gender, age, and place. Some people benefited from new employment opportunities, rising wages, and greater independence, while others experienced overcrowded housing, dangerous working conditions, and poor health.

Students who select answer B may be drawing on a long-standing interpretation associated with the work of Arnold Toynbee, or from cultural representations of the period, such as the novels of Charles Dickens and their film adaptations. These sources powerfully emphasise suffering, exploitation, and decline, and can lead students to assume that the Industrial Revolution made life uniformly worse for all groups.

Students who select answer A may have encountered more optimistic accounts that emphasise technological progress and rising living standards, but without recognising how uneven and delayed these improvements often were, particularly for women and children.

Students who select answer C may be treating the Industrial Revolution as a purely economic or technological process, underestimating the extent to which it reshaped everyday life, family structures, and patterns of settlement.

Students who select answer D are likely to have encountered more recent historical interpretations, such as those by Emma Griffin that challenge the idea of a single experience of industrialisation. Griffin argues that the Industrial Revolution should not be understood simply as a "darker period," nor as an uncomplicated story of progress, but as a complex and uneven process. As she suggests, its effects were felt differently by men, women, and children. While hardship was real, the period also marked the emergence of new forms of liberty and opportunity.

A teacher faced with a split set of responses can now make a better-founded decision. They might explicitly surface competing interpretations, model how historians weigh evidence, or clarify why the language of "everyone" is problematic in historical explanations. If many students select B, the teacher knows that the cultural narrative of unrelieved misery needs to be addressed directly. If A is the dominant choice, the focus shifts to unevenness and delay.

Examples such as this, alongside the English examples you are about to read from Miriam Hussain, help address a persistent misconception: that hinge questions are only suitable for factual recall or procedural subjects.

In reality, hinge questions can probe interpretation, nuance and disciplinary thinking, so long as the principles outlined in this chapter are adhered to. What matters is that the question stem and potential answers reveal how students are thinking and inform the teacher what they should do next.

Hinge Questions Spotlight: Miriam Hussain

Miriam Hussain is an English teacher, writer, and senior leader who believes that every child deserves access to high-quality education. She is committed to raising school standards and has spent her career serving in challenging contexts. As Vice Principal responsible for Quality of Education, Miriam's leadership experience includes roles such as Assistant Headteacher, Designated Safeguarding Lead and Chair of Governors.

Teaching is, without question, the most rewarding and the most challenging part of my job. Every lesson is an intricate act of transfer, taking a complex web of knowledge, understanding it deeply enough myself, and then communicating it clearly and effectively so that my students can make it their own. I currently teach two Year 11 classes and a Year 10 class, which requires planning. This process of teaching doesn't end once ''ve explained an idea; in fact, that's where the real work begins. It is not enough for me to teach knowledge; I must ensure it is understood, retrievable, and applicable, and that it forms part of a growing body of knowledge students can return to and build upon over time.

In the classroom, this means constantly monitoring the movement of knowledge from my explanation to students' understanding and, eventually, to their independent use. Checking for understanding is not simply about assessing what students know in the moment, but about ensuring the stability of that knowledge so that it becomes transferable across contexts and texts. Without that security, the bridge between what is taught and what is learned collapses.

Before introducing any independent practice or new knowledge, I must be confident that all students have grasped the key concept. This is not about speed but precision, ensuring that every learner, regardless of starting point, can confidently articulate and apply the essential knowledge before moving forward.

When teaching, hinge questions are invaluable. The following example is specific to *An Inspector Calls*; a play I have taught for the past

12 years. Hinge questions allow me to check not just that students know what Mr Birling says in his Act One speech, but why Priestley has crafted his words in that way and how this speech reveals key contextual and thematic ideas about progress, capitalism, and ignorance.

EXAMPLE 1: THE TITANIC

> **Why does Priestley include Mr Birling's reference to the Titanic being "unsinkable, absolutely unsinkable"?**
>
> A. To show Birling's optimism and confidence in technological progress
>
> B. To show Birling's ignorance and dramatic irony in Priestley's message
>
> C. To foreshadow the Inspector's arrival
>
> D. To present Birling as a man who values wealth over people

This question ensures students understand how context is used for effect. A common misconception is that Priestley shows Birling's optimism, when in fact he uses dramatic irony to undermine his authority and expose capitalist arrogance. If this misconception surfaces, I pause, reteach the context of 1912, and explicitly model how Priestley's irony serves his political purpose.

EXAMPLE 2: THE LABOUR STRIKES

> **What do Birling's comments about "Capital versus Labour agitations" reveal about his attitude toward social change?**
>
> A. He is concerned for workers' welfare
>
> B. He believes industrial progress will solve inequality
>
> C. He dismisses workers' rights and fears social disruption
>
> D. He supports fair pay and better conditions

This question tests a deeper understanding in which students can connect Birling's attitudes to Priestley's broader critique of capitalism. Misconceptions here are revealing: many students assume "progress" is always positive. When this happens, I revisit the historical context and unpack Priestley's socialist intentions before moving to written responses.

EXAMPLE 3: MR BIRLING'S CHARACTER

> **Which statement best captures Priestley's presentation of Mr Birling in this speech?**
>
> A. A wise father offering sensible advice
>
> B. A symbol of capitalist arrogance and complacency
>
> C. A man open to learning from his mistakes
>
> D. A victim of historical circumstance

This hinge question brings together earlier understandings of context, language, and theme, requiring students to connect Birling's words to Priestley's purpose. Students who can confidently explain the correct response, drawing on prior hinge questions, demonstrate not just comprehension but conceptual depth.

All of the example questions can be amended to increase complexity and challenge, but also adapted for easier access. Whilst the mini whiteboards will be the tool for students to write their answers, the routines for how this will be done need to be rehearsed so that these checks can be rapid.

What happens after the hinge question is as important as the question itself. The purpose is not to catch students out, but to surface misconceptions so they can be addressed immediately. If responses suggest uncertainty or misunderstanding, I stop and reteach, sometimes returning to a model, re-explaining a key term, or using retrieval to rebuild prior knowledge.

Routines are crucial for this to work. I set explicit expectations for using mini whiteboards when students write, when they show, and when they stay silent so that I can quickly gauge the whole class's understanding. Cold calling complements this process, ensuring every voice contributes to the learning, not just the confident few. David Didau (2024) highlights that hinge-point questions illuminate the threshold between misunderstanding and mastery.[44] That threshold is where I spend much of my teaching time working responsively, diagnosing gaps, and helping students cross from partial to secure understanding. Michael Chiles (*Powerful Questioning*, 2023) reinforces that clarity and precision in questioning are key to making this possible.[45] Tom Sherrington (*Rosenshine's Principles in Action*, 2019) similarly reminds us that frequent checks for understanding are not interruptions to learning; they are learning.[46] Good hinge questioning is born of thoughtful planning. I script my hinge questions in advance, identifying what knowledge they test and how I will respond to different outcomes. This means that my lessons are never rigid; they are responsive and purposeful.

Checking for understanding is not a procedural step; it is the beating heart of great teaching. It is how knowledge is transferred, secured, and built over time, and it all stems from planning.

11 Exit Tickets

Exit ticket Name: ____________________

1. How do you usually know how well a lesson has gone?

Choose the answer that **best matches** what you rely on the most:

A. My gut feeling as students leave the room, based on their behaviour, engagement, and how smoothly the lesson seemed to run.

B. A whole-class confidence check (for example, hands up, thumbs up/down, or red-amber-green cards).

C. What I infer later from marking students' books or written work in depth.

D. A small number of focused questions answered by every student at the end of the lesson that are quick to respond and quick to interpret.

2. A teacher marks students' books over the weekend and realises many misunderstood a key idea from Monday's lesson (5 days ago).

What is the main limitation of finding out this way?

____

____

3. Complete the sentence:

"The most useful end-of-lesson question is one that helps the teacher decide whether students are ready to..."

____

____

DOI: 10.4324/9781003657019-15

This deliberately self-referential exit ticket mirrors a familiar dilemma for teachers: how to know whether a lesson has gone well.

It is a question teachers reflect on daily, often quickly and intuitively. Many teachers will recognise a sense of success that accompanies a lesson in which students were compliant, the planned content was covered, and engagement appeared high. Yet, as outlined earlier in this book, these proxies, while not without merit, offer a limited window into how students' understanding is actually changing.

You might recall this observation from Graham Nuthall in Chapter 1:

> . . . in order to know if you have been effective, you must have some way of knowing what your students believed, knew, could do, or felt before you taught them and what your students believed, knew, could do, or felt after you taught them.[14]

Nuthall's point feels deceptively simple. We can only judge the effectiveness of teaching by examining its impact on students' thinking. The challenge, of course, resides in the second half of that statement. While teachers have some sense of what students knew before a lesson, gaining a reliable window into what students know, believe, or can do after instruction is far more difficult, particularly in a time-efficient manner that allows teachers to act swiftly.

Exit tickets offer one practical solution to this everyday teaching issue.

Exit tickets are a short sequence of questions that closely align with the learning objective and reveal how well students understand the core content. They typically consist of 1–3 carefully crafted questions that students complete independently in the last five minutes of the lesson, then hand in upon leaving. Teachers review the exit tickets shortly after and use this analysis to decide what should happen in upcoming lessons.

Exit tickets differ from other end-of-lesson routines, such as plenaries, because they are not about closure. They do not signal that learning is finished or that mastery has been secured. Instead, they provide a brief diagnostic window into students' thinking at a natural pause in instruction, allowing teachers to respond to misconceptions and gaps before they become embedded: typically at the start of the next lesson.[30]

A key point to keep in mind, which you will recall from Chapter 4, is that learning and performance are not the same thing. An exit ticket does not serve to measure learning. Instead, it makes students' thinking visible as they are in the process of learning, providing teachers with immediate insight into misconceptions and fragile understanding. Their strength lies in revealing patterns, recurring errors, partial understanding, or fragile knowledge that might otherwise remain invisible until much later, when the opportunity to intervene has passed.[2]

In this sense, exit tickets are not about the end of a lesson or measuring learning, but about shaping what happens next.

Designing Effective Exit Tickets

Poorly designed exit tickets yield vague or misleading information. Well-designed exit tickets do the opposite: they reveal what students have understood, where understanding remains fragile, and, therefore, what the teacher should do next. The following principles explain what makes this possible.

Align with the Lesson Objective

An effective exit ticket aligns precisely with the lesson's most important knowledge. A useful way of framing this is to ask: "If students take only one thing away from today, what should it be?"

The exit ticket should be designed to assess that point directly. Such a tight focus often requires restraint. There is a natural urge to assess everything covered in a lesson. Yet when exit tickets try to do too much, they become too onerous to review, and they often reveal very little. Exit tickets are far more useful when they reveal whether students have grasped the idea that everything else in the lesson depends on.

Aligning an exit ticket to the lesson objective places an important demand on lesson planning. A clear, well-framed lesson objective is a prerequisite for an effective exit ticket. A novel way to think about this comes from Heather Snodgrass via Doug Lemov's *Teach Like a Champion 3.0*.[2] She advises crafting the exit ticket before any other parts of the lesson. She points out that doing so helps sharpen her thinking about the most important content and improves alignment across her lesson.

To illustrate this principle, consider this Year 2 (ages 6-7) English exit ticket in which students are learning to use expanded noun phrases.

LO: To use expanded noun phrases to add detail to a noun.

Exit Ticket **Name: ____________________**

Add two describing words to each noun.

1. The ________________, ________________ butterfly flew away.
2. The ________________, ________________ dog sat on the mat.
3. I saw a ________________,________________ tree.
4. She held the ________________, ________________ box.

This principle of focusing on alignment also helps clarify what doesn't work well as an exit ticket. Prompts that ask students to rate their confidence, such as red, amber, or green self-assessments, have an intuitive appeal. Yet, as reviewed in Chapter 4, the Dunning-Krueger effect explains how self-report measures, such as confidence checks, are unreliable and have little diagnostic value. Such activities yield false confirmation and make it difficult for the teacher to know what to do next.

Keep it Short

An exit ticket is not an exam or quiz. Using 1-3 questions is most effective. The aim should be for students to complete the exit ticket in 3-5 minutes. Similarly, the teacher should be able to review and infer what to do next in approximately five minutes. Effective exit tickets capture a snapshot of understanding; they do not attempt to diagnose every aspect of content.

Questions should therefore be tightly focused, economical, and mapped to a single concept. When using more than one question, each should assess a single idea. Craig Barton cautions against questions that weave together several skills or concepts because, when students go wrong, it makes it more difficult to figure out why.[47] It makes the process far more time-consuming.

For an exit ticket to provide reliable information that informs timely instructional decisions, teachers must attend to its format.

Choose the Right Format

Exit tickets can contain open-ended and closed-ended questions. Each format has advantages. The key is to choose the format that makes it easiest to get the information you require.

You will recall from the previous chapter how diagnostic questions can be quick for students to answer and easy for teachers to review. Adopting the same principles from the previous chapter can make for an exit ticket with effective diagnostic properties. You could couple a diagnostic multiple-choice question with a short open-ended question that requires students to explain their choice. Such responses, especially when students select incorrect answers, can offer even more insight into their thinking.

Short, open-ended questions, such as single-sentence explanations or worked examples, can reveal students' thinking, but take longer to review. There is a trade-off here. These types of questions are likely to take twice as long to sample, but they can offer richer evidence of a more advanced understanding. It is possible to strike a balance by structuring open responses by using sentence stems or tightly constrained prompts that reduce variability while preserving insight.

A useful rule of thumb is to make it as easy as possible to obtain the information you need. Avoid overly complex tasks and remember that you are not trying to assess everything, only the most crucial ideas from the lesson's objective.

The following examples show how exit tickets can be adapted across subjects and implemented using a range of formats.

In French, the teacher might want to check students' ability to express future intentions.

Exit Ticket **Name:** ____________________

Complete each sentence with the correct form of the verb aller to create the near future tense (e.g., Je vais manger).

1. Demain, je _________ manger au restaurant.
2. Ce soir, nous _________ regarder un film.
3. Samedi, tu _________ jouer au foot avec tes amis.
4. Pendant les vacances, elles _________ visiter Paris.

The next example is inspired by Craig Barton, who suggests varying the format within an exit ticket. This might include a factual recall question, an open-response question to check procedural knowledge, and a student-generated task that requires students to construct their own examples.[47]

Exit Ticket **Name:** ____________________

1. Calculate the area of the triangle below.

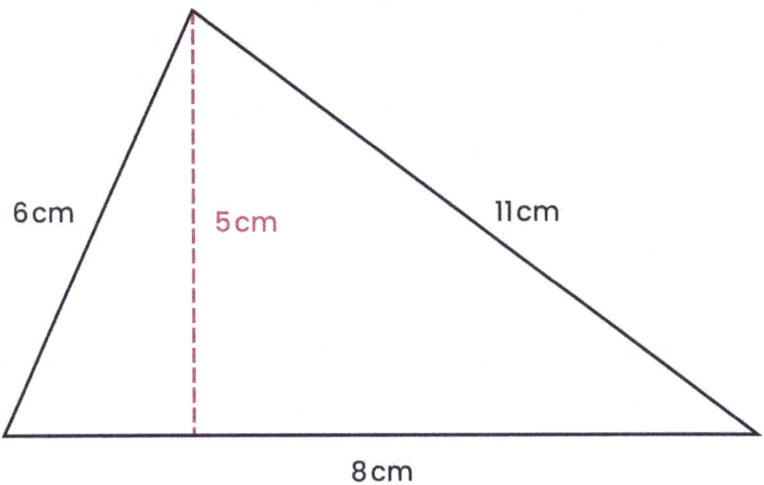

Figure 11.2 Triangle.

A. 20 cm^2 B. 40 cm^2 C. 24 cm^2 D. 25 cm

2. Calculate the area of a triangle with a base of 7.5 cm and a height of 4 cm.

3. A triangle has an area of 36 cm✣. Give three different combinations of base and height that would give this area.

Triangle 1
Base:_______cm Height: _______ cm

Triangle 2
Base:_______cm Height: _______ cm

Triangle 3
Base:_______cm Height: _______ cm

These next two examples draw on the brilliant writing activities from the seminal book *The Writing Revolution* (TWR) by Judith Hochman and Natalie Wexler.[48]

Using the *sentence expansion* strategy from TWR, the exit ticket can assess factual recall and whether students can use this to provide a structured account. The following example is from KS2 history (age 7-11) and concerns the Roman Empire's impact on Britain, specifically the construction of Hadrian's Wall.

To illustrate how the sentence expansion technique works, this example has been completed, with an expected response written in purple.

Exit Ticket **Name:** ____________________

Kernel sentence: Hadrian's Wall was built.

1. Fill in the notes below to recall the facts.

When: **In AD 122 during the Roman Empire**

Where: **Across Northern England**

Why: **To defend the Roman frontier from northern tribes**

2. Now, use your notes to write one long, detailed sentence.

In AD 122, the Romans built Hadrian's Wall across Northern England to defend their territory from the tribes in the North.

Another technique from TWR that can be effective as an exit ticket is *because, but, so*. The strategy is a cornerstone of TWR, moving students beyond simple recall. It is particularly effective as an exit ticket because, rather than posing a broad question that can take time to answer and analyse, it provides a structured sentence starter that requires students to process a single idea in three distinct directions. It requires students to think about causality, contrast, and consequence. Another benefit of this technique as an exit ticket is that its structure helps keep the focus tight and aligned with the lesson's core content, while still revealing how students reason about that idea.

In Year 8 geography (ages 12-13), students might study the rise of megacities in Asia. The following exit ticket checks students' understanding of a big idea that underpins much of the geography curriculum. Again, this example has been completed in purple to illustrate how the technique works.

Exit Ticket **Name:** ____________________

1. Complete the "Because, But, So" prompts below based on today's lesson.

   Sentence starter: Many people are moving from the countryside to cities like Mumbai . . .

   because **there are more reliable, higher-paid jobs available in the service and manufacturing sectors.**

   but **they often find that they lack the specific technical skills needed for the highest-paying roles.**

   so **the city's population is increasing by hundreds of people every single day.**

The final example is adapted from *Teach Like a Champion 3.0*. Doug Lemov illustrates how an exit ticket can combine a diagnostic multiple-choice question with plausible distractors and a short, structured, open-ended prompt.[2] The diagnostic question is an efficient and reliable way to sample students' thinking, provided the incorrect options are plausible. Including an open-ended justification adds another layer of insight, revealing the specific reasoning or misunderstandings students use to connect evidence to the underlying concept.

In *An Inspector Calls*, J.B. Priestley uses the character of Arthur Birling to represent the "hard-headed" capitalist views of 1912. This exit ticket checks if students can distinguish between Birling's misplaced confidence and the underlying dramatic irony.

Exit Ticket **Name:** ____________________

1. Which of the following quotes from Mr Birling's Act 1 speech show his overconfidence and lack of foresight? Circle all that apply:

   A. " . . . the Titanic . . . forty-six thousand eight hundred tons . . . and unsinkable, absolutely unsinkable."

   B. " . . . there's a lot of wild talk about possible labour trouble in the near future. Don't worry. We've passed the worst of it."

   C. "And in the future, Eric, when you have a daughter of your own, you'll understand why."

   D. " . . . a man has to make his own way - has to look after himself - and his family too, of course."

   Select one of the circled quotes and, in 2–3 sentences, explain how Priestley uses dramatic irony to make the audience doubt Mr Birling's judgement:

____

____

Clarity and Precision

Like hinge questions, aim for parsimony in the wording of your questions and options (when including a diagnostic question). If students are to understand and complete an exit ticket in under five minutes, the wording must be crystal clear. Students should be thinking about the content, not trying to decode the question's meaning.

The quality of the evidence you elicit from your exit ticket is contingent on its design. The preceding examples serve as a useful heuristic for achieving precision and clarity in exit ticket questions.

Make it Explicitly Low-stakes

The questions on your exit ticket should align with the lesson's core content. Another important consideration is students' perception of completing them. The message should be explicit: this is not a test, and students are not being judged.

Across all the checking-for-understanding routines outlined in this book, fostering a culture in which it is safe to make mistakes is crucial, and exit tickets are no exception. When students feel safe to get things wrong, they are more likely to attempt the questions. This, in turn, sharpens teachers' inferences, as the evidence they receive is more trustworthy and therefore more reliable.

Daisy Christodoulou argues that each lesson should end with a question that all students can get right.[39] On an exit ticket, such a question offers tight alignment to the intended learning objective and can be a real confidence boost for all students.

Design for Efficiency

The final principle relates to how responses are collected and reviewed. Since immediacy is important, routines for collecting and reviewing exit tickets should be as simple and efficient as possible.

There is no orthodoxy; you might use printed paper slips with the questions, sticky notes, or an online form. You might place a basket near the classroom door for students to leave their exit tickets as they leave the classroom. Select the approaches that make it as easy as possible to collect and review the exit ticket.

Another approach to improve efficiency comes via Harry Fletcher-Wood. In his book, *Responsive Teaching: Cognitive Science and Formative Assessment in Practice*, Fletcher-Wood suggests that teachers benefit from predicting likely student responses by writing answers they would expect from a high prior attainer, a student with a basic grasp of the key idea, and a student holding common misconceptions.[49] He argues that this process helps set a minimum benchmark for success, increases the likelihood that the exit ticket will surface the intended thinking, and provides a clearer indication of how long students are likely to need to complete it.

Implementing Exit Tickets

For exit tickets to lead to better-founded decisions, teachers need reliable evidence from them and efficient ways to sample responses and interpret patterns to determine the best way to respond.

Creating the Conditions for Valid, Usable Evidence

For exit tickets to serve their purpose and inform the teacher reliably, they must generate reliable information. This depends not only on the design of the exit ticket, as seen in the preceding paragraphs, but also on the conditions under which responses are generated and reviewed.

A simple yet important step is to ensure students complete their exit tickets independently. Allowing students to collaborate, copy, or seek reassurance from peers contaminates the quality of the evidence. The teacher is no longer seeing individual understanding that would allow them to support individual students; instead, they are seeing a composite of shared thinking.

For an exit ticket to guide instructional decisions effectively, it needs to reflect what each student can do. Without this, teachers risk drawing false positives, where students who have not yet grasped the material appear secure because they received a helping hand from a peer.

A second consideration is that exit tickets need to be quick to analyse at a class level. Teachers must be able to identify patterns swiftly if they are to intervene while student understanding is fragile. You will recall the exit ticket at the start of this chapter, which deliberately exposed some of the less-reliable ways teachers can end up using to judge the effectiveness of their teaching. One such approach is marking books, which, as all teachers know, can be incredibly time-consuming.

While careful marking has an important place in teaching, it typically means that knowledge gaps or recurring errors are identified much later than they might be through ongoing checks for understanding. The point of the comparison here is not to diminish the value of marking, but to highlight the advantage of a well-conceived exit ticket. When evidence is quick to sample, teachers have more time and cognitive space to decide how to respond when misconceptions or fragile understanding emerge.

Once you have designed the exit ticket in line with the principles set out in this chapter, and considered how to protect the validity of the evidence it generates, the next step is to decide how to sample responses and respond efficiently.

Sampling and Responding to Exit Tickets

Exit tickets lose their instructional affordance if they are not reviewed promptly. Ideally, they should be reviewed on the same day they are completed, or before the next lesson, so students can see how their responses meaningfully shape what happens next.

The aim here is not to read every response in depth. Instead, teachers should develop a simple, efficient routine to quickly identify patterns. One effective approach is to group responses into three broad categories: those that reflect secure understanding, those that suggest partial understanding, and those that reveal significant confusion. An initial scan and sort of this kind provides a sense of the class's overall understanding.

Once the broad picture is established, attention can then be focused on responses that show a partial or insecure understanding. The purpose here is to identify precisely what students are struggling with. Are they applying the method incorrectly? Confusing two related concepts? Omitting a key step?

From start to finish, the initial grouping and analysis should take no more than five to ten minutes, depending on the exit ticket's format and complexity.

At this point, the teacher can decide what happens in the upcoming lessons. When responses indicate that most students have a secure grasp of the lesson's core idea (80% or above), the teacher can proceed with confidence while planning tailored intervention for the small number who do not. Doug Lemov describes this as being *entrepreneurial with time*.[2] When understanding is secure, it is often better to schedule a retrieval task for a week later rather than spending too long revisiting the content, as the time can then be used to tackle areas that genuinely cause confusion.

If students' responses indicate that a substantial number have misunderstood the core idea (fewer than 40% answering the exit ticket correctly), this signals the need to address it directly at the start of the next lesson. Importantly, reteaching should not involve repeating the same explanation. Instead, it is more likely to involve a different representation, a new worked example that foregrounds a common error, and a short sequence of focused practice.

When exit ticket responses suggest a mixed understanding (40–80% of students answering correctly), it may indicate the class needs to return to the concept. It might be a case of using a different explanation or a contrasting example to address the confusion.

In other cases, it may be more effective to model how to solve a problem that students struggled with, explicitly foregrounding the decision points that sparked confusion. When taking this approach, it is important to follow up by providing a similar problem for students to complete to check whether the model has addressed the misunderstanding.

Another productive response is to use errors as the focus of a class discussion. Craig Barton suggests that teachers could present several responses to the exit ticket, one correct and the others reflecting common errors, and ask students to identify the correct answer and explain why the others are wrong.[47]

A final, and perhaps less familiar, approach is to ask students to write their names on the exit ticket and use their responses to inform groupings in the subsequent lesson. Dylan Wiliam suggests that teachers can use exit-ticket evidence to form homogeneous groups, providing intensive support for students demonstrating the greatest difficulty, or heterogeneous groups in which at least one student has a firm grasp of the content.[30]

An added benefit of this is that, because exit tickets are not formally marked, students do not know who produced the strongest responses. This can lead to a richer discussion within groups and helps surface and resolve misconceptions without attaching status or judgement to individual answers.

These sampling and follow-up moves keep the focus firmly on the lesson's core idea. Crucially, when students see that their exit ticket responses directly inform subsequent lessons, they begin to take the process more seriously. You can create further continuity by using a question from an exit ticket as a retrieval practice question at the start of the next lesson, either in the same form or slightly adapted.

Limits, Culture, and Common Pitfalls

Like all tools in a teacher's toolkit, exit tickets have limits and pitfalls that teachers need to be aware of to get the most from using them. Being clear about what they can and cannot do helps ensure they are used appropriately.

Learning and Performance

An important caveat when using them is that they capture performance during the learning process, not learning in the long term. As discussed multiple times in this book, success immediately after instruction does not guarantee durable learning. Students may produce correct answers at the end of a carefully structured and well-scaffolded lesson, only to forget the salient ideas days later. The learning versus performance distinction reminds us not to over-interpret exit tickets. Their role is to inform the next instructional steps, not to provide proof of learning.

Practical Constraints

A common pitfall is the end-of-lesson crunch. When time is tight, exit tickets can feel rushed or be dropped altogether. Over time, this can reduce their reliability and undermine their perceived importance. Teachers who use exit tickets effectively tend to plan for them, preserving a small but consistent window of time at the end of most lessons.

Another potential barrier is teacher workload. If a teacher teaches five lessons per day, and each class has an average of thirty students, that is 150 exit tickets to sample. If a teacher spent 2 minutes per exit ticket reviewing them, it would take 5 hours. Not practical. As emphasised earlier, exit tickets should not be marked exhaustively. Teachers should be able to sample a class set in 5–10 minutes by being strategic and focusing on patterns over precision.

It is worth noting that teachers should not be afraid to abandon exit tickets. As Craig Barton points out, exit tickets are not the only check for understanding technique in a teacher's repertoire, and there are multiple other points in an instructional sequence where a check will likely have occurred.[47] If one of these earlier checks reveals the lesson needs to take a different direction, because most students are struggling to understand, the teacher might choose to slow down to offer more support and practice. In this scenario, the teacher should not feel pressured to squeeze in the exit ticket at the end of the lesson, knowing it is unlikely to serve its intended purpose.

Student Buy-in and Classroom Culture

Exit tickets can also become performative if students do not know their purpose. When students complete them with no discernible follow-up, they are likely to disengage or treat the task superficially. Conversely, when teachers clearly use exit tickets to shape subsequent lessons, students take them more seriously, providing more reliable evidence for inference.

This links closely to classroom culture. Like all the checking-for-understanding routines in this book, exit tickets work best in environments where mistakes are normalised and where students understand that revealing uncertainty is helpful rather than something to be frowned upon. Maintaining a low-stakes approach, avoiding public judgement, and using responses respectfully all contribute to exit tickets providing teachers with more reliable evidence.

The value of exit tickets lies in the way they sharpen teachers' judgements about what should happen next. When crafted with care and reviewed efficiently, they provide a brief but powerful window into students' thinking at a moment when misconceptions are still malleable. In so doing, exit tickets should remind us that effective teaching is not defined by how smoothly the lesson went, but by how teachers intelligently respond to what their students do and do not understand.

Section 3: Checking for Understanding in Action Concluding Principles for Practice

1. **Each check for understanding should require every student to think.**

   Techniques such as cold calling, mini whiteboards, hinge questions, and exit tickets are effective because they create regular opportunities for all students to engage with the material. When participation is deliberately engineered rather than left to volunteers, teachers gain a more accurate picture of what students understand, not just what a confident minority is willing to share.

2. **Ratio increases the likelihood that all students are thinking at a desirable level of difficulty.**

   High-ratio classrooms provide frequent opportunities for every student to think, retrieve, explain, and decide. By increasing the proportion of students required to respond and the quality of thinking each response demands, teachers make it more likely that all students are engaged in productive cognitive effort, rather than passively observing others do the work.

3. **The quality of a check for understanding depends on its design.**

   Poorly designed checks generate noise; well-designed ones generate insight. Effective checks for understanding tightly align to core ideas, expose plausible misconceptions, and make reasoning visible. Simply asking more questions does not improve understanding unless those questions are doing the right diagnostic work.

4. **Checks for understanding are only as effective as the responses they provoke.**

   The real instructional leverage comes from how teachers respond to what each check for understanding reveals. Whether through immediate feedback, modelling, targeted practice, or planned reteaching, checking for understanding only improves learning when it meaningfully shapes what happens next.

5. **No single technique is sufficient; intelligent sequencing matters.**

   Each checking-for-understanding technique offers a different lens on student thinking and is most useful at particular moments in the instructional sequence. Cold calling, mini whiteboards, hinge questions, and exit tickets work best when used deliberately and in combination to build an increasingly accurate picture of understanding over time.

Section 3: Checking for Understanding in Action References

1. Willingham, D.T. (2009) *Why don't students like school?: A cognitive scientist answers questions about how the mind works and what it means for the classroom*. San Francisco: Jossey-Bass
2. Lemov, D. (2021) *Teach like a champion 3.0: 63 techniques that put students on the path to college*, 3rd ed. Hoboken, NJ: Jossey-Bass.
3. Rosenshine, B. (2012) "Principles of instruction: Research-based strategies that all teachers should know," *American Educator*, 36(1), pp. 12–39.

4. InnerDrive (2024) 'Thinking and participation ratios: How to maximise cognitive engagement," InnerDrive blog, 6 min read [online]. Available at: https://www.innerdrive.co.uk/blog/maximise-cognitive-engagement/ (Accessed: 14 November 2025.)
5. Lemov, D. (2017) "Bloom's Taxonomy – that pyramid is a problem," Teach Like a Champion blog, 3 April. Available at: https://teachlikeachampion.org/blog/blooms-taxonomy-pyramid-problem/ (Accessed: 14 November 2025.)
6. Wiliam, D. (2017) "[Tweet]", X, 8 May. Available at: https://x.com/dylanwiliam/status/849277989577789441 (Accessed: 15 November 2025.)
7. Boxer, A. (2019) "Challenge beyond Bloom's," A Chemical Orthodoxy – Schools, Science and Education, 23 October. Available at: https://achemicalorthodoxy.co.uk/2019/10/23/challenge-beyond-blooms/ (Accessed: 15 November 2025.)
8. Dallimore, E.J., Hertenstein, J.H., and Platt, M.B. (2019) "Leveling the playing field: How cold-calling affects class discussion gender equity," *Journal of Education and Learning*, 8(2), pp. 14–24.
9. Mccrea, P. (2024) "Orchestrating attention." Available at: https://snacks.pepsmccrea.com/p/orchestrating-attention (Accessed: 18 February 2025.)
10. Dallimore, E.J., Hertenstein, J.H., and Platt, M.B. (2013) "Impact of cold-calling on student voluntary participation," *Journal of Management Education*, 37(3), pp. 305–341.
11. Rosenshine, B. (2012) "Principles of instruction: Research-based strategies that all teachers should know," *American Educator*, 36(1), pp. 12–39.
12. Hendrick, C. (2025) "Making retrieval practice actually work: Seven essential principles for teachers to know," Carl Hendrick's Substack, [online]. Available at: https://carlhendrick.substack.com/p/making-retrieval-practice-actually (Accessed: 20 February 2025.)
13. Sumeracki, M.A. and Castillo, J. (2022) "Covert and overt retrieval practice in the classroom," *Translational Issues in Psychological Science*, 8(2), pp. 282–293.
14. Nuthall, G. (2007) *The hidden lives of learners*. Wellington: NZCER Press.
15. Morek, M., Heller, V., and Kinalzik, N. (2022) "Engaging 'silent' students in classroom discussions: A micro-analytic view on teachers' embodied enactments of cold-calling practices," *Classroom Discourse*, 13(4), pp. 731–749.

16. Doty, C.M., Geraets, A.A., Wan, T., Saitta, E.K.H., and Chini, J.J. (2019) "Student perspective of GTA strategies to reduce feelings of anxiousness with cold-calling." PERC Proceedings 2019, American Association of Physics Teachers.

17. Tofade, T., Elsner, J., and Haines, S.T. (2013) "Best practice strategies for effective use of questions as a teaching tool," *American Journal of Pharmaceutical Education*, 77(7), Article 155.

18. Kirschner, P.A. and Hendrick, C. (2020) *How learning happens: Seminal works in educational psychology and what they mean in practice*. Abingdon: Routledge.

19. Stahl, R.J. (1994) "Using 'think-time' and 'wait-time' skillfully in the classroom," ERIC Digest. Available at: https://www.eric.ed.gov (Accessed: 22 February 2025.)

20. Daslin, F.H. and Zainil, Y. (2020) "Teachers' use of wait time: A case study of questioning strategies in SMAN Padang," *Journal of English Language Teaching*, 9(4), pp. 718–732. Available at: http://ejournal.unp.ac.id/index.php/jelt (Accessed: 22 February 2025.)

21. Sherrington, T. (2017) *The learning rainforest: Great teaching in real classrooms*. Woodbridge: John Catt Educational.

22. Barton, C. (2024) "The one question to ask mini-whiteboard sceptics," *Eedi Newsletter*, 11 June. Available at: https://eedi.substack.com/p/the-one-question-to-ask-mini-whiteboard (Accessed: 20 October 2025.)

23. Walker, J. (2021) "Mini whiteboards, major outcomes!" The Literacy Blog, 14 July. Available at: https://theliteracyblog.com/2021/07/14/mini-whiteboards-major-outcomes/#:~:text=Writing%20on%20whiteboards%20enables%20children,they%20start%20learning%20to%20read (Accessed: 20 October 2025.)

24. Didau, D. (2022) "Using mini whiteboards in English," The Learning Spy, 9 October. Available at: https://learningspy.co.uk/english-gcse/using-mini-whiteboards-in-english/#:~:text=However%2C%20I%20suspect%20the%20issue,I%20think%20it%E2%80%99s%20possible (Accessed: 20 October 2025.)

25. Gardner, R., Heward, W. L., and Grossi, T. (1994) "Effects of response cards on student participation and academic achievement: A systematic replication with inner-city students during whole-class science instruction," *Journal of Applied Behavior Analysis*, 27(1), pp. 63–71.

26. Christle, C. A. and Schuster, J. W. (2003) "The effects of using response cards on student participation, academic achievement, and on-task behavior during whole-class math instruction," *Journal of Behavioral Education*, 12, pp. 147–165.

27. Randolph, J. J. (2007) Meta-analysis of the research on response cards: Effects on test achievement, quiz achievement, participation, and off-task behavior. *Journal of Positive Behavior Interventions*, 9(2), pp. 113–128.

28. Marsh, R. J., Cumming, T. M., Randolph, J. J., et al. (2023) "Updated meta-analysis of the research on response cards," *Journal of Behavioral Education*, 32, pp. 450–473.

29. Sherrington, T. (2012) "THE number 1 bit of classroom kit: mini-whiteboards," TeacherHead, 28 August. Available at: https://teacherhead.com/2012/08/28/the-number-1-bit-of-classroom-kit-mini-whiteboards/ (Accessed: 22 October 2025.)

30. Wiliam, D. (2011) *Embedded formative assessment*. Bloomington, MN: Solution Tree Press.

31. Barton, C. (2021) "Mini-whiteboards - part 2: Mini-whiteboard routines." Tips for Teachers, 14 July. Available at: https://tipsforteachers.co.uk/mini-whiteboards/#4-part-2-mini-whiteboard-routines (Accessed: 22 October 2025.)

32. Boxer, A. (2021) "To reduce 'choppy time' in lessons, use a front loaded means of participation and wait for golden silence.," Tips for Teachers, [online] Available at: https://tipsforteachers.co.uk/choppy-time/ (Accessed: 22 October 2025.)

33. Wiliam, D. (2023) "The best formative assessment processes often leave no written evidence; just a smarter decision by the teacher . . ." X, 21 May. Available at: https://x.com/dylanwiliam/status/1857576345355825464 (Accessed: 24 October 2025.)

34. Clear, J. (2018) *Atomic habits: Tiny changes, remarkable results: An easy and proven way to build good habits and break bad ones*. New York NY: Avery.

35. Schulz, T., Cividini-Motta, C., Cho Blair, K-S., and MacNaul, H. (2022) "A comparison of high-tech and low-tech response modalities to improve student classroom behavior," *Journal of Behavioral Education*, 31, pp. 243–264. doi: 10.1007/s10864-020-09393-3.

36. Hendrick, C. and Hughes, H. (2025) How teaching and learning happens - Checking for understanding. YouTube video. Available at: https://www.youtube.com/watch?v=1nUrX66nM4M (Accessed: 30 January 2026.)

37. Coe, R. (2015) "From evidence to great teaching.", paper presented at the ASCL Annual Conference, London, 20 March.

38. Wylie, C. and Wiliam, D. (2006) "Diagnostic questions: Is there value in just one?" Paper presented at the Annual Meeting of the American Educational Research Association, San Francisco, CA.

39. Christodoulou, D. (2016) *Making good progress? The future of assessment for learning*. Oxford: Oxford University Press.

40. Barton, C. (2025) *Tips for teachers: A guide to diagnostic questions*. Dunstable: Craig Barton.

41. Case, S.M. and Swanson, D.B. (2002) Constructing *written test questions for the basic and clinical sciences*, 3rd edn. Philadelphia: National Board of Medical Examiners.

42. Gierl, M.J., Bulut, O., Guo, Q., and Zhang, X. (2017) "Developing, analyzing, and using distractors for multiple-choice tests in education," *Educational Measurement: Issues and Practice*, 36(1), pp. 6–16.

43. D'Mello, S., Lehman, B., Pekrun, R., and Graesser, A. (2014) "Confusion can be beneficial for learning," *Learning and Instruction*, 29, pp. 153–170.

44. Didau, D. (2024) "Using hinge-point questions in English." Available at: https://learningspy.co.uk/tag/hinge-point-questions/ (Accessed: 28 October 2025.)

45. Chiles, M. (2023) *Powerful questioning: Strategies to deepen learning and check for understanding*. Carmarthen: Crown House Publishing.

46. Sherrington, T. (2019) *Rosenshine's principles in action*. London: John Catt Educational.

47. Barton, C. (2023) *Tips for Teachers: 400+ ideas to improve your teaching*. London: John Catt Educational Ltd.

48. Hochman, J. and Wexler, N. (2017) *The writing revolution: A guide to advancing thinking through writing in all subjects and grades*. San Francisco, CA: Jossey-Bass.

49. Fletcher-Wood, H. (2018) *Responsive teaching: Cognitive science and formative assessment in practice*. London: Routledge.

SECTION 4

Checking for Understanding and . . .

12 Checking for Understanding and SEND

You may have heard the phrase: "Good teaching for pupils with SEND is good teaching for all."[1] It should not be surprising, then, that checking for understanding has roots in special education research.

The practice of formative assessment, and by extension checking for understanding, stems from the pioneering work of Lynn and Douglas Fuchs (1986).[2] Their research in special education first demonstrated how systematically checking students' understanding and adapting instruction led to significant achievement gains.[2] Their meta-analysis of more than twenty studies showed an average effect size of +0.70. This gain is large enough to represent nearly an additional year of progress for students who received instruction shaped by systematic formative checks.

Their model of systematic formative evaluation was originally designed for students with SEND. Yet its utility has proven universal. Over time, this model evolved into the broader concept of formative assessment. Its origins were, and remain, profoundly inclusive. Checking for understanding may be in vogue now, but it draws directly from research from decades ago in special education.

The moral imperative that underpinned this early research is as important today as at its inception. Arguably, it is even more so now. The current UK picture for SEND reveals a system under strain: rising numbers of students with identified needs, delayed assessments, and a lack

DOI: 10.4324/9781003657019-17

of clarity about what truly inclusive education means.[3] Yet within this uncertainty, there is a consensus that inclusion begins with high-quality teaching and learning. The Education Endowment Foundation reminds us that no magic intervention replaces consistent, high-quality teaching that makes learning accessible for all.[1]

Checking for understanding is both a pedagogical and moral act. It embodies habitual curiosity: the teacher's continual commitment to seek evidence of every student's understanding. In classrooms where the teacher frequently checks everyone's understanding, confusion or misunderstanding does not exclude students from learning. The teacher first makes students' thinking visible. Then, they can adapt their instruction. What could be more inclusive?

So important is this work that inclusion is now explicitly included in the UK school inspection framework. Schools will now be judged on the extent to which they systematically identify learning gaps, address them swiftly, review adaptations, and make adjustments as needed. The framework also places strong emphasis on teachers' professional expertise, noting that "Teachers are expert at checking pupils' understanding and adapting their teaching, in the moment, to meet pupils' needs."[4]

The Graduated Approach

First outlined in the SEND Code of Practice (2014), the graduated approach established a clear expectation. Teachers should assess, plan, do, and review to meet students' needs through high-quality, inclusive teaching.[5]

Both checking for understanding and the assess-plan-do-review cycle are inherently formative processes. Each helps teachers decide on the next steps in instruction. These decisions are likely to be *better, or at least better founded*, than those made without the evidence elicited.[6]

The graduated approach is a cyclical process and a framework for improving provision over time. In the classroom, checking for

The graduated approach	Checking for understanding equivalent
Assess	Elicit evidence of understanding through cold calling, mini whiteboards, hinge questions or observation.
Plan	Interpret what the evidence shows and decide what to do next.
Do	Implement the next step: reteach, model again, provide more examples or proceed as intended.
Review	Recheck to see if learning is on track.

understanding loops are not prolonged sequences. Instead, they set the cadence of the lesson itself. Each time the teacher uses a check for understanding, it informs the next step and demonstrates a micro-version of the assess, plan, do, review model. The most effective teachers run these loops continually, keeping every student's learning on track.

At a policy level, the graduated approach requires teachers to provide bespoke support and to review its effectiveness regularly. At the classroom level, checking for understanding makes the support dynamic and responsive. Both approaches are parallel: each involves gathering evidence, making decisions, and adjusting support based on students' needs. The graduated approach zooms out to view learning over time, while checking for understanding zooms in to view it in real time.

This parallel matters because it makes the system more agile. When teachers check for understanding effectively, they become the first line of identification. Teachers who check and probe students' thinking often do not need to wait for formal assessments or SENCO feedback to know a student is struggling. A well-designed mini whiteboard session or a probing cold call discussion can reveal misconceptions. Even a brief observation can show processing delays or attentional barriers far earlier than paperwork would.

In this way, checking for understanding can serve as an early form of identification and intervention, supporting teachers to act on emerging needs before they crystallise into long-term difficulties. As Fuchs and Fuchs' work in the 1980s showed, the power of systematic formative checking lies in how teachers use evidence to adapt instruction in the moment. Their findings showed that when teachers engaged in the assess-plan-do-review loop routinely, students with SEND made significantly greater progress than those whose needs were reviewed only intermittently.[2]

Checking for understanding, then, transforms the graduated approach from an administrative cycle into a lived classroom habit. Each process depends on the other: the graduated approach establishes structure and accountability over time, while checking for understanding allows that structure to adapt and respond within each lesson. By explicitly intertwining these processes, teachers are less likely to separate assessment from teaching, recognising that continual assessment provides essential feedback for next steps.

This responsiveness also connects directly to the adaptive teaching model outlined in the next chapter. Before the lesson, teachers engage in **proactive adaptive teaching**. They anticipate variation, plan scaffolds, and design checks for understanding. During the lesson, those checks trigger **reactive adaptive teaching**. Teachers then make in-the-moment decisions about when to scaffold, when to stretch, and when to pause. After the lesson, teachers review the evidence, adjust planning, and refine future sequences.

Cognitive Foundations

Learning is the long-term retention of knowledge and the ability to apply it in new contexts. It is the result of the construction, partial forgetting, and reconstruction of knowledge and is influenced by how the mind perceives, processes, and stores information. When teaching students with SEND, these cognitive principles become especially important, as SEND students may process, store, or retrieve information differently.

Therefore, our checks for understanding should be particularly informed by these needs.

Working Memory: The Narrow Gateway of Learning

For learning to occur, new information must pass through working memory. When a task's cognitive demand exceeds this, students experience overload: learning stalls before information can be encoded into long-term memory.

For students with SEND, this bottleneck is often narrower. Gathercole and Alloway (2008) found that working-memory limits define many learning difficulties, especially in literacy and numeracy.[7] Too much input, listening, writing, recalling and decoding quickly overwhelms these students.

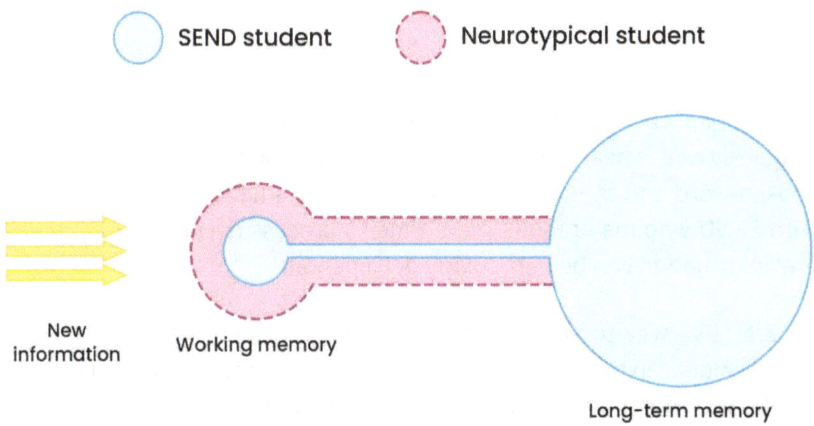

In contrast to the challenges described earlier, educational approaches have evolved. In the past, teachers were told that discovery learning was the gold standard. Too much teacher talk stifled creativity and curiosity, and the best learning happened when the teacher acted as a *facilitator*. Despite the intuitive appeal of unguided or minimally guided teaching, there is over half a century of empirical evidence refuting this approach. In their review of the research, Kirschner, Sweller, and Clark concluded that minimally guided instruction fails to account for how humans learn.[8] The limitations of working memory mean that novice learners cannot hold, manipulate, and integrate large amounts of information without explicit guidance.

More recent research, discussed by Carl Hendrick, strengthens this conclusion by showing that the costs of unguided learning are unevenly distributed.[9] For some students, particularly those with ADHD and dyslexia, discovery-based approaches impose additional cognitive demands that make learning less likely. Something Hendrick eloquently refers to as a discovery tax.

Despite overwhelming evidence, inquiry-based learning remains pervasive today. Supporters of such approaches argue that explicit instruction is uninspiring and involves too much teacher talk or lecture-style teaching, even though it is one of the EEF's SEND Five-A-Day recommendations. Done properly, nothing could be further from the truth. Cognitive science tells us that too much unbroken exposition to content risks producing the transient information effect. This is when the information presented fades as quickly as it is heard or seen, leaving no trace for students to revisit. The spoken word and the teacher's slides are problematic here. For students with SEND who may require more time to process new material, ephemeral information can be particularly detrimental.

An effective way to address the transient information effect is to capture key ideas in graphical or written form. Teachers record concepts on the board, model processes visually, or provide worked examples for students to refer to. These methods externalise information, reducing the strain on working memory.

However, the balance required introduces a new challenge. The more information there is, the more likely it is that students' working memory is overloaded. An overcrowded slide or an overly detailed model can split attention and create what cognitive science calls extraneous load. This occurs when students expend unnecessary effort to overcome poor instructional design, thereby diverting working memory resources that could be better spent on learning. Once again, the solution risks becoming the problem.

Enter chunking. Special education has long recognised that chunking information into smaller, meaningful units can reduce the amount of information students must process at any one time. Chunking allows students to experience success incrementally, building confidence and fluency as they progress.

However, even chunking has limitations. Students who benefit most from segmented information are often at the greatest risk of overload when presented with too many chunks. Each new chunk competes for working memory resources, and earlier segments can easily slip from memory before students can make connections. Once again, the solution becomes the problem.

To address these challenges, consider the space between each chunk as a genuine opportunity. Each segment must include deliberate, cumulative checks for understanding: short opportunities for students to rehearse, retrieve, and articulate what they have just learned. We can now frame checking for understanding as a way of mediating students' limited working memory.

The main message here is to check for understanding more frequently. Each check allows students to rehearse and refine their thinking, improving memory as they retrieve and apply the ideas. Therefore, do it more often.

Cognitive Load and Attention

Cognitive Load Theory highlights the need for teachers to manage two specific kinds of cognitive load.[10] Intrinsic load is determined by the complexity of the material, while extraneous load results from poor instructional design. Effective checking for understanding reduces extraneous load and helps working memory focus on learning.

For example, to check students' understanding of a science process, use a clear, simple diagram and focus on one variable at a time. This isolates the concept you are checking. In contrast, if you ask students to interpret dense text or multi-step data and answer conceptual questions too soon, your checks risk confusing understanding with cognitive endurance. Thus, the way checks are structured has direct implications for student learning.

Ensuring effective checks for understanding is especially critical for students with SEND, who are more susceptible to extraneous load. Well-designed checks focus attention on intended learning, optimising intrinsic load, and reducing distractions.

Attention is the gatekeeper of learning.[11] If attention falters, information cannot enter working memory in the first place. Students with attention difficulties, including those with ADHD, may appear disengaged when in fact their attention systems are under strain. In this context, checking for understanding can serve as an attentional reset by refocusing students and clarifying expectations. For example, "Take a minute to study this diagram before I ask you some questions." This front-loaded instruction gives students advance warning that the upcoming questions depend on their attention to the information in the diagram.

Distinguishing between attention and genuine understanding is essential. Students who appear attentive may still misunderstand, whereas distracted students can grasp the main ideas. Teachers should avoid assumptions and use checks for understanding that probe students' thinking, such as asking for explanations of their reasoning to reveal conceptual depth.

Schema Development

Checking for understanding reveals whether students have the necessary schema to accommodate new learning. For instance, if students fail to understand what particles are, they will struggle to grasp evaporation beyond surface-level associations, such as "water disappearing."

For students with SEND, fragmented or unstable schemata can distort understanding. A student with developmental language disorder (DLD) might misinterpret key vocabulary ("energy," "change," "flow"). Checks for understanding, therefore, serve a diagnostic function: they help identify where schemata need to be stabilised or restructured before new material can take hold.

Pre-teaching key vocabulary, using visual representations, and prompting retrieval of prior learning all support schema development and make subsequent checks more valid.

Long-term Memory and Retrieval

Learning is not a one-off event. The more actively students think with and about content, the more likely they are to remember it.

Checking for understanding contributes to this process in two ways. It gives the teacher feedback on what is currently understood. Additionally, it enhances learning through rehearsal and fluency with the material. Each check can reinforce memory traces and signal what still needs consolidation.

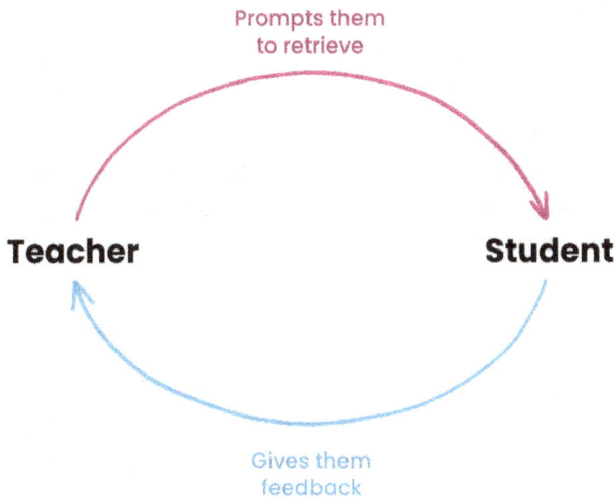

For students with SEND, retrieval needs to be frequent, varied, and supported. Short, low-stakes checks spread over time are more effective than single, high-pressure tests. Spaced practice, even brief bouts, has been shown to stabilise knowledge that might otherwise decay over time.

Routines and Checking for Understanding

Routines are the cornerstone of inclusive classrooms.[12] They create the psychological safety necessary for students to participate, teeing them up for success. Once routines become ingrained, students' working memory is free to expend on learning rather than deciphering expectations. This is particularly critical for students with SEND.

Building on the importance of routines outlined previously, let's revisit cold calling and mini whiteboards. By examining how routines support these strategies, we see how routines become the fabric of inclusive classrooms. When anchored in consistent, predictable habits, these techniques are reliable tools for eliciting evidence of understanding while reducing students' uncertainty. This ensures that the voices and thinking of every student inform the teacher's decision-making, not just a handful.

Cold Calling

When used thoughtfully, cold calling broadens participation and signals that every student's thinking matters. The key is to build a culture that draws students in, rather than catching them out. *Teacher SEND Handbook* highlights how predictable routines, extended processing time, and varied response options support student learning.[5] With effective routines, cold calling achieves these outcomes.

Mini Whiteboards

Mini whiteboards can be considered a routine for inclusion in their own right. By allowing all students to express their ideas without the pressure of public performance, they democratise classroom dialogue. *Teacher SEND Handbook* highlights the importance of accessible response formats and predictable routines. Mini whiteboards, used properly, embody both.

Cold Calling

Instructional consideration	Routines to run:
Students with speech, language and communication needs (SLCN) or autism may need additional time to process language and organise their response.	**Pre-cueing or batched cold calling**: Offer a brief, neutral cue before calling, such as, "I'll come to you next, Sam." This helps students focus their thoughts without reducing cognitive demands. **Wait time**: Consistently use it and, when needed, extend it. It may be uncomfortable to pause for 10 seconds between asking a question and choosing a response, but with routine practice, this discomfort will ease and help students organise their thinking. **Visible questioning**: Present key questions visually to clarify language and ease working memory demands.
For students experiencing anxiety, autism, or social communication challenges, unpredictability can hinder participation.	**Establish norms**: Embed cold calling into classroom culture. As detailed earlier, clarify its purpose, stress that each voice matters, and assure students they need not fear mistakes or forgetfulness. **Normalise error**: Value thought and effort. "That's an interesting idea, let's build on it together." **Warm call**: Have students record their answer on a mini whiteboard first. Then give reluctant responders advanced notice that you want them to share their response.

(Continued)

Instructional consideration	Routines to run:
For students with dyslexia, DLD, or auditory processing difficulties, complex, multi-part questions or figurative language can overwhelm working memory and obscure understanding.	**Simplify syntax**: Ask single questions and avoid multiple clauses. **Concrete first**: Start with a concrete example or image before moving to abstraction. **Rephrase supportively**: If a student hesitates, restate the question in simpler language rather than giving them the answer. This maintains their independence while lowering linguistic demand.
For students with ADHD, cold calling can act as an attentional anchor.	**Cold call frequently**: Use dynamic cold call moments to re-engage attention without overwhelming students. **Track participation**: Use a seating plan to log who has been called on, ensuring equitable participation and reducing over-reliance on frequent responders. **Layered recall**: Occasionally revisit earlier contributions in the lesson. "Let's return to Zara's contribution from earlier. How does that link to this new idea?" This reinforces retrieval and validates contributions over time.

Mini Whiteboards

Instructional consideration	Routines to run:
Students with ADHD, dyspraxia, or motor coordination difficulties may struggle to think, write, and manage resources at once.	**Start with a predictable sequence:** Use routines from the MWB chapter in this book to reduce uncertainty. **Model routines**: Break MWB routines into steps. Demonstrate each step deliberately. Simply instructing students to hover their board is insufficient when introducing MWBs. **Standardise the format**: Clearly specify how students should present answers and model this presentation.
Students with dyslexia, DLD, or literacy difficulties may have their understanding obscured by slow writing or spelling.	**Train students to write big**: Model, using both examples and non-examples, how to write answers in large, legible print. **Model brevity**: For students with profound writing difficulties, encourage varied response modes such as diagrams, sketches, and symbols to surface conceptual understanding. Use such scaffolds responsively, withdrawing them as proficiency develops. **Preload vocabulary**: Display key terms on the board for students to use rather than recall spelling. As before, gradually withdraw.

(Continued)

Instructional consideration	Routines to run:
For students with social anxiety, autism, or low confidence, public performance can increase stress. The goal is to foster a psychologically safe environment where every response matters.	**Develop a predictable show-scan routine**: Provide instructions for how and when students will reveal answers, such as in set groups (back row, middle row, etc.) at a consistent time, to ensure all students know what to expect. **Silent scanning**: The teacher scans for patterns before commenting. The focus is on collective trends, not individual mistakes. **Neutral feedback**: Use phrases like "I'm seeing lots of . . . " or "Some of us are thinking that . . . " to depersonalise error.
Students with ADHD or attention regulation differences can be overwhelmed by multi-step questions or instructions.	**Front-load the means of participation**: As explored earlier in the book, this routine involves giving participatory instructions before asking the question. Doing so helps manage students' attention. **Tell students not to rub out their work**: Work on a student's mini whiteboard might include a worked example, which is sufficient to support their working memory when working independently. **Clear physical signals**: Use specific gestures or clear verbal cues, such as raising a hand or saying "whiteboards down," to guide transitions and reduce distractions.

SEND Spotlight: Sarah Robertson

Sarah Robertson has spent more than two decades working across different settings, experiences that have given her a deep understanding of how teachers can create inclusive learning that reaches every pupil. Her work centres on helping educators strengthen their practice, designing professional development that blends practical strategies, coaching, and reflective learning to improve outcomes for pupils with SEND. Through her collaborations with schools and professional development hubs, she supports staff at all levels in building confidence, refining classroom practice, and embedding approaches that ensure all learners are understood, supported, and able to thrive. Her ongoing involvement in regional SEND and maths networks continues to deepen her commitment to equity and effective teaching that makes a lasting difference.

Essential for Some, Useful for Most and Accessible for All

What do these three things have in common?

- A dropped kerb;
- Talking Tins;
- A minifigure at the bottom of a Lego instruction book that moves from page to page.

Each of these examples was intentionally designed to support a particular group of people in completing a task more independently and to check their understanding. While they are essential for some, they have proved useful for most and accessible for all. This principle, designing with inclusion in mind, can be applied directly to how we check understanding in our classrooms.

Inclusion by Design

When we plan, select, and implement strategies to check understanding, we should choose approaches that are accessible to everyone and essential for some students, particularly those with SEND. Intentional decision-making, both proactive and reactive, ensures that inclusion is embedded within our lesson design rather than bolted on afterwards.

Inclusion by design can also mean planning for multiple ways for students to demonstrate their understanding. It involves selecting strategies that enable every student, including those with SEND, to participate confidently, communicate their thinking, and demonstrate what they know.

The Education Endowment Foundation *Special Educational Needs in Mainstream Schools* (2021) guidance report and the *Five-a-day High-quality Teaching Principles* offer clear, evidence-based expectations for how we support students with SEND. Although checking for understanding is not listed as a stand-alone recommendation, the guidance highlights three essential components that inform our practice: ongoing assessment, responsive teaching, and understanding students' needs and barriers, all of which shape how we plan and deliver inclusive checking for understanding strategies, many of which are detailed in this book.

Knowing Our Students

In every classroom, we are constantly gathering information about our students, how they respond, what they understand, where they struggle, and how they learn best. A holistic understanding of each learner's strengths and barriers is crucial. It is beneficial to have effective ways to share this knowledge with all the adults who work with these students.

When everyone understands that every child should have the opportunity to think deeply, participate, and express what they have learned, our checking-for-understanding strategies become far more meaningful, targeted, and effective, and expectations for all students increase.

Schools gather a great deal of information about students' strengths, barriers, and interests on the SEND register. However, with so much data, it is not always possible to match the "perfect" strategy to each student every time to check their understanding. It would be unrealistic to expect a teacher to check for understanding in 30 different ways for 30 different students. Instead, by looking at the most effective strategies for most students, we can apply a "best bets" approach that helps the majority succeed.

For example, if I knew that the main broad area of need in my classroom was communication and interaction, I might consider strategies such as using non-verbal cues (e.g., holding up A, B, C, D cards to answer multiple-choice questions), providing sentence starters for partner work, or using a pictorial board of common responses that students can point to.

By knowing the broad area of need for the students in our class, whether cognition and learning, communication and interaction, social, emotional, and mental health, or sensory and physical, we can select the strategies most likely to be effective. This ensures students feel able to share and communicate their understanding in ways that work for them.

Why Hand Raising Doesn't Tell the Whole Story

I want to invite you to reflect on how effective hand raising is as a strategy that includes all students. In my experience, it is one of the most common classroom practices I see and one that teachers are confident using across all subjects: asking a question and inviting students to raise their hands, often with little or no thinking time. Yet beneath this seemingly simple action lies a complex internal process that varies from student to student.

Many students rapidly make both conscious and unconscious decisions before responding, and these internal thoughts may significantly influence whether they participate. They may wonder whether they will get the answer right, whether they have misunderstood the question, or whether they can even remember it. Some students know the answer but cannot retrieve the word they want, or they worry about saying it incorrectly. Others fear making a mistake in front of their peers or compare themselves to classmates who they believe may give a "better" answer.

Some students need more processing time, are still organising their thoughts, or become distracted by noise, anxiety, or sensory discomfort. Some assume the teacher will not choose them, feel unsure about the expected length or type of response, or recall a previous negative experience of answering in class.

These hidden cognitive and emotional processes show that a raised hand does not always reflect understanding, confidence, or readiness to contribute, highlighting the importance of using more inclusive, responsive ways to check understanding for all learners, including those with SEND.

The "Thought Bubbles" We Don't See

Visualising the invisible "thought bubbles" above students' heads helps us understand why relying heavily on this method can be unreliable and not inclusive for all. It provides powerful insight into the internal barriers students may be navigating and offers valuable information on which strategies may be more appropriate.

Recognising what students' barriers are and what they are thinking and feeling enables us to choose strategies that provide more accurate, inclusive insights into their understanding. By noticing these barriers and sharing our observations with others (including the student), we can select approaches that genuinely support learning, reduce anxiety, and allow all students to demonstrate what they know in ways that work for them.

Some of the internal questions students may be thinking:

- Will I get the answer right?
- What if I've misunderstood the question?
- I can't remember the question.
- I know the answer, but can't find the word I need.
- I understood it a second ago, but now it's gone.
- I'm worried about getting it wrong in front of everyone.
- I need more time to think.
- What if I stutter or get stuck?
- I can picture the answer, but can't explain it.
- I don't like raising my hand; it's uncomfortable.
- Is the teacher expecting a long answer or a short one?
- Someone else will know this better than me.
- I'm thinking about something that's worrying me.

13 Checking for Understanding and Adaptive Teaching

By now, it is likely to be apparent that teaching is a complex endeavour. A classroom, at its core, is a space filled with young people who differ in their prior knowledge, learning propensities, and pace of progress. All teachers will confront this reality, and the challenge lies in stretching all students, teaching to the top, avoiding holding anyone back, while ensuring they support those struggling to overcome fragile starting points.

The solution to this problem was once called differentiation: a well-intentioned framework designed to make teaching more inclusive of all students' needs. Yet, in a classic case of system-over-sense, the solution gave rise to an entirely new problem. Differentiation was reduced to "**all, most, and some**" learning objectives, resulting in diluted expectations, fragmented classrooms, and, rather than narrowing the learning gap, this approach risked widening it.

As Alex Quigley so eloquently puts it:

> If we are setting simple tasks for struggling pupils, but complex tasks for high prior attainers, how are they ever meant to catch up? [13]

So poorly understood and badly implemented by leaders, differentiation led teachers to decide in advance which students could perform which tasks, inadvertently capping some students' learning.[14] The

DOI: 10.4324/9781003657019-18

implicit message was clear: we expect less of some of you than of others. The result was a decline in motivation, lower effort, and weaker outcomes.[15]

If differentiation teaches us anything, it is that even the most well-intentioned solutions can unravel when misunderstood or applied mechanically. This is why leaders, teachers, and support colleagues must be cautious when turning to the next proposed remedy: adaptive teaching.

Adaptive teaching is just as seductive as differentiation once was. It promises responsive instruction that meets students where they are. Yet without recognising the central role of checking for understanding in this process, it too risks being reduced to surface-level routines that fail to deliver the inclusive learning environments we strive for.

To move beyond rhetoric, view adaptive teaching as a process rather than a posture. Its effectiveness rests on the dynamic interplay between two elements: the scaffolds that support students as they learn and the checks for understanding that help gauge whether those scaffolds are too heavy or too light. Together, they create a feedback loop that increases the likelihood of successful adaptation. Let's unpack these claims.

In her brilliant book, *Demystifying Adaptive Teaching*, Jade Pearce defines adaptive teaching as providing sufficient support and challenge to meet the needs of all students.[16]

Pearce suggests that adaptive teaching unfolds across three phases: before, during, and after instruction. Each phase reflects the formative assessment process of eliciting, interpreting, and using evidence to guide next steps, while also highlighting the interplay between checking for understanding and scaffolding. It is therefore helpful to view adaptive teaching as a cyclical process, one that aligns with the iterative feedback loops at the heart of formative assessment.

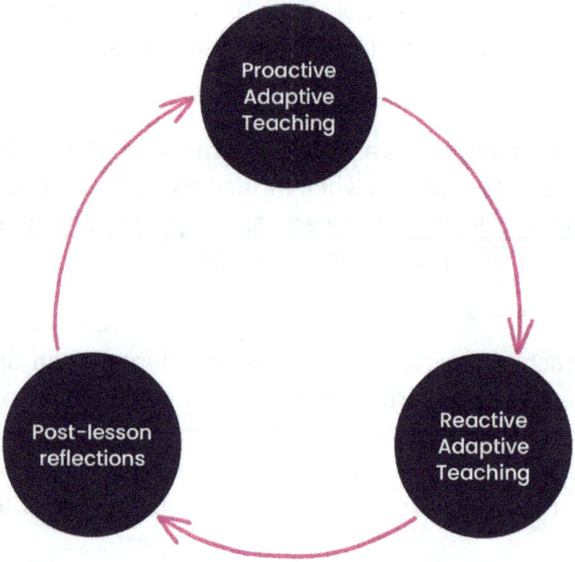

The Three Phases of Adaptive Teaching

Before the Lesson: Proactive Adaptive Teaching

Before the lesson, teachers anticipate variation. They plan how to support and challenge students based on students' prior knowledge, evidence from exit tickets, and information from other sources, such as SEND student passports. This is often referred to as **proactive adaptive teaching**: planning potential scaffolds and intentionally designing opportunities to gather meaningful evidence resulting in better-founded decisions.

At this stage, the teacher carefully considers the intended learning by asking themselves, "Where do I want my students to get to?" "How will I know when they are there?" "How can I help them get there?" The teacher designs checks for understanding, such as hinge questions, to identify likely misconceptions. The teacher also considers which concepts are most demanding, who might find them challenging, and what scaffolds are most likely to help.

During the Lesson: Reactive Adaptive Teaching

During the lesson, teachers respond to what checks for understanding reveal. This is the act of reactive adaptive teaching. As Ball and Fairlamb note, while scaffolding involves planning for potential barriers, it also requires in-the-moment adaptation, since it is impossible to anticipate every student's needs. They argue that ongoing checks for understanding should determine the extent and type of scaffold to use.[14] As seen in Chapter 6, these checks create what Dylan Wiliam calls *moments of contingency*: hinge points where instruction can pivot, pause, or extend depending on what the evidence shows.[17]

Post-lesson Reflection

After the lesson, teachers reflect on the evidence elicited. They might use exit tickets to decide who needs further support, who is ready for greater challenge, and what content requires reteaching or resequencing. This is an adaptation as curriculum refinement. In this way, adaptive teaching contributes to improving learning over time, thereby constituting part of the formative assessment loop. It also reinforces that checking for understanding is not merely a window into students' thinking but also a mirror reflecting the quality of our instructional decisions.

In essence, adaptive teaching is a process of making decisions that rely on evidence from checking for understanding to calibrate the extent and type of scaffolding students need. As Pearce says, effective adaptive teaching is a process of checking, reflecting, and responding. In this view, checking for understanding provides the insight, while scaffolding offers the instructional response. The intersection of the two occurs where adaptive teaching takes place. It is about using what we learn about students' understanding to decide what support to provide, when to offer it, and when to remove it.

The Venn diagram shows the relationship between checking for understanding and scaffolding in the adaptive teaching process. However, the active ingredients of scaffolding and checking for understanding are

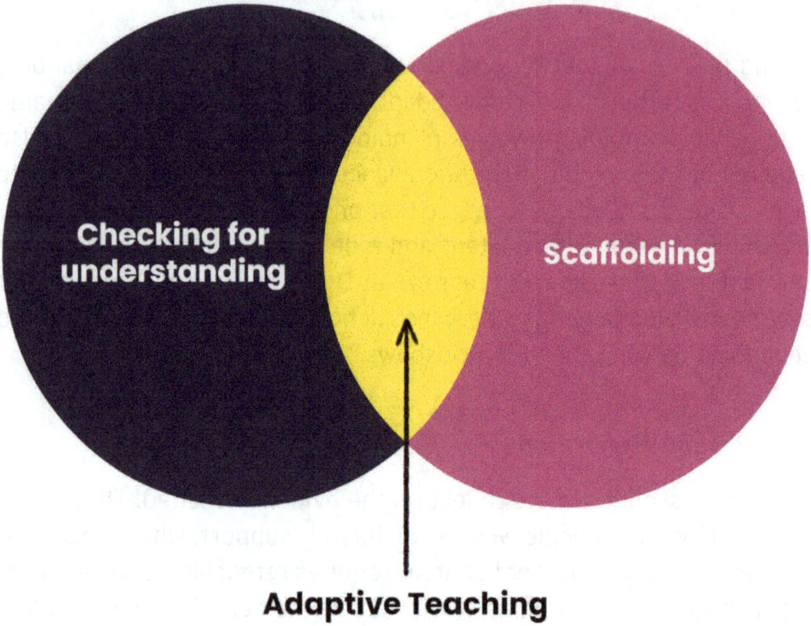

more nuanced. In workshops on adaptive teaching and scaffolding, Sarah Robertson, Deputy Director of the Learn SEND Hub, emphasises the importance of having an exit strategy, a plan for gradually reducing support as students' understanding deepens. Scaffolding is a metaphor for assistance that is carefully built up and then withdrawn as students' proficiency develops. Scaffolds are not supposed to be permanent. This matters for three main reasons:

1. **The gradual release of responsibility for learning from teacher to student promotes independence.**

   When support remains in place indefinitely, students may become overly reliant on it and struggle once it is withdrawn, particularly in assessment conditions. However, some students require permanent support such as assistive technology, adapted materials, or access arrangements. These are not scaffolds but essential, legally recognised forms of reasonable adjustment that ensure equitable participation and foster genuine inclusion.

Scaffolds, by contrast, are temporary instructional supports designed to fade as students' competence grows. While both reduce barriers to learning, their purposes differ: scaffolds promote the development of independent mastery, whereas permanent supports guarantee ongoing accessibility.

2. **Keeping scaffolds in place for too long can trigger what cognitive science labels the expertise reversal effect.**

   To understand this phenomenon, consider a familiar example. When learning to drive, an instructor might place small symbols on the wing mirrors to help a learner align the car with the curb while parking. For a novice driver, these visual cues provide concrete reference points that support spatial judgements. However, once the learner becomes proficient, the same symbols may become a distraction, drawing attention away from the now-automatic ability to judge distance and position the car accurately. What once supported knowledge acquisition can become a hindrance, competing for working memory capacity needed for the task at hand.

3. **When scaffolds provide too much support, students may only engage with content at a surface level, leading to shallow learning and weak retention.**

   Remember Dan Willingham's aphorism: "Memory is the residue of thought."[18] In other words, what students remember depends on what they are required to think about. If a scaffold removes too much of the cognitive challenge, students may not need to think deeply enough to encode the material meaningfully. Conversely, if a scaffold provides insufficient support, students may become overwhelmed by the complexity or volume of information, leading to cognitive overload.

Many educators invoke Vygotsky's zone of proximal development (ZPD) to explain this balance: the space between what students can do independently and what they can achieve with guidance. While this idea has intuitive appeal, it is often misappropriated.[19] ZPD was conceived as a developmental theory, not as a day-to-day teaching formula.

In practice, the ZPD is best viewed as a heuristic, a helpful but imperfect guide for considering the relationship between challenge, support, and learning. It is unrealistic to expect teachers to pinpoint it precisely for every student or every task. Instead, scaffolds must be calibrated in real time through ongoing checks for understanding. Without these formative checks, teachers have little reliable evidence to judge the extent or type of support required, or which students need it most.

The I do We do You do modelling structure offers a valuable lens through which to examine how checking for understanding and scaffolding operate interdependently within adaptive teaching.

I Do, We Do, You Do: Why it Works

The I do We do You do model embodies the worked example effect; the idea that students learn best when teachers manage students' cognitive load through modelling, structured practice, before gradual independence. It works because it aligns with human cognitive architecture: novice learners benefit from seeing an expert's thought process before attempting to use the knowledge themselves.

> **I do**: Teacher explanations and models make their expert schema visible.
>
> **We do**: Guided practice offers students the opportunity to rehearse the knowledge while the teacher manages cognitive load.
>
> **You do**: Independent practice helps students consolidate their understanding.

The structure provides a roadmap to independence by gradually transferring responsibility for learning to the student. Done well, it can reduce anxiety as students get the support they need when grappling with an unfamiliar and new concept.

The Non-linearity of Learning

Despite its widespread use, the structure is often misinterpreted as a linear formula, reduced to a step-by-step sequence to be completed once per lesson.[20] In total disregard of the cognitive science underpinning this model, some schools mandate that the structure reflect the lesson format itself, as though learning happens so neatly.

Such interpretations are naive. Imposing the model in this way does not honour the nuance of individual domains. In a maths lesson, students might work through multiple cycles of I do, We do, You do. Conversely, in history, where students answer questions about utility sources, it would be unrealistic to expect them to learn to analyse sources and write about them independently in a single lesson.[20]

Implementing I do, We do, You do in this way will likely give you consistency, but learning is too messy. Concepts vary in complexity; students' prior knowledge varies; and misconceptions can surface unexpectedly. Teachers often feel pressure to move on in the name of content coverage. Mary Myatt points out that meaningful learning requires staying with concepts long enough for students to make connections, see patterns and practise retrieval. Deep understanding takes time, and progress depends on what students know securely, not on how many topics have been covered.[21] The consequences of moving on too soon are often disproportionate and felt more significantly by the most vulnerable students.

The Role of Checking for Understanding

It is better to think of the structure as a continuum. A model where learning alternates dynamically between teacher input (I do), guided practice (We do), and short bursts of independent practice (You do), with the sequence moving back and forth rather than progressing in a strict linear fashion. Teachers use checks for understanding to decide when to revisit earlier stages or move forward, ensuring that students are ready to progress. Without evidence, transitions between phases become arbitrary. Moving on too soon risks leaving some students behind, and failing to move on risks hindering independence.

Viewing the model as a continuum reflects the reality that students rarely have the prerequisite knowledge to engage in lengthy or

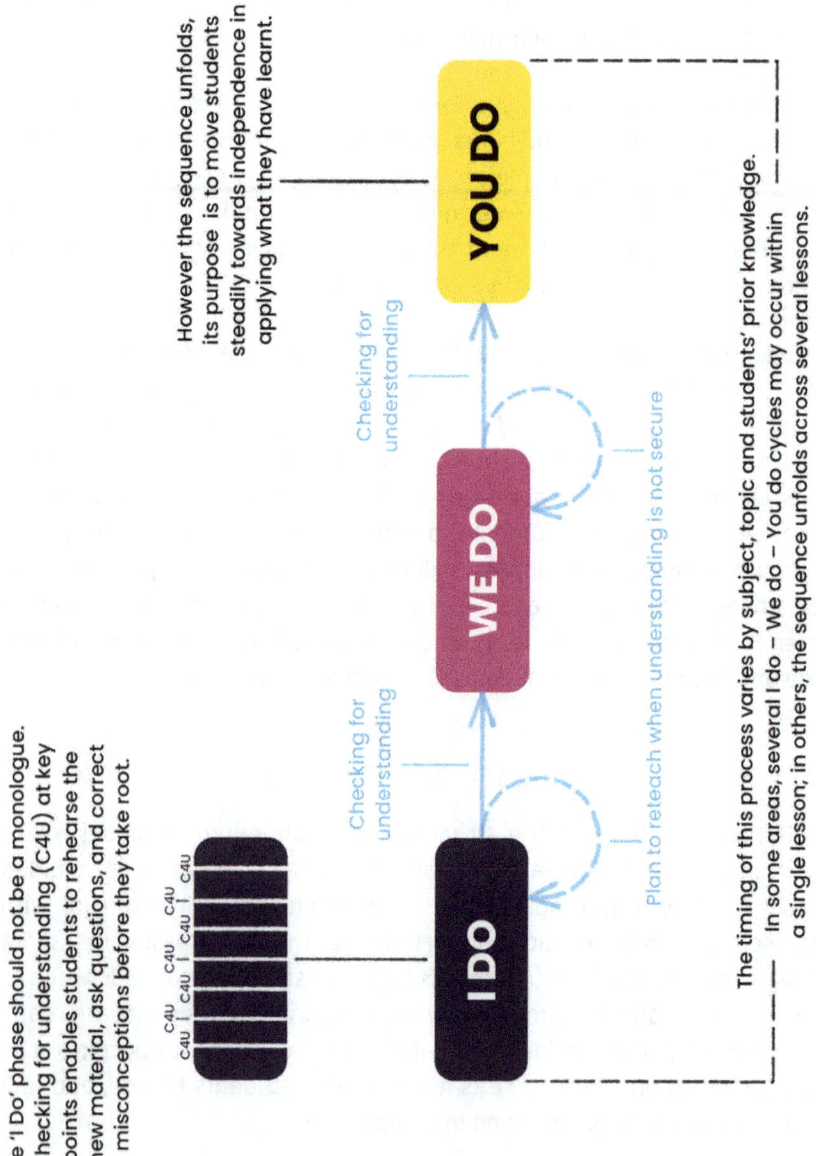
The 'I Do' phase should not be a monologue. Checking for understanding (C4U) at key points enables students to rehearse the new material, ask questions, and correct misconceptions before they take root.
C4U
C4U
C4U
C4U
C4U
C4U
I DO
WE DO
YOU DO
Checking for understanding
Checking for understanding
Plan to reteach when understanding is not secure
However the sequence unfolds, its purpose is to move students steadily towards independence in applying what they have learnt.
The timing of this process varies by subject, topic and students' prior knowledge. In some areas, several I do – We do – You do cycles may occur within a single lesson; in others, the sequence unfolds across several lessons.

sustained independent practice within a single lesson. In many cases, this cycle will span multiple lessons, gradually building toward greater independence as students deepen their mastery of foundational skills and knowledge. Teachers should plan how they will check for understanding at each stage and expect to revisit earlier stages in response to these checks. Repetition and re-teaching play an integral part in this process. When checks for understanding indicate that students are not yet ready to move on, teachers should provide immediate remediation through new models, explanations, and examples. In this way, the I do, We do, You do structure operates as an iterative loop in which evidence guides teachers' decision-making.

Some teachers worry that the back-and-forth movement between phases impedes their ability to cover the curriculum. Dylan Wiliam says it is a professional decision to cycle back or to move on. He describes some elements of the curriculum as being important but not consequential to students' progress. Conversely, some concepts are absolute prerequisites for meaningful learning. It is a decision that all teachers must make at some point. Wiliam pointedly asserts that it would be unprofessional to make such a decision without first determining what students know.[22]

14 Checking for Understanding and the Early Years by Rachel Ashfield

Rachel Ashfield is the Director of Early Education at RISE Multi Academy Trust, where her work focuses on leading strategic and school improvement across EYFS and KS1. She supports schools and leaders in strengthening EYFS practice and developing high-quality early years provision, and she has designed and implemented the trust's EYFS curriculum. Her work includes promoting effective phonics and early reading practice, supporting the implementation of phonics schemes, and championing a love of reading.

Checking for understanding, as with many other elements of teaching, may look slightly different within an EYFS environment, but the underlying principles remain the same. Early education plays a vital role in shaping a child's future. During the first years of life, the brain develops more rapidly than at any other time, making young children especially receptive to learning, having a profound and lasting impact. Quality early education nurtures language, thinking, and social-emotional skills through meaningful interactions and play. These early experiences build a strong foundation for lifelong learning, positive behaviour, and overall well-being, preparing children to succeed both in school and beyond.

Building on this foundation requires careful attention in the early years. Without identifying and addressing misunderstandings, gaps in knowledge, or underdeveloped skills, practitioners risk building on weak foundations, allowing small errors to persist. These gaps may widen gradually

DOI: 10.4324/9781003657019-19

at first, but their impact grows as new learning is layered onto fragile foundations. If such gaps are not closed early on, children are more likely to fall behind later, when catching up becomes increasingly difficult.

Within the EYFS, checking for understanding cannot be carried out through formalised methods such as tests, as seen in later schooling. Instead, it is embedded within everyday practice as an ongoing, continuous process that develops over time. Every observation, interaction, and activity provides a valuable insight, allowing practitioners to deepen their understanding of each child's learning. Checking for understanding does not end at the conclusion of a direct teaching input. If new learning is to become embedded, practitioners must observe how confidently and automatically children retrieve and apply their knowledge, skills, and behaviours as they engage in continuous provision, play, and everyday routines. It is through this transition, from input to application, that practitioners can determine whether learning has genuinely connected to existing knowledge structures or whether gaps and misconceptions remain.

Within our trust, we found that practitioners were effective at checking for understanding during direct teaching; however, this knowledge was not consistently used to shape learning opportunities within the provision. There was a need for greater intentionality in considering how information gained through checking for understanding during direct teaching could be deliberately further developed within the classroom environment. Building on existing CPD around the enabling environment, we explored strategies and principles to strengthen this link, ensuring that the learning environment is carefully and strategically tailored to meet individual needs. Discussions focused on strengthening provision through thoughtful enhancements and carefully selected resources within continuous provision, refined interactions, and purposeful adult placement,. This ensured that children had repeated opportunities to practise and consolidate learning, deepen their understanding, and transfer knowledge and skills across different contexts.

These key strategies are further discussed in the rest of this chapter.

Linking Prior Knowledge to Provision

To maximise the impact of provision and ensure it supports children in embedding their learning, practitioners must deliberately consider how learning from direct teaching is woven into the environment. This requires intentional decisions about how provision shapes teaching and learning experiences so that children are supported to revisit, practise, and apply new knowledge and skills.

Careful selection of resources within continuous provision is essential. Resources should directly support children's skill development and provide opportunities for them to demonstrate, practise, and extend their understanding. This does not mean limiting children's access to high-quality resources or placing a ceiling on learning. Children should continue to engage with activities that motivate and challenge them. Instead, practitioners must understand which scaffolds or resources best support a child at their current stage of development, while also enabling access to materials that promote next steps as understanding deepens.

Effective continuous provision and thoughtful enhancements create opportunities for children to retrieve and apply new learning in flexible and meaningful ways. This strengthens understanding and enables practitioners to observe whether children are making secure connections between new learning and prior knowledge. This process is just as important as the initial instruction itself. Practitioners should regularly reflect on the purpose of enhancements and the reasoning behind resources in provision to ensure they are supporting children to embed and consolidate learning. Providing plentiful opportunities for practise is essential if learning is to become secure.

By analysing the components of learning and identifying what children may be missing, confused about, or not yet fluent in, practitioners can pinpoint precisely what support is required. This analysis informs intentional decisions about how adult guidance can be woven naturally into play and how the environment can be adapted to strengthen understanding. For example, during a handwriting session, a practitioner may notice that a child is struggling to form letters due to underdeveloped gross and fine motor skills. By checking for understanding in the moment, the adult can plan for the provision to support prewriting skills, such as using hole punches, creating spaces in which to vertically mark make, large blocks to manoeuvre and manipulate and squeezing and rolling playdough. The adult can position themselves to offer targeted guidance. This ensures the child has repeated opportunities to practise the skill in a supportive context, consolidating learning and developing the physical foundations for handwriting.

Assessment, therefore, must directly inform the design of provision and the ways in which children's learning is supported. In this way, checking for understanding becomes the bridge between curriculum intent and classroom enactment.

High-quality Interactions: Conversations and Responsive Questioning

High-quality interactions are fundamental to supporting learning and checking for understanding in the Early Years Foundation Stage. This is not about adults talking more, but about engaging in meaningful interactions that promote learning. Two key approaches underpin effective interactions: engaging in back-and-forth exchanges that extend communication and thinking, and using scaffolding to support children in completing tasks they cannot yet complete independently. Across our trust, practitioners were supported to develop effective interactions through the ShREC approach (Share attention, Respond, Expand, Conversation) (EEF).[23] Through purposeful and responsive engagement, adults can observe and listen to children as they explore, play, and communicate, gaining insight into what they know, understand, and can do. By using open-ended questions, modelling language and concepts, and engaging in sustained shared thinking, practitioners can uncover children's reasoning, identify misconceptions, and recognise when skills or knowledge are secure, thereby enabling them to see not just what a child does, but why and how they think.

EXAMPLE 1

If children have been taught new vocabulary through a shared story or adult-led discussion but are not yet using these words independently, practitioners might enhance the book nook or small-world area with props linked to the text and visual vocabulary prompts. Adults can then position themselves within the play to model the language, repeat key words in context, and encourage children to use them meaningfully during their play. This allows practitioners to see whether children can retrieve and apply new vocabulary and to offer further support or extension as understanding becomes more secure.

EXAMPLE 2

During a counting or sorting activity, a child may be grouping objects but is unsure how to organise them efficiently. An adult can prompt the child's thinking by asking, "I wonder how many red ones are there compared to blue ones?" or "I wonder what would happen if we put all the big blocks together?" These questions encourage the child to reason, compare, and make independent decisions. At the same time, the adult observes understanding and provides guidance, such as modelling language, repeating key vocabulary in context, and encouraging children to use it meaningfully during play when necessary. This allows practitioners to check the child's mathematical thinking further and extend learning in the moment.

Importantly, effective interactions allow adults to respond in the moment; they can clarify misunderstandings immediately, rephrase or model concepts in new ways, extend learning when understanding is secure, and provide scaffolding where needed. This real-time responsiveness is central to checking for understanding, ensuring that children receive an appropriate level of support and challenge to support their progress. Ultimately, high-quality interactions create a learning environment that is responsive, inclusive, and centred on the child, enabling both cognitive and emotional development to flourish.

Targeted Adult Placement

To further check for understanding and gain insight into children's learning, practitioners must consider how adults position themselves within the learning environment. Adults should avoid being static or supervising from the edges and instead be present, purposeful, and responsive.

Children build understanding by connecting new information to what they already know, forming a mental framework of their learning. Without timely guidance, misconceptions can easily arise, especially when concepts are unfamiliar or prior knowledge is limited. Intentional adult placement enables practitioners to notice understanding as it unfolds, respond in the moment, and intervene thoughtfully to extend children's thinking in meaningful ways. This may involve positioning an adult alongside specific children following an input, or directing children towards areas of provision designed to deepen thinking and prevent missed learning opportunities.

It is also crucial to ensure all children have access to adult interaction, not just those who seek it. Children who are less verbally confident, or those with limited prior exposure to language, are at greater risk of being overlooked and may require more intentional checks to assess their understanding. Differences in starting points do not indicate differences in potential, but rather differences in prior opportunity. Many children with low starting points thrive when provided with appropriate support, scaffolding, and repeated opportunities to practise.

Strategic adult placement also enables practitioners to identify gaps in children's conceptual or linguistic foundations and to address them before they become barriers to future learning. By carefully checking for understanding and responding thoughtfully, adults can scaffold prior knowledge and ensure that all children have access to the same ambitious and inclusive curriculum. Starting points should inform, not limit, teaching, enabling every child to reach their potential without imposing an artificial ceiling on learning.

15 Checking for Understanding and Oracy by Nikki Sullivan

Nikki is a deputy headteacher at Beckfoot School in Bradford, with experience across both pastoral and academic senior leadership roles in the UK and Asia. Alongside her in-school role, she contributes to her trust's central team as Trust CPD Programmes Lead.

Nikki presents at educational events in the UK and internationally and regularly contributes to books, journals, and other professional publications. In October 2025, she published her first co-authored edubook, Unlocking Oracy, in partnership with Inner Drive.

Passionate about fostering a love of professional learning, Nikki also shares reflections and practical insights on her blog: https://lovetotalktandl.wordpress.com/

I love mini whiteboards. I think they are an irreplaceable tool within the classroom, maximising participation and enabling the teacher to check the understanding of each student. That being said, I think checks for understanding that lean upon oracy, that is to say, which lean upon verbal responses, can be overlooked.

When making decisions in the classroom about which strategies to deploy, we need to consider their relative affordances. Mini whiteboards enable us to check the understanding of each student, but, in isolation, do not allow us to dig into the thinking behind those responses. Additionally, where there is a wider range of acceptable responses, and

DOI: 10.4324/9781003657019-20

especially where responses are naturally longer, mini whiteboards cannot all be read quickly, thereby removing one of the affordances of this approach - its efficiency.

As teachers, we need a range of checking-for-understanding tools in our toolkit so that we can utilise the right strategy for the right reasons at the right time. If I only have a hammer, it works well for a nail, but not for a screw. Oracy-based strategies expand our toolkit. They allow us to surface thinking, test meaning, and probe misconceptions in ways that written checks alone cannot.

Partner Talk as a Diagnostic Tool

Doug Lemov's turn-and-talk or think, pair, share are often described as participation strategies.[24] In terms of participation ratio, when we set students off, we instantly have 50% of our class engaging in the generative act of verbalising their ideas, followed by the other 50% in turn.

In addition, used deliberately, partner talk functions as a diagnostic tool. Purposeful circulation during these discussions enables us to hear responses from multiple students. As students talk, the teacher listens for:

- common errors or misconceptions;
- partial or insecure understanding;
- language that suggests meaning is forming outside the acceptable range;
- strong explanations that can be used to model thinking.

This listening informs what happens next. A teacher may:

- pause the class to address a widespread misconception;
- select a response to share and build upon;
- pull responses together into a "We do" written response, before moving on with the lesson.

In this way, partner talk does not sit in isolation. It is woven together with other questioning strategies, including written responses and individual questioning, as part of a responsive checking-for-understanding approach.

One of the other huge benefits of partner talk is that it requires students to not only articulate their thinking but also actively listen to the thinking of another student. Set up well, partner talk puts positive cognitive demand on the listener who is getting the opportunity to interrogate their own understanding based on the thoughts of a fellow student. It can be helpful for students to initially offload their thinking to an *external memory field* (Donald, 1991), such as a mini whiteboard or exercise book, so that their working memory does not become overloaded when they are listening to their partner.[25]

Teachers can strengthen this further by asking students to:

- explain how their thinking changed after discussion;
- justify why they kept their original answer;
- respond directly to a partner's idea when sharing with the class.

Listening, in this sense, becomes a form of assessment for both the student and the teacher.

The "Third Turn" and Asking a Range of Questions

Here, we begin to see the range of question types we encounter in a lesson, and how the kinds of questions we ask are better served by different questioning strategies.

In *Unlocking Oracy* (2025), we describe how "Coe et al. (2020) explain how quality questioning forms part of a dialogue where students are not only engaged but stretched. Students not only rehearse or recall but also give explanations, justifications, and elaborations" (p. 91).[26,27]

This links to the power of what Alexander (2020) explains as the "third turn".

> [T]eacher talk moves that encourage students to elaborate their own and each other's ideas [which] have particular potency (Alexander, 2020, p. 114).[28]

These "talk moves" are reflected in the work of Michaels and O'Connor (2012), in which, once a student has shared their answer (in partner talk, on a mini whiteboard, or via cold call), teachers follow up with questions to further explore their thinking and encourage deeper thinking.[29] To keep the participation ratio high, these follow-up questions, or talk moves, can be bounced out to the whole class before the teacher decides whether to return to the original student or bounce to a fellow class member. For example:

- "Can you say more about that . . . *thinking time* . . . name of student?"
- "Can you give an example . . . *thinking time* . . . name of student?"
- "Is that always the case . . . *thinking time* . . . name of student?"

Avoiding Common Pitfalls

When using oracy to check understanding, there are risks to be mindful of:

- **Empty talk**: Talk must be supported by subject knowledge. Students cannot talk their way to new content, but they can talk their way to a stronger understanding of the content they have been taught. Norms need to be established whereby students utilise subject-specific vocabulary and, in doing so, enable us to check for understanding in how they are using this language.
- **Unchecked misconceptions**: Student-to-student talk must be monitored. Without sufficient circulation and follow-up, incorrect ideas can spread and become reinforced.
- **Transience of talk**: Spoken ideas disappear. Teachers need to decide when thinking should remain exploratory and when key ideas need to be captured in a more permanent form.

- **Uneven participation**: Clear routines for who speaks, who listens, and when roles switch help to keep the participation ratio high.

What This Means for Classrooms

Using oracy to check understanding is not about replacing written work or abandoning established strategies. It is about making students' thinking visible in moments where written checks fall short.

In a study from Sedova and Sedlacek (2023), not only did they find that students with greater verbal participation outperformed those with greater silent engagement, but they also found that 7% of students in the study did not speak at all over the course of two lessons.[30] Therefore, not only should we be utilising strategies which lean upon speaking and listening because of the role they play in making students' once invisible thoughts available for us to evaluate, and not only because the generative process of talk is linked to progression in learning, but also because we want to ensure our students are in schools in which their voices are heard.

Section 4: Checking for Understanding and . . . Concluding Principles for Practice

1. **Checking for understanding is a matter of cognitive equity.**

   Inclusive teaching is about more than access, support, or goodwill. It is about ensuring that instructional approaches do not impose avoidable cognitive burdens that make learning harder for some students than others. Well-designed checks for understanding reduce unnecessary cognitive demand and allow all students to direct their effort towards learning itself.

2. **Adaptive teaching depends on evidence.**

   While teachers must plan proactively for variation, effective adaptation happens in response to what students actually understand in the moment. Checking for understanding ensures adaptive teaching is a responsive process, enabling teachers to calibrate support, challenge, and pace based on evidence rather than assumption.

3. **Scaffolding is only effective when it is calibrated and temporary.**

   Scaffolds are instructional supports designed to help students succeed with tasks they cannot yet complete independently. Their purpose is to promote independence, not replace it. Checks for understanding provide the feedback teachers need to judge when scaffolds are necessary, when they should be adjusted, and when they can be withdrawn.

4. **Learning improves when checks for understanding are embedded across time.**

   Whether in the early years, during modelling and guided practice, or through talk-based routines, checking for understanding is most effective when it is woven throughout instruction. Frequent, low-stakes checks allow teachers to identify fragile understanding early, strengthen schema through retrieval and rehearsal, and prevent small gaps from becoming enduring barriers.

5. **No single strategy can meet all needs; professional judgement lies in selection and combination.**

   Cold calling, mini whiteboards, exit tickets, partner talk, and observational checks each offer different insights into students' thinking. Their power lies in the thoughtful combination of different techniques. Effective teachers select and sequence checks for understanding to generate the most useful evidence when it matters most.

Section 4: Checking for Understanding and . . . References

1. Davies, K. and Henderson, P. (2020) *Special educational needs in mainstream schools: Guidance report*. London: Education Endowment Foundation.
2. Fuchs, L.S. and Fuchs, D. (1986) "Effects of systematic formative evaluation: A meta-analysis," *Exceptional Children*, 53(3), pp.199–208.

3. House of Commons (2024) *Special educational needs and disabilities (SEND) support in England: A review*. London: UK Parliament.
4. Department for Education (n.d.) Schools inspection toolkit. Available at: https://assets.publishing.service.gov.uk/media/68b9a6b8b0a373a01819fe4b/Schools_inspection_toolkit.pdf (Accessed: 17 October 2025.)
5. National Association for Special Educational Needs (NASEN) (2024) *Teacher SEND handbook* [PDF]. Available at: https://asset.nasen.org.uk/Teacher%20SEND%20handbook%2030th%20January%202024.pdf (Accessed: 11 October 2025.)
6. Black, P. and Wiliam, D. (2009) "Developing the theory of formative assessment," *Educational Assessment, Evaluation and Accountability*, 21(1), pp. 5–31. https://doi.org/10.1007/s11092-008-9068-5.
7. Gathercole, S.E. and Alloway, T.P. (2008) *Working memory and learning: A practical guide for teachers*. London: Sage.
8. Kirschner, P.A., Sweller, J., and Clark, R.E. (2006) "Why minimal guidance during instruction does not work: An analysis of the failure of constructivist, discovery, problem-based, experiential, and inquiry-based teaching," *Educational Psychologist*, 41(2), pp. 75–86.
9. Hendrick, C. (2025) "Does explicit instruction work for students with learning difficulties?" Blog post, 13 June. Available at: https://carlhendrick.substack.com/ (Accessed: 31 January 2026).
10. Sweller, J. (2011) "Cognitive load theory," *Psychology of Learning and Motivation*, 55, pp. 37–76.
11. McCrea, P. (2025) "Orchestrating attention." Snacks. Available at: https://snacks.pepsmccrea.com/p/orchestrating-attention (Accessed: 17 October 2025.)
12. McCrea, P. (2025, 14 March) "The power of routines." Snacks. Available at: https://snacks.pepsmccrea.com/p/the-power-of-routines (Accessed: 17 October 2025.)
13. Quigley, A. (2024) Adaptive teaching: Scaffolds, scale, structure and style. Alex Quigley, 13 April. Available at: https://alexquigley.co.uk/adaptive-teaching-scaffolds-scale-structure-and-style/ (Accessed: 4 October 2025.)
14. Ball, R. and Fairlamb, A. (2025) *The scaffolding effect: Supporting all students to succeed*, 1st edn. London: Routledge. doi:10.4324/9781003467069.

15. Roberts, M. (2022) *The boy question: How to teach boys to succeed in school*. Routledge.

16. Pearce, J. (2025) *Demystifying adaptive teaching: How to teach to the top*. London: Routledge.

17. Wiliam, D. (2016) *Leadership for teacher learning: Creating a culture where all teachers improve so that all students succeed*. West Palm Beach, FL: Learning Sciences International.

18. Willingham, D.T. (2009) *Why don't students like school?: A cognitive scientist answers questions about how the mind works and what it means for the classroom*. San Francisco: Jossey-Bass.

19. Didau, D. (2017) "Problems with the 'zone of proximal development.'" Learning Spy. Available at: https://learningspy.co.uk/featured/problems-zone-proximal-development/ (Accessed: 9 October 2025.)

20. The Educational Imposters (2025) "I/we/you: Use with caution." [Blog] 2 June. Available at: https://theeducationalimposters.wordpress.com/2025/06/02/i-we-you-use-with-caution/ (Accessed: 19 October 2025.)

21. Myatt, M. (2021) "The curse of content coverage." [Blog] 9 Jan. Available at: https://www.marymyatt.com/blog/the-curse-of-content-coverage (Accessed: 19 October 2025.)

22. Wiliam, D. (2011) *Embedded formative assessment*. Bloomington, MN: Solution Tree Press.

23. James, F. (2025) *The ShREC approach*. EEF. Available at https://educationendowmentfoundation.org.uk/early-years/the-shrec-approach (Accessed: 1 May 2026.)

24. Lemov, D. (2021) *Teach like a champion 3.0: 63 Techniques that put students on the path to college*, 3rd ed. Hoboken, NJ: Jossey-Bass.

25. Donald, M. (1991) *Origins of the modern mind: Three stages in the evolution of culture and cognition*. Cambridge, MA: Harvard University Press.

26. Sullivan, N., Heaton, K., and Lowde, L. (2025) *Unlocking oracy: Enhancing student learning and personal development*. London: Routledge.

27. Coe, R., Rauch, C., Kime, S., and Singleton, D. (2020) *Great teaching toolkit: Evidence review*. Evidence Based Education. Available at: https://f.hubspotusercontent30.net/hubfs/2366135/Great%20Teaching%20Toolkit%20Evidence%20Review.pdf.

28. Alexander, R. (2020) *A dialogic teaching companion*. London: Routledge.

29. Michaels, S. and O'Connor, C. (2012) *Talk science primer*. Cambridge, MA: TERC.

30. Sedova, K. and Sedlacek, M. (2023) "How vocal and silent forms of participation in combination relate to student achievement," *Instructional Science: An International Journal of the Learning Sciences*, 51(2), pp. 343-361.

Closing Thoughts

This book centres on a deceptively simple question: **What are they thinking?** It is a question that many teachers don't ask themselves often enough. Not because they are bad teachers, but because they feel pressured to keep the lesson going and to cover the curriculum. They worry about how leaders might judge the quality of their teaching if students answer questions incorrectly. And in some cases, leaders have yet to establish a culture in which teachers are empowered to grapple with what the science of learning tells us about how learning actually happens.

This book demonstrates that even when teachers pause and reflect on this question, answering it with any degree of confidence is far from straightforward. Learning is not directly observable, tempting though it is to believe otherwise. What teachers observe in the classroom, such as answers, behaviours, confidence, and silence, can only ever offer a partial window into what students truly understand.

Teaching, then, is an inferential act. Teachers make decisions in conditions of uncertainty, drawing on incomplete and sometimes misleading evidence. It might not be possible to eliminate that uncertainty, but we can find ways to work within it more intelligently. Check for understanding serves to support that work. It helps teachers bypass reassurance and assumptions in favour of better-founded judgements about what

DOI: 10.4324/9781003657019-21

students know, what they are struggling with, and, crucially, what needs to happen next.

A central message of this book is that checking for understanding is not a moment in the lesson, nor a routine that teachers insert at fixed intervals. Instead, it is a way to orient attention to student thinking and treat it as the primary driver of instructional decisions. Cold calling, mini whiteboards, hinge questions, and exit tickets are powerful because of what they make possible: broader participation, deeper thinking, clearer evidence, and more responsive teaching.

When participation relies on a few confident volunteers, the evidence teachers gather is invariably insufficient. Confident volunteers, correct responses, engaged students, and a smooth lesson flow all create the illusion of learning, while masking fragility elsewhere. Designing checks for understanding that require all students to think and respond enriches the quality of information available to the teacher. When done well, checks for understanding reveal patterns, misconceptions, and emerging understanding.

Crucially, while learning and performance are not the same thing, and checking for understanding is diagnostic rather than a measure of learning, it plays an important role in the learning process. Each time students retrieve information, explain their thinking, or commit to an answer, they are rehearsing and refining their understanding. Such moments shape attention, regulate cognitive load, and promote the encoding of new knowledge. In this sense, checking for understanding acts as the connective tissue between what is taught and what students learn, helping to dissolve the artificial boundary between teaching and assessment.

At the same time, no check-for-understanding routine can guarantee that it will, with absolute certainty, lead to improved learning. Instead, the benefits are probabilistic. Increasing the likelihood that each check yields a better-founded decision requires teachers to design checks carefully, use them thoughtfully, and consider how they respond to the information they gather. Two teachers can ask identical questions, yet one gains greater clarity about what her students are thinking, while the other is left with little more than false assurance. The difference lies in how intentionally all students are included in the thinking and how thoughtfully the evidence is then acted upon.

This is why the ideas, practices and techniques explored in this book deserve careful attention. Not because they are complex, but because they are consequential. Developing expertise in checking for understanding takes time, reflection, domain-specific knowledge, and professional dialogue. It involves learning to craft better questions, interpret responses more cautiously, and act on evidence more deliberately. For teachers and leaders alike, this is less about adding new initiatives and more about strengthening the mechanisms through which teaching already happens.

Ultimately, checking for understanding is a matter of responsibility. It reflects a commitment to noticing when students are unsure rather than assuming they are fine, to responding while learning is evolving rather than after it has failed to endure. It asks teachers to shift effort from retrospective correction to in-the-moment adjustment, where it has the greatest impact.

There will never be a complete or final answer to **What are they thinking?** But asking it seriously and creating the conditions that help us answer it better change what teaching makes possible. When teachers cultivate habits of curiosity and attend closely to students' thinking, and when schools nurture conditions for that work to flourish, learning becomes more visible, teaching becomes more responsive, and success becomes more attainable for all students.

Index

www.ingramcontent.com/pod-product-compliance
Lightning Source LLC
LaVergne TN
LVHW010644270826
846615LV00023B/203
* 9 7 8 1 0 4 1 1 0 8 2 3 8 *